the New Wine Country
Cookbook

OTHER BOOKS BY BRIGIT BINNS

The Cook & the Butcher

Whole Beast Butchery (coauthor, with Ryan Farr)

How to Roast a Lamb (coauthor, with Michael Psilakis)

Mr. Sunday's Soups (coauthor, with Lorraine Wallace)

The Relaxed Kitchen

The Low-Carb Gourmet

The Palm Restaurant Cookbook

The Tavern on the Green Cookbook (coauthor)

Cuisine Naturelle: Modern French Classics (coauthor,
    with Jean-Francois Meteigner)

Cowboy Cocktails (coauthor, with Grady Spears)

Rockenwagner! (coauthor, with Hans Rockenwagner)

The Patina Cookbook (coauthor, with Joachim Splichal and Charles Perry)

Jody Maroni's Sausage Kingdom Cookbook

Polenta: 40 Recipes for All Occasions

WILLIAMS-SONOMA TITLES

Let's Do Brunch

The Weeknight Cook

The New Slow Cooker Cookbook

Bride & Groom Entertaining

Pizza and Other Savory Pies

Food Made Fast: Salad

Food Made Fast: Small Plates

Cooks Collection: Sauce

Cooks Collection: Breakfast

Cooks Collection: Hors d'Oeuvre

American Christmas (coauthor)

Complete Grilling Cookbook (coauthor)

the New Wine Country
Cookbook

RECIPES FROM CALIFORNIA'S CENTRAL COAST

BRIGIT BINNS

PHOTOGRAPHY BY COLIN CLARK

Andrews McMeel
Publishing, LLC
Kansas City · Sydney · London

Andrews McMeel Publishing, LLC
an Andrews McMeel Universal company
1130 Walnut Street, Kansas City, Missouri 64106

www.andrewsmcmeel.com

13 14 15 16 17 SHO 10 9 8 7 6 5 4 3 2 1

ISBN: 978-1-4494-1912-7

Library of Congress Control Number: 2012952340

Design: Diane Marsh
Photography: Colin Clark
Digital/Photo Assistant: David Lincoln and Weber Shih
Food Stylist: Valerie Aikman Smith
Food Stylist Assistant: Brigit Binns
Prop Stylist: Brigit Binns

www.brigitbinns.com

ATTENTION: SCHOOLS AND BUSINESSES

Andrews McMeel books are available at quantity discounts with bulk purchase for educational, business, or sales promotional use. For information, please e-mail the Andrews McMeel Special Sales Department: specialsales@amuniversal.com

To Casey, for finding it within his warm,
New England–loving heart to cherish this
part of California almost as much as I do.

Contents

Introduction

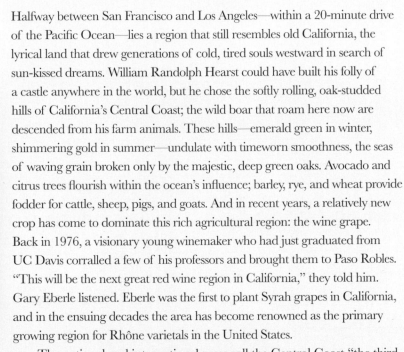

Halfway between San Francisco and Los Angeles—within a 20-minute drive of the Pacific Ocean—lies a region that still resembles old California, the lyrical land that drew generations of cold, tired souls westward in search of sun-kissed dreams. William Randolph Hearst could have built his folly of a castle anywhere in the world, but he chose the softly rolling, oak-studded hills of California's Central Coast; the wild boar that roam here now are descended from his farm animals. These hills—emerald green in winter, shimmering gold in summer—undulate with timeworn smoothness, the seas of waving grain broken only by the majestic, deep green oaks. Avocado and citrus trees flourish within the ocean's influence; barley, rye, and wheat provide fodder for cattle, sheep, pigs, and goats. And in recent years, a relatively new crop has come to dominate this rich agricultural region: the wine grape. Back in 1976, a visionary young winemaker who had just graduated from UC Davis corralled a few of his professors and brought them to Paso Robles. "This will be the next great red wine region in California," they told him. Gary Eberle listened. Eberle was the first to plant Syrah grapes in California, and in the ensuing decades the area has become renowned as the primary growing region for Rhône varietals in the United States.

The national and international press call the Central Coast "the third wine region of California" and "the next wine country." Arguably, the heart of this fast-growing wine-and-food destination, which stretches from Monterey in the north to Santa Barbara in the south, is the once-dusty town of Paso Robles, where tasting rooms, boutiques, and world-class restaurants have replaced sleepy junk shops and farm-supply stores. Now, sleek sports cars share the road with pickup trucks and horse trailers, as wine country tourists increasingly choose this "new" wine region over Tuscany and Bordeaux (too expensive), or Napa and Sonoma (too crowded *and* too expensive). To add to the excitement, the area has attracted a younger, rollicking gang of winemakers, often called the "Rhône Rangers," who tip their hats to convention, then break rules with wild abandon. You'll get to know some of the local winemakers, ranchers, and farmers in 25 intimate profiles. Most of these folks take pride in being known as coming from "the non-Napa." There is an uncommon, longstanding family connection to the land that has stood the test of time—the landscape and terroir seem conducive to keeping people on their land for generations. Yes, there are newcomers—more with every passing year and glowing article—but these people are circling the wagons, settling down for keeps. You could call it "Tuscany with cowboys."

emerald green in winter, shimmering gold in summer

I was born and raised in Southern California, but the land of my birth no longer exists. This sprawling state attracted too many people in search of the good life and, in most of the state, the weight of their needs has erased the dream they came to find. It's only in the center of the state, just a little too far for commuting—but close enough for luscious long weekend escapes—that my California lives on. After decades in Spain, Italy, England, and the United States Northeast, I have finally come home. Surrounded by the bucolic landscapes, rich resources, and sensational wine of my new/old home state, my intention now is to cook, sip, and revel in the bounty of the Central Coast. To share this intense joy with you in my 25th cookbook is not only an obvious choice, but a great honor. I have written a love letter to the food, wine, and cowboy spirit in this golden corner of my home state.

MY CALIFORNIA

The California of my youth was a place of dirt roads and clean beaches, boundless optimism, and unlimited parking. The wheaten hills were soft and smooth, crafted by millennia of shifting tectonic plates, pounding surf, and capricious winds, not by a plastic surgeon's knife. Paradise had yet to be paved. In the 1960s, I was lucky enough to spend perhaps the happiest times of my childhood on a breathtakingly beautiful piece of the California coast: the legendary, inaccessible Hollister Ranch. I count myself immensely lucky to have grown up in the Golden State, one of the few second-generation Californians in a rapidly growing sea of newcomers.

In *Where I Was From*, Joan Didion's love letter to old California, she quotes the doyenne of another huge landholding family, Joan Irvine Smith: "I can see California as it was and as we will never see it again." I believe the Central Coast is the only place where that mythic California is still—just barely—visible. I can't imagine any more wonderful place to eat, drink, and be married.

ABOUT THE RECIPES

There is good reason why early immigrants from the Mediterranean flocked to this area and made their livelihoods from the land. The gentle climate mirrors both the Mediterranean and the Middle East, and the (then) abundance of water allowed huge swaths of the state to be cultivated in fruit, vegetables, and livestock. Foodways were borrowed from all the disparate immigrants who flocked here, interwoven with a casual simplicity born from the ability to live mostly out of doors—surrounded by delicious abundance.

The rich bounty of ingredients grown and produced in the Central Coast reads like a litany of the best foodstuffs in the world.

CHEESE: goat's, sheep's, cow's milk

CITRUS: oranges, lemons, limes, grapefruit, Buddha's hand citron, kumquats

FINFISH: halibut, rockfish, sole, sand dabs, anchovies, sardines

FRUIT: grapes, figs, olives, persimmons, plums, pomegranates, strawberries, tomatoes

HERBS: lavender, rosemary, thyme, wild fennel, tarragon, sage

MUSHROOMS: boletus, black trumpet, candy caps, chanterelles, oyster, shiitake

NUTS: almonds, pistachios, walnuts

PASTURE RAISED MEAT: beef, Berkshire pork, goat, lamb

POULTRY: chicken, duck

SALMON: king, coho, sockeye

SHELLFISH: abalone, clams, crab, lobster, mussels, oysters, shrimp

VEGETABLES: artichokes, avocados, garlic, greens, radicchio

My recipes showcase these ingredients, all of them identified with the lush and sunny heartland of California—truly, the land of milk and honey. This is rustic, wine-friendly, and wine-inclusive cuisine, with a large selection of filling little bites to partner with extended sipping. In locavore-friendly style, chapters are organized by the provenance of the ingredients. Recipes are tailored to the home cook yet have a sophisticated, wine-savvy sensibility. Think Chuck Williams meets Suzanne Goin, with James Beard looking benevolently over their shoulders.

RECIPE NOTE: For decades, cookbook recipes have used standard, large eggs in order to ensure consistency, but pasture raised eggs come in all sizes. A large egg, sans shell, weighs 2 fluid ounces, or equals 4 tablespoons (1 ounce/2 tablespoons of egg white, and 1 ounce/2 tablespoons of egg yolk). So if a recipe calls for 5 egg whites, you should measure out 5 fluid ounces/10 tablespoons of egg white.

RECIPE NOTE: For quantities of butter 2 tablespoons or less, salted or unsalted make no difference, at least in my opinion. In larger quantities (if it matters) I have specified.

ABOUT THE WINE PAIRINGS

I live in a community where wine is taken very, very seriously. I often tell visitors that people here "eat, drink, think, and talk wine during most of their waking hours."

Pairing wine with food is an art, not a science—and it should always allow room for a small element of humor. This is, after all, not brain surgery, and drinking wine should, at the end of the day (right around magic hour) be all about enjoyment.

I have spent a lifetime pursuing my own passion: food. When it comes to wine, I know what I like, but my understanding is less developed. So I asked some hugely talented people in the wine and food world here to lend a hand, and was lucky enough to lure in a really spectacular wine gang. For each dish, there are two choices: one from the Central Coast, and one from somewhere else in the world. Where no specific vineyard is designated, grapes may be either 100 percent estate produced, sourced from multiple vineyards, or a combination. For blended (cuvée) wines, grape varieties are given in descending order of content.

Ali Carscarden is a master sommelier and proprietress of the sophisticated wine shop 15°C, in Templeton, and she gives very detailed choices in one of the most important chapters in the book: Magic Hour Grazing. Sonja Magdevski, winemaker at Casa Dumetz (her tasting room is the hottest spot in the captivating little town of Los Alamos), had arguably the toughest job: matching wines with vegetable and fruit dishes. She stepped deliciously outside the box with her tempting lineup. Cris Cherry grew up in a restaurant family, and his restaurant Villa Creek was one of the first places one could taste an array of global wines in the formerly dusty cow town of Paso Robles. He supplied the pairings for the From the Field and Barnyard chapter with the unflinching approach of a man who really knows his stuff. Stephan Asseo, owner-winemaker of L'Aventure (and a former chef) is a fierce lover of both fish and exquisite red wines. I knew that asking him to make the pairings for the From the Sea chapter would produce some eye-opening surprises, and I was right. Wes Hagen, winemaker at Clos Pepe, wears his passion for wine and food on his sleeve and came up with gutsy choices in the From the Ranch (meat) chapter, giving me a subtle dig for adding a citrus note to a braised beef dish. Chris and Shandi Kobayashi, of the locavore mecca restaurant Artisan, in Paso Robles, tackled the local choices for the dairy chapter with savvy and enthusiasm, asking me to supply the wine choices from elsewhere. And for the From the Wood-Fired Oven chapter, Frank Ostini and Anne Twigg of the Hitching Post II restaurant, in Buellton (made infamous in the region-altering film *Sideways*), plumbed the oaky-smoky depths of our region's biggest wines.

Enjoy!

CHAPTER 1

Magic-Hour Grazing

In wine country, "magic hour" refers to that golden, relaxed time between the activity of the day and dinner. We like to stretch it out to more than just an hour, and that means every host needs a trusty repertoire of delicious, user- and wine-friendly snacks. Cheese is a natural partner for wine, and you'll see a lot of it in this chapter. Christina Maguire (Rinconada Dairy, in Santa Margarita) makes some of the finest. Antonio Varia (chef-owner of Buona Tavola Italian restaurant, in Paso Robles) began making small-batch cured meats under the name Allesina in 2010. Using no nitrates or preservatives, he creates to-die-for salumi, sausages, and a decadent, soft salami spread called n'duja. If you are simply too relaxed to contemplate cooking (even one of the many simple preparations in this chapter), then a selection of perfectly ripened honest cheeses and salumi will take you happily through the golden hour to dinnertime.

Wine pairings by Ali Carscarden of 15°C

Sheep's Cheese Gougères

These crisp little puffs are like rich, cheese-flavored air. If you have some dry-aged ham on hand (serrano, prosciutto, Virginia country ham), split a gougère like a sandwich and put a little sliver of ham in the middle. You'll thank me. The make-ahead bonus here: Let the finished dough (called *pâte à choux*, in French) stand, covered, for up to an hour before forming and finishing the cheesy puffs.   MAKES ABOUT 30 SMALL PUFFS

Preheat the oven to 425°F and line a baking sheet with parchment paper. (Or use nonstick baking sheets.)

In a saucepan, combine the milk, water, butter, salt, and a bit of pepper. Place over high heat and simmer until the butter is melted. Remove from the heat and dump in the flour all at once; immediately stir energetically (and constantly) until the mixture pulls away from the sides of the pan and starts to look smooth, 1 to 2 minutes. Return the pan to the heat for 1 minute, continuing to stir vigorously; remove again and let rest for about 3 minutes.

Add the eggs, one at a time, stirring quickly and thoroughly to fully incorporate each one before adding the next. The batter will first appear lumpy, but after a minute or so will become thick, shiny, and smooth. Add the rosemary and cheese; stir until fully blended. (At this point, you may cover the pan and let the dough stand for up to 1 hour before finishing the puffs.)

Using two teaspoons, make approximately 1-tablespoon mounds on the prepared baking sheet, leaving about 1 inch between the mounds.

Bake for 10 minutes, then turn the oven down to 375°F and bake for 20 to 25 minutes more, until the puffs are doubled in size and a lovely golden brown all over, including the sides. Serve warm. (Or reheat the cooled cheese puffs in a low oven for 5 to 10 minutes before serving; don't overdo it or they will be very dry.)

¼ cup whole milk

¼ cup water

4 tablespoons unsalted butter, cut into cubes

¼ teaspoon fine sea salt

Freshly ground black pepper

½ cup all-purpose flour

2 eggs

¾ teaspoon minced fresh rosemary

¾ cup grated Central Coast sheep's cheese, or a young pecorino or Manchego (about 3 ounces)

CENTRAL COAST: Clavo Vermentino "Voluptuous," Paso Robles
FARTHER AFIELD: Costamolino Vermentino, Sardinia, Italy

Melon Wedges with Orzo and Blue Cheese Salad

Neon orange melon lends visual spark to the creamy white pasta mixture, while earthy blue cheese is a fantastic partner for the cool, sweet fruit. If your event calls for plated appetizers, simply cut crosswise circles of melon, remove the seeds, and place a large scoop of the cheesy salad in the center. The salad may be made up to 8 hours ahead; the melon wedges may be cut, covered with plastic wrap, and refrigerated for up to 4 hours. MAKES ABOUT 40 BITES

6 ounces mild blue cheese, at room temperature

3 tablespoons fresh lemon juice

2 tablespoons Dijon mustard

½ cup heavy cream

2 large shallots, finely chopped (about ½ cup)

1 celery rib, finely diced

¼ cup finely chopped fresh flat-leaf parsley

Freshly ground black pepper

4 ounces orzo (or use small elbow macaroni)

1 small ripe cantaloupe

Bring a large pan of lightly salted water to a boil for the orzo. In a large bowl, combine the blue cheese, lemon juice, and mustard. Mash with a fork until the cheese is broken up but still quite lumpy. Whisk in the cream and then add the shallots, celery, and parsley. Mix well and add black pepper to taste. Taste for salt and add a little, if necessary.

Cook the orzo in the boiling water until al dente, according to the package directions. Drain in a colander and then rinse thoroughly with cold water to remove excess starch. Shake the colander well, and toss the drained pasta with the cheese mixture.

Slice the cantaloupe in half crosswise and scoop out all the seeds. Cut each half into ½-inch rounds and then trim away the outer peel, leaving a large, flat doughnut shape. Cut each circle into 6 equal wedges. (There will be some off cuts from the ends that are not usable; eat them!)

Place the cantaloupe wedges on a large platter and top each with about a tablespoon of the pasta salad.

CENTRAL COAST: Bodegas M Albariño, Paso Robles
FARTHER AFIELD: Paco & Lola Albariño, Rias Baixas, Spain

Rainbow Radishes
with Anchovy Butter

Radishes are served with sweet butter throughout France, from Provence to Paris. Tart and cool radishes are perfectly paired with rich and creamy butter. At the farmer's market, look for white, black, French Breakfast, and Misato Rose radishes. Every day it seems there are new (old) radishes to feast our eyes and taste buds upon.

The radishes may be refrigerated, uncovered, for up to 2 hours before serving. Here, the quality of the butter is crucial; please use French or Irish butter, or cultured butter, or goat butter. If you don't have a piping bag, use a heavy plastic bag, like a zip-top one: Push the softened butter firmly into one lower corner of the bag, twist the top, and snip about ½ inch off the corner of the bag. Squeeze the butter through the small corner opening. SERVES 8 TO 10

In a small bowl, stir together the butter, anchovies, and 1 teaspoon of the dill until evenly combined. Spoon the butter into a pastry bag fitted with a small tip, forcing the butter down as far as possible toward the tip end of the bag before twisting the top closed. Chill for at least 30 minutes and up to overnight. (If refrigerated overnight, return to room temperature for 20 minutes before piping.)

Arrange the cold, halved radishes on a platter with the cut sides up. Pipe a small dollop of the butter in the center of each half. Scatter with the remaining 1 teaspoon dill, and pass at once. (If likely to stand on a party table for more than 30 minutes, place the radishes on a bed of crushed ice.)

CENTRAL COAST: Il Campo "White," Paso Robles (Tocai Fruliano, Moscato Bianco from vineyards next to my house, and Chardonnay from the famed James Berry Vineyard—A.C.)
FARTHER AFIELD: Gini Soave Classico, Soave, Italy

½ cup (4 ounces) best-quality unsalted butter, softened

1½ tablespoons minced anchovies

2 teaspoons finely chopped fresh dill

16 radishes, washed, stem and root ends trimmed flat, and halved crosswise, very cold

Warm Sheep's Milk Ricotta and Tomato Tartlets

Old way: Make brioche dough from scratch in order to bring the rich goodness of butter to these delicately cheesy, bite-size confections (elapsed time: 3 hours). New way: Drench little circles of tortilla in melted butter for the exact same effect (elapsed time: 10 minutes). Never used mini muffin pans as a shortcut to casually elegant finger food? It's time to invest in a couple of 24-cup tins. (A nonstick surface is unnecessary with this level of butter content, but probably a good investment for all the other things you'll do with this piece of equipment!)   MAKES 48 BITES

In a bowl, combine the ricotta, shallot, chives, half the parsley, ½ teaspoon salt, and plenty of pepper. Use a fork to whisk until evenly blended.

Preheat the oven to 350°F. Use a 2-inch cookie cutter to cut 8 or 9 rounds from each of the tortillas; you should have about 48 rounds. In a baking dish, drench the tortilla rounds in the melted butter, turning to be sure all sides are evenly coated. Press each circle down firmly into the cups of mini muffin pans (or small tartlet pans). Bake for 8 to 10 minutes, until just starting to turn golden. Set aside in their pans to cool briefly. Leave the oven on (or you may prepare the shells ahead of time and warm the tartlets just before serving time).

Spoon 1 mounded teaspoon of the ricotta mixture into each tartlet shell and top with a pinch of the sun-dried tomatoes. Return to the oven for a few minutes just to warm through. Transfer to a platter, scatter the remaining half of the parsley over all, and serve immediately.

NOTE: Sheep's milk ricotta can be hard to find; if it's not available, whisk about ½ cup finely grated Manchego into 8 ounces of whole-milk ricotta.

CENTRAL COAST: Tablas Creek "Patelin Blanc," Paso Robles (Grenache Blanc, Viognier, Roussanne, Marsanne)
FARTHER AFIELD: Faury Saint Joseph Blanc, Northern Rhône, France

10 ounces whole-milk ricotta, preferably sheep's milk (see Note)

1 small shallot, very finely chopped

3 tablespoons finely snipped fresh chives

3 tablespoons finely chopped fresh flat-leaf parsley

Fine sea salt and freshly ground black pepper

6 (8-inch) flour tortillas

¾ cup (6 ounces) salted or unsalted butter, melted

3 ounces plump and juicy sun-dried tomatoes, cut into small dice

Caramelized Onion, Anchovy, and Sun-Dried Tomato Pissaladières

A favorite in the south of France, pissaladière is a no-cheese French take on pizza that scales untold heights of deliciousness due to the rich flavor of puff pastry. These powerfully tasty little squares can stand up to a big wine, like a GSM (local-speak for the Rhône-style Grenache-Syrah-Mourvedre blend).

Be sure to thaw the puff pastry for 1 to 2 hours, at room temperature. For this recipe, you will not be rolling the pastry out any farther, so all you have to do is remove it from the package and unfold. If you caramelize the onions and thaw the pastry ahead of time, these morsels can be on the platter and in guests' mouths in 20 minutes. If you are anti-anchovy, substitute oil-cured black olives, pitted and quartered. MAKES TWENTY-FOUR 2-BITE PIECES

2 tablespoons extra-virgin olive oil

1 tablespoon butter

2 large sweet onions (about 2 pounds), trimmed, halved lengthwise, and slivered

Fine sea salt and freshly ground black pepper

2 sprigs fresh thyme

4 garlic cloves, very finely chopped

About 1 pound frozen puff pastry (two 10 by 15-inch sheets), fully thawed

8 to 9 ounces (about 1½ cups) plump, juicy sun-dried tomatoes, cut into julienne strips

12 to 24 oil-packed anchovies, well drained and halved lengthwise

1½ tablespoons capers

1 egg, lightly beaten

5 to 7 leaves fresh basil, torn into small pieces

Warm the olive oil and butter in a large frying pan over medium-low heat. Add the onions, season with ¾ teaspoon salt, ¼ teaspoon pepper, and the thyme; stir together. Cover and cook very gently until tender and juicy, about 30 minutes. Stir occasionally but not too often; a steamy environment is crucial. Uncover the pan and continue to cook gently, now stirring more frequently, until all the excess moisture has evaporated and the mixture resembles a thick jam, 10 to 15 minutes longer. Stir in the garlic and cook for 1 to 2 minutes more, just to release the aroma. Remove the remains of the thyme sprigs.

Line two large baking sheets with baking parchment (or use nonstick baking sheets).

Unfold the puff pastry sheets, and with a long, sharp knife, cut each one into 3 rectangles, cutting along the fold lines. Cut each rectangle cross-wise into 4 squares, to yield a total of 24 squares of pastry. Transfer 12 squares to each baking sheet. Spread a spoonful of the onion mixture in the center of each rectangle, smoothing it flat, and top with a few slivers of sun-dried tomato. Arrange one or two anchovy strips (to taste) on the top and place a few capers on either side of the anchovy.

Refrigerate for 15 minutes while you preheat the oven to 400°F (ideally, set to convection mode).

Brush the exposed edges of each rectangle with the beaten egg. Bake for 12 to 15 minutes, until the pastry edges are golden brown and nicely puffed. Scatter with a few little pieces of basil and serve at once.

CENTRAL COAST: Clesi Malvasia, Monterey
FARTHER AFIELD: Fieudi Fiano d'Avellino, Avellino, Italy

Rosemary-Tangerine Breadsticks with Orange Salt

These are absolutely essential nibbling for an extended afternoon of wine tasting. Why make your own breadsticks? Because they simply sing with the flavor of citrus and rosemary, just like a rocky hillside on the Central Coast just above the retro-beachy town of Cayucos. If Hawaiian orange salt is unavailable, substitute smoked black salt, sea salt flakes, or even kosher salt.

MAKES 32 BREADSTICKS

1 envelope (¼ ounce) active dry yeast

1 teaspoon sugar

1 cup warm water (about 110°F)

¼ cup extra-virgin olive oil, plus more for brushing the dough and for serving (optional)

11¼ ounces bread flour (2¼ cups), or more as needed

½ cup semolina flour

Finely grated zest of 1 tangerine or orange

1½ teaspoons finely chopped fresh rosemary

1 teaspoon fine sea salt

1 egg, lightly beaten with a pinch of salt

Hawaiian Alaea (orange) salt or sea salt, for sprinkling

In a large measuring cup, combine the yeast, sugar, and ½ cup of the water and stir to dissolve. Let stand for about 10 minutes, or until the yeast mixture forms a frothy head. Stir in the remaining ½ cup water and the olive oil.

In the bowl of a food processor, combine the flour, semolina, zest, rosemary, and sea salt and pulse to combine. With the motor running, add the yeast mixture through the feed tube in a steady stream; take about 10 seconds to pour it in. Process for 10 seconds more, by which time the dough should form a rough mass on the stem. If the dough is too wet and forms a mass right away, remove the cover and sprinkle 2 tablespoons of bread flour on the dough. If it is too dry and has not formed a ball on the stem within 15 seconds, sprinkle with 1 to 2 teaspoons water. Process for 10 seconds more. Let stand with the cover on for 20 minutes.

Pulse for 5 seconds more, then turn out onto a lightly floured surface. The dough should be slightly soft but not sticky. Cover with a clean plastic bag and let rest for 20 minutes.

Generously oil a rimmed baking sheet. Begin stretching, pushing, and pulling the dough with your fingertips and the heel of your hand into an 8 by 12-inch rectangle. This will take a little while—the dough will be tight at first, so give it a chance to relax. Transfer the dough to the prepared baking sheet and brush the top of the dough with oil. Cover with the plastic bag and allow to rise in a warm, draft-free place for about 45 minutes, or until puffy.

continued on page 12

Preheat the oven to 400°F.

Transfer the dough to a cutting board (do not flour the board) and cut it crosswise into 4 equal sections. Cut each section crosswise into 8 little strips and roll each one under the palms of your hands into a thin rope about 12 inches long. Transfer to the oiled baking sheet, forming curlicues if desired. Brush with the beaten egg and sprinkle each one with orange salt.

Bake for 15 to 20 minutes, until slightly golden. Do this in batches if necessary, keeping the unrolled strips covered and rolling them out just before baking. Serve warm with a little dish of your best extra-virgin olive oil, or cool on racks and serve at room temperature.

NOTE: The breadsticks will keep in an airtight container for up to 2 weeks. To serve after they have been stored for a few days, reheat at 350°F on a dry baking sheet for 10 to 15 minutes.

CENTRAL COAST: L'Aventure Rosé (Syrah, Cabernet Sauvignon)
FARTHER AFIELD: Trinquevedel Tavel Rosé, Southern Rhône, France

Smoky Sizzled Almonds

Paso Robles was the almond capital of the world for generations. Many of the almond trees that were once ubiquitous have been torn out to make room for grapevines, and the wood now stokes hearty and aromatic fires during the brief but intense chill of winter. These addictive, value-added nuts are my kind of party food—practically all you have to do is the shopping! Plus, the almonds may be prepared way ahead of time. SERVES 6 TO 8

Combine the smoked paprika, ground chipotle, and salt in a heatproof bowl. Place a large skillet over medium heat and add the butter and olive oil. When the butter foam has subsided, add the almonds and stir occasionally for 6 to 7 minutes, until aromatic and beginning to brown (they will make little popping noises). Dump the almonds and all the oil into the spice-salt mixture and keep tossing until the salt has dissolved (this will take a minute or three).

Serve warm, or let cool completely, tossing every 5 minutes or so. Toss once again right before serving to distribute the spicy oil. (Or, cool and place in an airtight container, then freeze for up to 3 months. Thaw in the same container, then spread on a baking sheet and toast for 15 minutes in a 275°F oven to re-crisp before serving warm or at room temperature.)

CENTRAL COAST: Denner Vineyards Rosé, Paso Robles (Mourvedre, Grenache, Counoise)
FARTHER AFIELD: Muga Rosé, Rioja, Spain

¾ teaspoon smoked paprika

½ teaspoon ground chipotle or 1½ teaspoons hot or mild pure chile powder

2 tablespoons coarse sea salt

2 tablespoons butter, preferably cultured or Irish

¼ cup extra-virgin olive oil, preferably from the Central Coast

1 pound (about 2½ cups) whole raw almonds

Rancho La Viña Walnuts and La Nogalera Walnut Oil

Farming is a dying art form in the United States. A hundred years ago, 95 percent of the population had a connection to the land. Today, that number is 1 percent. Jose Baer, president of Rancho La Viña in the Santa Rita Hills, understands this implicitly. He is the fifth generation to take over the family business since 1869, and his primary goal is simply to continue farming. He organically farms 2,800 acres of heirloom tomatoes, zucchini, snap peas, green beans, and various other vegetables (as well as some Pinot Noir vines). But his walnut trees are his top concern. Between the Santa Rita Hills and the Santa Ynez Valley, Baer farms a total of 250 acres of walnuts. He is one of the last of his kind to tend the heritage varieties of Concord, Placentia, Payne, and Lompoc that have fallen out of favor to the newer, larger, lighter, and more durable commercial varieties, such as Chandler.

The United States is the world's second-largest producer of walnuts, and California grows 99 percent of the crop, yet you'd be hard pressed to find a commercial grower who has even heard of the varieties Baer still nurtures. Known as coastal varieties, they are smaller, darker, and packed with intense flavor. Most of his youngest trees are 50 years old. What has saved them thus far is the booming popularity of the farmer's markets in central and Southern California, where people can actually taste the difference. "This has allowed us to hang on to our last trees," Baer says. "These walnuts are grown in the similar climate as world-class grapes in our area. The cool, coastal climate allows for greater flavor development."

In the past, Baer and other walnut ranches in this area sold only by contract to the Diamond nut company. When the company went public, he and a few others opted out of the cooperative. This somewhat frightening new independence allowed the growers to explore the opportunity to add value to their product and connect directly with consumers. Fellow coastal walnut ranchers Art Hibbits and Mary Jane Edalatpour were the first to try their hands at walnut oil. After intensive research, tasting, and testing, their first batch was so delicious and promising that they joined forces with Baer to grow their walnut oil concept. Today the steady growth of their La Nogalera walnut oil is fueled by their passionate desire to remain farmers and protectors of their treasured heritage walnut trees, some of the last of their kind. Future generations deserve the chance to appreciate these ancient trees.

Known as coastal varieties, they are smaller, darker, and packed with intense flavor.

Harvesting walnuts—and getting them to the consumer—is no easy task. First, the trees are shaken and the walnuts, which are covered in a protective green outer husk, fall to the ground. A large sweeper comes through and collects the walnuts into bins, which are then shipped to processors, who remove the outer green shell as well as the wrinkled inner shell that surrounds the coveted walnut meat. For fresh walnuts sold through Rancho La Viña, the raw walnuts are then packaged and kept in cool storage.

The walnuts destined for oil are shipped to an oil processor, where they are toasted, crushed, and pressed with an artisan hydraulic press (this is known as the French process; it's similar to a bladder press in the wine-making world). Again, similar to the best wine, only the free-run and lightly pressed oils are used for the La Nogalera line, to avoid any possible bitterness. This process also removes the need for any chemicals or additives—all that's in the bottle is pure, unadulterated walnut oil from coastal heritage walnut trees.

The perfect way to enjoy both the walnuts and the oil? Take a yummy tip from Edalatpour for a truly irresistible combination: Crush toasted walnuts over a bowl of vanilla ice cream and top it with drizzled La Nogalera walnut oil.

IF YOU VISIT:

The best place to experience Rancho La Viña walnuts and La Nogalera walnut oil is through local farmer's markets, specifically in Santa Barbara, Santa Monica, Ojai, and Hollywood. (Find a full listing here: www.cafarmersmarkets.com.)

You may also purchase online, at www.lanogalerawalnutoil.com.

Black Olive
and Pine Nut Biscotti

When I made these cheese-a-licious adult "cookies" for a Christmas open house, they disappeared in a minute flat. Lesson learned: Double the recipe. Shatteringly crisp and as powerful as the surf at San Simeon after a storm, they'll have you reaching for a glass of wine with some sun-kissed muscle.   MAKES 36 TO 40 BITES

4 cups all-purpose flour,
plus more for dusting

2 teaspoons baking powder

2 teaspoons fine sea salt, plus a pinch

1¼ cups finely grated Grana
Padano or best-quality Parmigiano-
Reggiano, finely grated

½ cup pine nuts, finely chopped

½ cup oil-cured black olives,
pitted and minced

½ teaspoon coarsely ground black
pepper, plus more for seasoning

¾ cup (6 ounces) cold unsalted
butter, cut into ½-inch cubes

4 eggs

1 cup whole milk

Place the oven racks in the upper and lower thirds of the oven and pre-heat it to 350°F.

In a food processor, combine the flour, baking powder, salt, 1 cup of the cheese, the pine nuts, olives, and the pepper. Pulse briefly to combine, then scatter the butter evenly over the top and pulse in short bursts until the mixture resembles coarse, crumbly meal. Whisk 3 eggs with the milk, drizzle evenly over the mixture, and pulse briefly to form a soft dough.

Turn the dough out onto a lightly floured surface and divide into 4 equal pieces. Using well-floured hands, form each piece into a slightly flattened log about 12 inches long, 2 inches wide, and ¾ inch high. Carefully transfer 2 logs to a large, ungreased baking sheet, placing them about 3 inches apart. Repeat with the remaining logs and another baking sheet.

Whisk the remaining egg with the pinch of salt, then brush a little egg over each log; sprinkle the tops evenly with the remaining ¼ cup cheese and a little more pepper. Bake, rotating the sheets 180 degrees and switching their positions in the oven halfway through cooking, until the logs are pale golden and firm, about 30 minutes total. Let cool slightly, about 10 minutes.

Reduce the oven temperature to 300°F.

Carefully transfer a warm log to a cutting board and use a bread knife to cut ½-inch-thick slices on the diagonal; transfer the slices to a baking sheet in a single layer. Repeat with the remaining logs. Bake until crisp, 35 to 45 minutes total, turning over once about halfway through. Ideally, cool the biscotti on racks to keep them nice and crisp, for about 15 min-utes, although cooling them on the baking sheets is fine.

If not serving immediately, layer between sheets of parchment paper and store in an airtight container for up to 7 days. To serve, re-crisp the biscotti on a baking sheet at 350°F for 5 minutes, not more than 1 hour before serving time.

CENTRAL COAST: Villa Creek "White," Paso Robles (Grenache Blanc, Roussanne, Picpoul Blanc)
FARTHER AFIELD: Janasse Côtes du Rhône Blanc, Southern Rhône, France

White Anchovies with Cool Endive Salad on Crostini

Increasing the level of appreciation for white anchovies has been a personal PR campaign of mine since I lived in Spain in the 1990s. Juicy, mild, plump, and ever-so-gently acidic, they are to standard anchovies as a dip in the Pacific is to a hot mud bath. (Both are nice, in their way, but they couldn't be less alike.) Luckily, Pier 46 in Templeton and Di Raimondo's in downtown Paso Robles always have some on hand. Do not substitute standard anchovies.   MAKES 28 BITES

2 large or 3 small, unblemished heads Belgian endive (about 8 ounces)

Finely gated zest of 2 Meyer lemons or 1 standard (Eureka) lemon

¼ cup coarsely chopped fresh flat-leaf parsley

4 tablespoons best-quality extra-virgin olive oil, preferably a green and fruity variety

Freshly ground black pepper

1 (8-ounce) French or sourdough baguette, cut into ½-inch slices (about 28)

Fine sea salt

⅓ cup store-bought or homemade mayonnaise

1½ teaspoons fresh lemon juice (Meyer or standard)

1 large garlic clove, minced or pushed through a press

¼ teaspoon smoked paprika

3 ounces mild Spanish white anchovies (available at specialty markets and Web sites such as www.latienda.com; sometimes called *boquerones en vinaigre*)

¼ to ½ teaspoon Hawaiian Alaea (orange) salt

With a sharp knife, quarter the endive lengthwise and trim away the core. Thinly sliver each quarter crosswise. In a metal mixing bowl, combine the endive, lemon zest, parsley, 2 tablespoons of the olive oil, and plenty of pepper. Toss thoroughly to combine. Cover and refrigerate for 1 hour to chill.

Preheat the oven to 350°F.

Arrange the baguette slices on a baking sheet and brush lightly with the remaining 2 tablespoons olive oil; season lightly with salt and pepper. Bake for 10 to 15 minutes, until golden. Transfer to a serving platter and let cool for 10 minutes. Whisk together the mayonnaise, lemon juice, garlic, and smoked paprika. Spread each piece of bread with a little of the mayonnaise mixture and mound a spoonful of the salad on top of each.

Quarter the anchovies lengthwise and drape 3 or 4 slivers across each spoonful of salad. Scatter each crostino with a few grains of orange salt to taste and serve immediately.

CENTRAL COAST: Zocker Grüner Veltliner, Edna Valley
FARTHER AFIELD: Hiedler Grüner Veltliner, Kamptal, Austria

Shatteringly Crisp Fried Zucchini Blossoms with Truffle Salt

Before I realized that the terrain of California's Central Coast is as close as you can get to Tuscany without leaving the USA, I spent several summers in a row in the Chianti region of Tuscany. In the Oltrarno neighborhood of Florence is a little restaurant called Cinghiale Bianco, where I experienced the crispest, most elemental and ethereal squash blossoms imaginable. The secret? Simple and true and honest: Don't stuff them. The delicate walls of the blossom can't stand up to a heavy stuffing and easily turn soggy. An empty blossom is light and innocent, with no heavy baggage—like Liv Tyler in *Stealing Beauty*.

MAKES 18 STUFFED BLOSSOMS

Pour the club soda into a bowl. In a sifter or sieve, combine the flour, cornstarch, and sea salt; sift this into the club soda and whisk until evenly blended. The mixture should be the consistency of thin pancake batter. Add a little more soda, if necessary, to thin. Cover and refrigerate for 45 minutes.

Meanwhile, gently pull open the tops of the zucchini blossoms and pull out the orange pistils (they're bitter).

Line a platter with a flattened brown paper grocery bag or baking parchment, and throw on some lemon wedges.

Fill a tall, heavy pot halfway full with a mix of half canola oil and half olive oil (or prepare a deep fryer); heat the oil to 350°F. Dip and roll a blossom in the batter, making sure to coat it well. Using the stem as a handle, very carefully submerge it in the hot oil and hold for about 10 seconds before you let it go (this allows the batter to seize, and stops the blossom from sticking to the pot). Proceed with dipping and frying the blossoms; as soon as one is golden brown, remove with a skimmer and allow to drain briefly for a few seconds, then transfer to the platter to drain. Sprinkle with a little truffle salt, and pass the blossoms as they are finished. This way, you can squeeze a little lemon over each blossom immediately before eating (if you squeeze too early, the lemon juice will make the coating soggy).

CENTRAL COAST: Ranchero Cellars "Chrome," Paso Robles (Grenache Blanc, Viognier)
FARTHER AFIELD: E. Guigal Condrieu, Northern Rhône, France

7 ounces club soda, or as needed

⅔ cup all-purpose flour

3 tablespoons cornstarch

1½ teaspoons fine sea salt

18 zucchini blossoms, ideally with a length of stem still attached

1½ lemons, cut into wedges, for serving

Canola oil, as needed

Extra-virgin olive oil, as needed

Truffle salt, for serving

NOTE: This is an interactive dish that should be attempted early in the evening only. Hot oil doesn't mix with anything beyond the first glass of wine.

Ancient Peaks

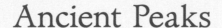

I was bouncing around in a dusty pickup truck, midway through a tour of one of the most historically important ranches in this corner of the great state of California, the former Spanish land grant known as Santa Margarita ranch. Inside the truck, it was cool as the air conditioner did its noisy job; outside, the dry, 101°F heat baked 14,000 acres of iconic California peaks and pasture. Here in the calcium-rich soil you can still spot huge, clearly visible oyster shells—from the days when the entire area was ocean bottom, millions of years ago. And the relative newcomers to this ancient land: 1,000 acres of thriving vineyards, dotted with towering oak trees.

About 10,000 years ago, this plateau was occupied by two tribes: the Chumash and the Salinans. In the late 1700s, the Spaniards erected one of the first stone-and-mortar buildings in the territory, the Asistencia de Cortona, which still stands today. It was destined to become a mission, providing a needed link between the missions in San Luis Obispo and San Antonio. Santa Margarita became the breadbasket for missions up and down the coast, shipping grain, cattle, sheep, and hogs from Santa Barbara to Monterey. Mexico secularized the missions after seceding from Spain in the 1820s, and anyone who was a member of the "lucky sperm club" was granted huge swathes of land. One of the many stewards of this land, Joaquin Estrada (the governor's nephew at the time of secession), was a Spaniard, a Mexican, and an American—all in one lifetime.

For 200 years, this was open rangeland. In 1999, the ranch was bought by Rob Rossi, and later his partners Doug Filipponi and Karl Wittstrom. The new owners understood the ravages wrought by continuous grazing, and they began to rotate the cattle that have always been the lifeblood of this ranch. Rotational grazing allowed tiny oak trees to grow under the majestic oaks that have stood here for hundreds of years. More important, it allowed green and nutritious native grasses to thrive. Healthy, antibiotic-free, grass-fed cattle are the result.

Here in the calcium-rich soil you can still spot huge, clearly visible oyster shells . . .

Grapevines had been cultivated and wine made here since the time of the mission, but in 1999 the Mondavi family developed an ambitious plan. They bought a 35-year lease from the partners and planted more than 900 acres of vines, at 908 plants per acre with 8 by 6-foot spacing. But then came 9/11, and the wine business faltered—the Mondavis eventually lost control of the land. The partners bought back the lease and began grafting Sauvignon Blanc, Chardonnay, Roussanne, Pinot Grigio, Riesling, Petit Verdot, Grenache, and Pinot Noir onto the original six varietals.

"We initially sold all of the fruit from Margarita Vineyard, but we could taste what other winemakers were doing with it," says owner Karl Wittstrom. "It was pretty obvious that this was a special vineyard, and that's what inspired us to establish Ancient Peaks Winery, and to become vintners as well as vine growers."

Along with award-winning winemaker Mike Sinor, the partners set out to aggressively pursue the potential first imagined before the most recent turn of the century. "I grew up a mile from the edge of this amazing ranch, and worked here back in 1977," says owner Doug Filipponi with awe and respect. "I can't believe I'm raising cattle and making wine here now." Wittstrom's daughter Amanda is VP of sales and marketing (photo above). The ranch employs about 75 people on any given day. There is *always* something going on.

There is no more perfect way to experience the stunning beauty of this ranch than to hop on the new zip line and skim silently across the tops of the historic oaks, between those ancient peaks. And then, of course, sip a glass of their excellent wine at magic hour (the light and gorgeously bracing Pinot Noir rosé is my own favorite).

IF YOU VISIT:

The Ancient Peaks tasting room is located on the main drag in the tiny, charming town of Santa Margarita. It's open every day from 11 a.m. to 5:30 p.m. (Fascinating) vineyard tours are every Saturday at 1:30 p.m.

The spectacular, not-to-be-missed zip line takes off Thursday through Sunday at 10:30 a.m., 1 p.m., and 3:30 p.m. Reservations at (805) 438-3120.

www.margarita-adventures.com

www.ancientpeaks.com

Instant Gravlax with Pomegranate Molasses and Fig Balsamic Vinegar

Californians have been serving salmon for dinner since 1925, which was also the year my grandmother emigrated from New York. But in recent years, we've come to understand that access to salmon is a luxury—one that must increasingly be earned via sustainable methods and periodically by full restraint. Farmed salmon may tempt with its price, but please refrain: The texture is most often unappealingly mushy, the coloring artificial, and the flavor pale by comparison with wild fish. Cherish wild Pacific Coast salmon whenever you can. This dish showcases the best salmon in pure and simple form, with no need to wait for the gravlax to "cure." Please don't attempt it with farmed fish. MAKES ABOUT 40 SMALL BITES

1¼ pounds wild salmon (small end pieces are fine)

½ cup extra-virgin olive oil

2 tablespoons fig balsamic vinegar or other rich and fruity balsamic vinegar

2 tablespoons pomegranate molasses/syrup (available at well-stocked and Middle Eastern markets)

2 tablespoons fresh lemon juice

Fine sea salt and freshly ground black pepper

36 to 40 pumpernickel cocktail squares

About ¾ cup (6 ounces) lightly salted butter, preferably cultured or Irish, softened

Black lava salt (optional)

Seeds from 1 pomegranate

Sprigs from a small bunch of fresh dill, torn into small pieces

Freeze the salmon on a plate for 30 to 40 minutes, to make it easier to slice.

In a medium shallow decorative glass or ceramic bowl (or on a small platter), whisk together the olive oil, vinegar, molasses, lemon juice, ½ teaspoon salt, and plenty of pepper. With a long, flexible, very sharp knife, slice the salmon thinly and evenly. Add the salmon slices to the bowl and toss with tongs to distribute the "cure" evenly. Cover with plastic wrap and refrigerate for 30 minutes.

Evenly spread each pumpernickel square with a little butter and arrange the squares on a large platter. Scatter the salmon with the lava salt, pomegranate seeds, and dill, and place the bowl of salmon next to the platter (or at one end, if your platter is long enough). Serve with small tongs, so each guest can mound a small pile of salmon on each pumpernickel square (or, you can assemble the squares yourself and arrange them on a large platter).

CENTRAL COAST: Daou Chardonnay, Paso Robles
FARTHER AFIELD: Olivier Savary Chablis, Burgundy, France

Roquefort and Rhône in Radicchio Cups

I admit that at first this dish was all about alliteration. Had it not worked out beautifully, I would have pronounced it history. But late on a hot summer afternoon, my talented culinary buddy Renaud L'homme helped me find the ratio and flavor loudly pronounced "Keeper!" by all the sophisticated palates then present.

The radicchio "cups" need not be formed from a full-size leaf—any portion of the leaf will do, as long as it's a concave shape that will hold a little mound of the salad mixture. If the only leeks you can find are big and fat, substitute about 2 tablespoons minced shallot (about 1 medium) or red onion. The assembled cups may be refrigerated for up to 1 hour. If you do this, let them stand at room temperature for about 10 minutes before serving, to awaken the flavors. SERVES 6 TO 8

In a small saucepan, simmer the wine until it's reduced to 1 to 2 tablespoons of syrupy liquid. Let cool (the liquid will thicken even more).

Once the liquid has cooled, whisk in ¼ teaspoon salt, plenty of pepper, the sugar, vinegar, and the two oils. In a bowl, combine the leek, figs, pears, walnuts, and Roquefort. Drizzle the vinaigrette over the top and fold together gently to blend and evenly coat with the vinaigrette.

Remove and discard any blemished leaves from the outside of the radicchio. Separate the largest outer leaves/pieces carefully, keeping them relatively intact. You should have about 18 cupped leaves (save the smaller, inner leaves for a salad). Arrange the cups on a platter and mound about 2 tablespoons of the salad into each cup. Refrigerate for up to 1 hour, if desired; but remove from the fridge 5 to 10 minutes before serving.

CENTRAL COAST: Claiborne & Churchill Riesling, Edna Valley
FARTHER AFIELD: Kuentz Bas Riesling, Alsace, France

1 cup Rhône-style red wine, such as a blend of Grenache, Syrah, and Mourvedre

Fine sea salt and freshly ground black pepper

¼ teaspoon sugar

1½ tablespoons red wine vinegar

¼ cup extra-virgin olive oil

2 tablespoons walnut or pistachio oil

1 small young leek, white part only, minced

4 ripe fresh figs, stemmed and finely diced

2 firm-ripe pears, peeled, stemmed, cored, and finely diced

½ cup coarsely chopped walnuts

4 ounces Roquefort or other blue cheese, crumbled

1 large or 2 medium heads radicchio

Raw Oysters with Saffron and Sauvignon Blanc Granita

On luscious, seemingly decades-long summer afternoons in Paso Robles, the gentle breeze blows soft and hot, like a caress. If the dry heat becomes just a little too much, here's a prescription: Slide a few of these icy-briny-winey mouthfuls down your throat, take a sip of chilled, effervescent wine, and immediately jump in the pool. You'll be chilled on the inside, cool on the outside, and primed for another seductive dose of delicious warmth. MAKES 40 OYSTERS ON THE HALF-SHELL

In a small saucepan, bring the wine to a boil over medium heat and simmer for 5 minutes. Remove from the heat and add the saffron. Let cool to room temperature, then stir in the lemon juice, salt, sugar, and black pepper. Pour into a large metal roasting pan and freeze for 30 minutes.

Scrape with a fork to flake the ice, then freeze for 30 to 45 minutes more, scraping the ice crystals every 15 to 20 minutes until the granita is pale and fluffy.

Line one or two large platters with crushed ice and arrange the oysters on top. Spoon a teaspoon or so of the saffron-flecked granita over each oyster and scatter with a little black lava salt; serve immediately.

CENTRAL COAST: Derby sparkling Pinot Noir, Paso Robles
FARTHER AFIELD: Julien Fouet Crémant d'Loire, Loire Valley, France

GRANITA
2½ cups Central Coast Sauvignon Blanc or other flinty white wine such as Muscadet or Sancerre

Pinch of saffron threads

2 teaspoons fresh lemon juice

¼ teaspoon fine sea salt

¼ teaspoon sugar

Freshly ground black pepper

TO SERVE
40 live oysters, shucked and on the half-shell

Black lava salt or *fleur de sel*

Smashed Avocado Toasts with Sun-Dried Tomato Jam and Black Lava Salt

Neon green avocado, brick red jam (pesto), and black lava salt make for striking contrast on these simple, fresh, and brightly flavored snacks. They are ridiculously easy to throw together at the last minute if you have ripe avocados—which most Californians do. In fact, this dish was created when my friends Steve and Gisela, new owners of Inn Paradiso in Paso Robles—a boutique inn that's at once stylishly eclectic, secluded, and luxurious—asked me to bring an appetizer to a last-minute dinner party.

MAKES ABOUT 28 BITES

2 tablespoons butter

3 tablespoons extra-virgin olive oil

1 (8-ounce) French or sourdough baguette, about 2 inches in diameter, cut into about 28 (⅓-inch) slices

Fine sea salt and freshly ground black pepper

2 ripe avocados, preferably Hass

2 to 2½ tablespoons fresh lime juice

2 to 3 teaspoons minced red onion

1 tablespoon finely chopped fresh basil

⅓ cup best-quality store-bought sun-dried tomato jam or pesto

1 tablespoon finely snipped chives

Black lava salt, for finishing (or best-quality sea salt)

Preheat the oven to 350°F. Melt the butter with the olive oil in a small saucepan over low heat. Arrange the baguette slices on a baking sheet and brush the tops with the butter-oil mixture; season lightly with salt and pepper. Bake for 10 to 15 minutes, until just golden. Transfer to a serving platter.

Halve and pit the avocados and scoop the flesh into a medium bowl. Add 2 tablespoons of the lime juice, 2 teaspoons of the red onion, the basil, ¼ teaspoon salt, and a little pepper. Mash and fold with a fork until well blended and almost smooth. Taste for seasoning and add additional lime juice, red onion, salt, and pepper to taste.

Spread a thick layer of the avocado mixture onto each piece of toasted bread, then place a small dollop of the tomato pesto in the center of each. Scatter with chives and place a few grains of lava salt over the avocado on either side of the tomato pesto. Serve at once.

CENTRAL COAST: Giornata Barbera, Paso Robles
FARTHER AFIELD: Massolino Barbera, Piedmont, Italy

Abalone, Avocado, and Kumquat Seviche

Abalone had all but disappeared from California's coast when I was a kid. Now, thankfully, it's back, and mostly due to the efforts of the Abalone Farm, on the coast below Cambria, just between Harmony (population: 20) and the crazy-adorable, antiques-heaven beach town of Cayucos. Abalone is chewy and briny, a little like octopus, and notoriously hard to tenderize—a spear-fishing Web site gives this delicate advice: "Wrap it in a clean T-shirt or pillowcase, and whack it with a two-by-four."

Luckily, almost every fishmonger who carries abalone will take care of this process for you; you can also find detailed instructions from Brad Buckley of the Abalone Farm on page 144. SERVES 6

Freeze the abalone for about 20 minutes, to make it easier to dice. With a very sharp knife, cut the abalone into ¼-inch slices, then again crosswise into ¼-inch dice.

In a glass or ceramic bowl, combine the abalone, lime juice, orange juice, sea salt, red pepper flakes, and Tabasco. Toss gently and cover. Refrigerate for at least 3 hours and up to 6 hours, tossing every hour.

When ready to serve, fold in the jicama, red onion, and kumquats. Just before serving, pit, peel, and cut the avocado into small dice; add to the bowl and fold in gently. Spoon into wine glasses, drizzle each with a teaspoon or so of olive oil, and scatter with a pinch of black salt. Serve with a spoon.

CENTRAL COAST: Laetitia sparkling, Arroyo Grande Valley
FARTHER AFIELD: J Lasalle Brut Champagne, France

8 ounces cleaned and pounded abalone

½ cup fresh lime juice (from 3 to 4 limes, depending on their juiciness)

¼ cup fresh orange juice

¾ teaspoon fine sea salt

Pinch of red pepper flakes

3 dashes Tabasco sauce, or to taste

½ cup peeled and finely diced jicama

¼ cup finely diced red onion

⅓ cup thinly sliced kumquats

2 small ripe avocados

Best-quality extra-virgin olive oil, for drizzling

Hawaiian black lava salt, for sprinkling

Alma Rosa Winery and Vineyards

The legend is true. Richard Sanford drove around the Santa Ynez Valley with a thermometer jerry-rigged into the bumper of his old Mercedes in the late 1960s looking for the perfect environment in which to establish a vineyard. His goal was to seek communion with the earth after returning home from Vietnam, and in the process he started a revolution. Pinot Noir was the object of his ardor. While in the service, a Navy buddy had shared with him a Volnay from the Côte d'Or, and the sensation still lingered on his lips. "It was like velvet," he says, remembering the moment.

As a geography major from UC Berkeley, Sanford understood the nuances of topography and climate. He studied a hundred years' worth of climate data from France and California to interpret the dynamics involved in growing grapes. He scoured the Central Coast, mapping temperature readings at each stop. He found his place of paradise on an old bean field along Route 246 in the transverse mountain range of Santa Ynez that gulfed open toward the Pacific Ocean. This geographic anomaly, which runs east-west rather than north-south like most ranges in California—allows the cool maritime influences from the Pacific Ocean to moderate an otherwise hot and dry region.

In planting his first grapevine in 1970 in the western Santa Ynez Valley, Sanford rewrote the template for Pinot Noir production in the state. From his first vintage in 1976, Sanford's goal has always been to create elegant, well-balanced wines expressing the beauty of what is now the preeminent Santa Rita Hills American Viticultural Area. Today, Sanford has had a hand in planting hundreds of acres of vines throughout the Central Coast, mentored dozens of winemakers and vineyard managers, and arguably continues to influence every aspect of California wine production. In 2012, the Culinary Institute of America inducted Sanford into their Vintners Hall of Fame, an honor recognizing those who have helped California become the center of the American wine industry.

He found his place of paradise on an old bean field along Route 246 . . .

In 1981, when Sanford and his wife, Thekla, left Sanford & Benedict Vineyards to create Sanford Winery, they planted all of their vineyards in alignment with the principles of organic agriculture, starting with the Rancho El Jabali vineyard, followed by La Rinconada and La Encantada; all are now heavyweights in the California Pinot Noir world. By 2000, all of Sanford's estate vineyards had been certified organic—the first in Santa Barbara County. "Both Thekla and I believe it is the responsible thing to do: to leave our land better than we found it for future generations," he says.

Over the years, the Sanfords have deeded 130 acres of oak woodland to a conservation easement, actively worked to sustain the area's once diminishing bluebird population, regularly used native wildflower plantings around the vineyard to attract a diversity of insects, and used owl boxes to naturally control rodent populations. They have even worked with conservationists on their properties to reestablish peregrine falcons, which have now repopulated abandoned nesting sites throughout the area. For this work and more, the Sanfords have been honored by the Environmental Defense Center as environmental heroes.

Renewal and growth is a theme for this husband-and-wife team, and in 2005, when they left their namesake Sanford Winery to create Alma Rosa Winery and Vineyards, they went even further in dedicating their new venture to all ways sustainable. "Nature and agriculture in sustainable harmony" is their mantra. It is evident in their bottle and closure choice, their building materials, and business relationships. Asked what has kept him going all these years, Richard smiles. "It was all I knew how to do. It's been hugely gratifying and hugely challenging. Each year, we have a new opportunity to make things better, and I am always thinking of new ways to do so."

IF YOU VISIT:
The Alma Rosa tasting room is located off of quiet Santa Rosa Road, which winds it way through the Sanfords' home ranch of Rancho El Jabali. Many of you may recognize it as the first stop in the wine-infused road trip through the Santa Ynez Valley in the movie *Sideways*. It is certainly a place of serenity, where the adobe buildings look up into the big blue sky.

Daily, 11 a.m. to 4:30 p.m.

7250 Santa Rosa Road
Buellton, CA 93427

www.almarosawinery.com

Roasted Potato and Chorizo Skewers

Hands down the best-ever snack with drinks, in my humble opinion, is this classic, which is inspired by the rustic tapas bars of Spain, where I lived for three years in the '90s. These tasty morsels are best served warm—if they cool off too much, just return them to the baking sheet, toothpick and all, and warm for 5 to 10 minutes in a very low oven (140° to 150°F). Think forty bites is plenty for a crowd? Think again. Try using partially stripped rosemary stems instead of toothpicks. The woody scent is like a soft Californian kiss. MAKES ABOUT 40 BITES

In a steamer set over rapidly boiling water, blanch the potatoes for 11 to 13 minutes, until the tines of a fork will just pierce the top ¼ inch of the surface. Drain and rinse under cool water to stop the cooking.

Cut each potato in half crosswise, and score the cut side of each with the tines of a fork.

Preheat the oven to 375°F and place a large rimmed baking sheet on a rack in the lowest position.

Combine the potatoes, olive oil, salt, pepper, and oregano in a large bowl and toss together until evenly coated. Transfer the potatoes to the hot baking sheet and jiggle the pan to distribute them evenly. Roast, turning the potatoes with a metal spatula every 10 to 12 minutes, for about 30 minutes, until very crisp and golden.

While the potatoes are roasting, heat a large nonstick or cast-iron skillet over medium-high heat. Add the chorizo half-circles and brown, turning occasionally with tongs, until golden and slightly crisp, about 5 minutes. Remove from the heat. When cool enough to handle, place a slice of chorizo on top of each roasted potato half and secure with a toothpick. Place the skewers on a platter and squeeze a little lime juice over the top before serving.

CENTRAL COAST: Hearst Ranch Tempranillo, Paso Robles
FARTHER AFIELD: Pago Florentino Tempranillo, Ribero del Duero, Spain

1½ pounds small red or white potatoes

3 tablespoons extra-virgin olive oil

1 teaspoon fine sea salt

1 teaspoon freshly ground black pepper

1 teaspoon dried oregano

6 to 7 ounces cured chorizo, sliced about ½-inch thick, slices halved crosswise

1 lime, quartered

Smoked Trout, Horseradish, and Apple Polenta Wedges

My very first cookbook, published in 1996, was called *Polenta* and featured 40 recipes for polenta. I'm *still* coming up with new ways to feature the golden grain: soft, sliced, grilled—it's an artist's canvas. What I like best about "hard" polenta dishes is that they can be prepared almost completely ahead of time (always one of my signatures, since I prefer chatting to chopping when there are people around). SERVES 10 TO 12

2 cups instant polenta (one 13.2-ounce package)

Chicken stock, for cooking the polenta

Whole milk, for cooking the polenta

4 tablespoons unsalted butter

⅔ cup freshly grated Parmesan

SALAD
8 ounces smoked trout, skin and bones removed, finely chopped

2 small apples, such as Gala or Fuji, peeled, cored, and cut into ⅛-inch dice

¾ cup coarsely chopped walnuts

¼ cup mayonnaise, plus more if needed

2 to 3 teaspoons prepared horseradish, as desired

2 teaspoons fresh lemon juice

Fine sea salt and freshly ground black pepper

2 tablespoons finely chopped fresh dill or finely snipped fresh chives

The night before serving (or, in the morning): Cook the polenta in a large heavy saucepan according to the package instructions, substituting an equal quantity of stock and milk for the water. Energetically stir in the butter and Parmesan until they are evenly distributed. Remove from the heat and immediately spread into pans, as follows: Working quickly, rinse a 12 by 17-inch rimmed baking sheet (or two smaller pans) with cold water and shake dry. Mound the polenta in the pan and, working quickly, use a spatula repeatedly dipped in hot water to spread the polenta into an even layer about ½ inch thick. Cover the pan with a clean kitchen towel and let rest for at least 1 hour at room temperature and up to 24 hours in the refrigerator.

Remove the polenta from the refrigerator about 1 hour before serving, to bring it to room temperature. With a round-bladed knife, cut the polenta into thirds lengthwise. Then cut each long rectangle crosswise every few inches, on the diagonal, into triangles. Transfer the triangles to one large or two smaller platters.

To make the salad, combine the smoked trout, apples, walnuts, mayonnaise, horseradish, lemon juice, and ¼ teaspoon salt in a large bowl. Add black pepper to taste and stir together with a fork until evenly blended. The salad should clump slightly; add a little more mayonnaise, 1 teaspoon at a time, until the salad holds together, if necessary. Mound about 1 tablespoon of the salad onto each polenta wedge and scatter with a little dill. Serve within 30 minutes of assembly.

CENTRAL COAST: Jack Creek Chardonnay "Concrete Blonde," Paso Robles
FARTHER AFIELD: Château Pouilly Pouilly Fuissé, Burgundy, France

Smoky Pork and Pimentón Pinchitos

In Spain, every little roadside grocery sells cubes of marinated *pinchitos*, ready to skewer and grill at a moment's notice. Here, you'll need to plan ahead, especially for the best flavor. Search out pork with nice marbling, ideally from a local butcher. Standard supermarket pork, especially lean cuts like loin and tenderloin, can dry out and toughen easily. If there's any exterior fat, don't trim it off—it will add to the sizzle and flavor and will burn off on the grill anyway. MAKES 24 TO 26 SMALL SKEWERS

To make the marinade, combine the wine, oil, paprika, salt, black pepper, garlic, bay leaves, and red pepper flakes in a large bowl. Whisk well, then add the pork and toss to coat evenly. Cover and refrigerate for at least 6 hours and up to 12 hours.

Soak 26 medium (6- to 8-inch) bamboo skewers in water for 15 to 20 minutes (or, use small metal skewers). Prepare a charcoal or gas grill for medium-high-heat grilling, or place an oven rack in the top position and preheat the broiler to high heat.

Lift the pork cubes from the marinade and let them drain in a colander while you assemble the skewers. Thread 3 or 4 cubes of pork onto each skewer; push the cubes snugly together and concentrate them near the pointy end, so they'll be easy to nibble off.

If you're grilling, fold a 12-inch length of aluminum foil in half lengthwise to create a strip that will lie flat directly on the grill surface underneath the blunt ends of the skewers, preventing them from catching fire. If using a broiler, wrap about 3 inches of the blunt ends with foil.

Dab the pork dry with paper towels, so the meat will sear nicely. Grill (or broil) the *pinchitos*, turning as needed to sear all sides, until golden brown, firm, and sizzling, 1½ to 2 minutes on each side. Transfer the skewers to a platter. Squeeze some lemon juice over and scatter with the smoked salt; serve at once.

CENTRAL COAST: Windward Vineyard Estate Pinot Noir, Paso Robles
FARTHER AFIELD: Brickhouse Pinot Noir, Oregon

⅓ cup dry white wine, such as Sauvignon Blanc

⅓ cup extra-virgin olive oil

2 teaspoons smoked paprika (pimentón)

1 teaspoon fine sea salt

¾ teaspoon freshly ground black pepper

2 large garlic cloves, minced or pushed through a press

2 fresh bay leaves, torn into small pieces (or 1 dried bay leaf, crumbled)

Large or small pinch of red pepper flakes, as desired

1¼ pounds boneless pork loin or tenderloin, cut into ¾-inch cubes

1 lemon, cut into wedges

Large pinch of smoked salt, such as Halen Môn brand or red alder–smoked salt

Pasolivo

The limestone-rich soils and Tuscany-like climate—crisp fall nights and warm summer days—that have attracted grape growers and winemakers from all over the world are also perfect for olives.

Olive trees were first planted on what is now Willow Creek Olive Ranch, out on the pastoral Vineyard Drive west of Paso Robles, almost 20 years ago. Today, about 45 acres are planted with 6,000 trees and a dozen varieties including Frantoio, Leccino, Pendolino, Lucca, Moraiolo, Mission, Manzanillo, Sevillano, and Ascolano olives. The trees flourished, and today the farm produces the award-winning Pasolivo olive oils.

Pasolivo's trees have been organically farmed for more than six years, although for various complex reasons the farm is not certified organic. Every bit of olive paste left over from production is utilized. After pressing, it's spread between the rows, to help with weed management. Weeds are mown down to avoid the need for weed killers. Yes, doing it organically takes more money and time, but the shepherds of this land believe strongly in being very careful with its stewardship.

The foreman, Catalino Rivera, has been with the ranch since its inception, and there are now three generations of the Rivera family living on the ranch. Catalino has a visceral, instinctive connection to the trees and the land. "We don't use a pneumatic tree shaker; we pick by hand into buckets," he says. The cast of characters at harvest changes every year, but it always includes local winemakers because olives are harvested after grapes. Catalino manages the pickers, anywhere from 50 to 100 people a day, and also prepares the harvest feast out in the orchard.

Farming is just a part of the process. Producing oil is also demanding and time consuming. While a ton of grapes will produce roughly 150 gallons of fermentable juice, a ton of olives yields a mere 25 to 40 gallons of oil. "Unlike wine, which splashes merrily into the press pan, olive oil just drip, drip, drips. It can take hours or even days to press a single lot. During harvest, the press is operating around the clock."

Although production is still small (3,000 to 5,000 gallons a year, depending on the weather), the quality is generally acknowledged to be excellent. Including Pasolivo, all three winners at the 2007 Los Angeles County Fair—the biggest olive oil competition in the United States—were from the Central Coast.

Pasolivo is the ranch's signature blend of five Tuscan olives—it's earthy, herbaceous, peppery, and slightly bitter, like a big bowl of greens. The California Blend brings together two California varieties— Mission and Manzanillo—and tends to be a little more grassy. Olio Segreto ("secret oil" in Italian) is made from trees initially thought to be Kalamata but apparently mislabeled by the nursery. This oil is rustic, earthy, and big. The citrus olive oil blends—made using all natural oils extracted from the citrus peels—include lime, tangerine, and lemon, and are radically wonderful drizzled on grilled protein and vegetables, and in vinaigrettes.

All the oils are on the intense end of the spectrum. In the sunny yellow tasting room, you can taste all the oils, either by chugging a small shot of oil or dipping fresh bread into the oil and perhaps sprinkling it with sea salt. Tasting room team Jillian and Suzanne have been here for seven years and recognize more than half the visitors.

There are plans to expand its kitchen garden and create more ways for visitors to experience the relationship between fresh produce and olive oil. "Last year, we pulled tomatoes warm from the garden, sliced them up, and served them to customers drizzled with olive oil and sprinkled with sea salt. It was such a hit!" says Jillian.

All the oils are on the intense end of the spectrum.

IF YOU VISIT:
Tasting room open daily, 11 a.m. to 5 p.m.

8530 Vineyard Drive
Paso Robles, CA 93446

(805) 227-0186

www.pasolivo.com

Little Soy- and Orange-Glazed Short Ribs

When magic hour grazing expands to take up the bulk of the evening, as it often does here in wine country, it's crucial to have filling finger food on hand to keep guests from getting tipsy. Short ribs aren't usually finger food, but this clever presentation—a carnivore's delight—makes it simple and nonmessy to pick up a rib like a beefy lollipop and nibble happily away. If you braise the ribs a day in advance, or early in the day, this becomes an incredibly easy dish. Just cool the ribs to room temperature after the initial braising, then cover and refrigerate for up to 6 hours—or even overnight. Bring to room temperature for about 1 hour before continuing. SERVES 10 TO 12

6 to 6½ pounds bone-in beef short ribs, cut in half crosswise into 1½-inch lengths (have the butcher do this, unless you are handy with a bone saw)

Fine sea salt and freshly ground black pepper

3 tablespoons canola or vegetable oil

3 garlic cloves, minced or pushed through a press

⅓ cup fresh orange juice

3 tablespoons tamari or low-sodium soy sauce

1 tablespoon blackstrap molasses

2½ cups beef broth or stock, homemade or store-bought

1 cup gutsy red wine, such as Zinfandel or Syrah

Finely grated zest of 2 oranges, preferably removed with a Microplane grater

3 tablespoons minced fresh flat-leaf parsley

Preheat the oven to 325°F. Trim the short ribs of excessive fat and season quite generously all over with salt and pepper.

Place a large heavy roasting pan over medium-high heat, and add the oil. When the oil is hot, sear the ribs until browned on all sides, turning with tongs (do this in two batches, if necessary, to avoid overcrowding). Set the ribs aside on a platter. Decrease the heat to low and add the garlic. Sweat the garlic gently for about 5 minutes, or until completely tender, then stir in the orange juice, tamari, molasses, beef broth, and wine. Return the ribs to the pan with the bone sides up and cover the pan with aluminum foil, crimping the edges. Transfer to the oven and let the ribs braise for about 2 hours, until very tender but not yet falling off the bone (you'll need the bone to use as a handle when nibbling).

Remove from the oven and increase the oven temperature to 400°F. Transfer the ribs to a rimmed baking sheet, bone sides down. (Save the braising liquid for a future soup or bean dish.) Roast until crisp and golden brown, about 15 minutes.

Transfer the ribs to a serving platter and scatter with the orange zest and parsley.

CENTRAL COAST: J Dusi Zinfandel, Paso Robles
FARTHER AFIELD: Catena Luca Malbec, Mendoza, Argentina

Radicchio and Monterey Jack Quesadillas with Fresh Fig Salsa

Almost three-quarters of the American crop of radicchio is grown within California's borders—the legacy of early Italian immigrants who, legend has it, told their children, "No radicchio, no America."

Many fans of the scarlet heads, both round and elongated—as in the Treviso variety—may not yet be acquainted with the earthy sweetness that results from cooking radicchio (halved or quartered heads, charred on the wood-fired grill, are a revelation!). Here, one of California's favorite cheesy snacks gets a Mediterranean transformation.

MAKES 18 WEDGES

FRESH FIG SALSA
1 cup diced (¼-inch) fresh California figs

¼ cup finely diced red bell pepper

1 scallion, trimmed and finely chopped

1 tablespoon fresh lime juice

Dash of green or red Tabasco sauce

¼ teaspoon fine sea salt

Freshly ground black pepper

QUESADILLAS
2 tablespoons extra-virgin olive oil

1 head radicchio, quartered, cored, and thinly slivered

1 garlic clove, minced or pushed through a press

1¼ teaspoons minced fresh rosemary

Salt and freshly ground black pepper

1 tablespoon balsamic vinegar

2 tablespoons unsalted butter, melted

6 large flour tortillas

3 ounces soft fresh goat cheese, crumbled

9 ounces Monterey Jack, coarsely grated

To make the salsa, combine all the ingredients in a bowl. Taste for seasoning, and adjust as needed.

To make the quesadillas, in a skillet, warm the olive oil over medium heat. Add the radicchio, garlic, rosemary, ¼ teaspoon salt, and a good pinch of pepper. Sauté until golden brown and limp; stir in the vinegar and remove from the heat.

Set the melted butter, tortillas, radicchio, and cheeses (combined in a bowl) near the stove. Place a flat griddle or a large cast-iron or nonstick skillet over medium-high heat and brush the pan with some of the melted butter. Place a tortilla in the pan and immediately scatter with one-third of the cheese mixture, leaving a little border around the edge. Top with one-third of the slivered radicchio and place a second tortilla on top; brush the top with a little more butter. Cook until the cheese begins to liquefy and the underside is mottled brown, occasionally pressing down gently with a wide metal spatula, 3 to 5 minutes. Turn over with the spatula and cook until the other side is golden, about 2 minutes longer. Transfer to a large baking sheet and keep warm in a low oven while you make the remaining quesadillas the same way.

Transfer to a cutting board and use a large, sharp knife to cut each quesadilla into 6 equal wedges. Fan the wedges out on a platter and top each with a little fig salsa; serve at once.

CENTRAL COAST: Ambyth Counoise, Templeton (slightly chilled)
FARTHER AFIELD: Marcel Lapiere Morgon, Beaujolais, France

CHAPTER 2

From Garden and Orchard

Today, the California gold rush has more to do with precious carrots and leeks than metal. Our rich bounty of ingredients, all grown and produced on the Central Coast (or slightly inland) reads like a litany of the best foodstuffs in the world: artichokes, avocados, garlic, greens, radicchio, oranges, lemons, limes, grapefruit, Buddha's hand citron, kumquats, grapes, figs, olives, persimmons, plums, pomegranates, strawberries, and tomatoes. Herbs like lavender, rosemary, and thyme grow wild. There are mushrooms: boletus, black trumpet, candy caps, chanterelles, oyster, shiitake; and nuts: almonds, pistachios, and walnuts.

In the lush Santa Ynez Valley, organic farmer Shu Takikawa (The Garden of . . . . .) has had a huge influence on the smaller farmers who stock and populate the farmer's markets of the region. Shu's leeks—each one with literally a foot and a half of mild, tender white—are literally

fought over. Shu's daughter-in-law Noey (Yes Yes Nursery) grows all his seedlings, and Shu taught Los Olivos local Jacob Grant (Roots Family Farm) everything he knows. Now, Jacob's carrots are considered the sweetest in the land.

Once again, California's bounty springs from its rich soil. But no matter where you live, you can bring the bounty of your own region to the table with these earthy, seasonally conscious dishes.

Wine pairings by Sonja Magdevski, journalist and winemaker at Casa Dumetz

Fennel and Persimmon Salad with Pistachios

This simple salad is a riot of color and texture, just perfect for serving alongside a grilled piece of chicken. Being an unapologetic carnivore, I'd add prosciutto to this gorgeous dish. It's still plenty perfect without the pork, however. Fuyu persimmons are edible and delicious when firm, unlike the Hachiya persimmon, which must be soft enough to scoop with a spoon before its severely astringent tannins are tamed. If Hachiya persimmons are available to you, use them for spooning over goat's milk yogurt for breakfast, or on slightly sweetened ricotta for dessert (not for this salad).

SERVES 6 TO 8 AS A FIRST COURSE OR SIDE DISH

VINAIGRETTE
2 tablespoons champagne vinegar or white wine vinegar

1 teaspoon Dijon mustard

½ teaspoon fine sea salt

¼ teaspoon freshly ground black pepper

6 tablespoons walnut oil (or if available, pistachio oil)

2 large fennel bulbs, trimmed, quartered, and cored

2 ripe Fuyu persimmons, top leaves trimmed off, halved lengthwise

1 cup shelled, roasted, and salted pistachios, coarsely chopped

1 cup loosely packed fresh flat-leaf parsley leaves (or fennel fronds), coarsely chopped

To make the vinaigrette, whisk together the vinegar, mustard, salt, pepper, and nut oil in a large bowl.

Sliver the fennel quarters crosswise and add to the bowl. Sliver the persimmon halves lengthwise and add to the bowl along with two-thirds of the pistachios and two-thirds of the parsley. Fold together until all the ingredients are evenly coated with the vinaigrette. Mound onto a platter or individual serving plates, and scatter with the remaining pistachios and parsley. Serve at once.

CENTRAL COAST: Flying Goat "Goat Bubbles" Crémant, Sierra Madre Vineyard, Santa Maria Valley
FARTHER AFIELD: Sparkling Vouvray, Loire Valley, France

Grilled Caesar Salad

Historical documents seem to confirm that the most popular salad ever in the history of the planet was invented in Tijuana, only a stone's throw from California. Leave it to the Californians to decide it would be better on the grill. This recipe may seem counterintuitive, but trust me when I say that the romaine hearts spend only a heartbeat on the hot grill, picking up a divine smokiness and just a hint of wilt. I'm on the fence about the traditional accompaniment of croutons—if you like them, forgo the store-bought variety and instead toast some thick slices of rustic country bread brushed with the best olive oil and seasoned with good sea salt and fresh pepper; after toasting, rub them with the cut side of a plump, firm garlic clove.

SERVES 4

In a mini prep or standard food processor, pulse the garlic until finely chopped. Add ½ teaspoon salt, plenty of pepper, the egg yolk, anchovies, lemon juice, mustard, vinegar, and Worcestershire sauce. Pulse until pureed, then add the oil and pulse until thoroughly emulsified. Refrigerate until serving time.

Prepare a charcoal or gas grill—or a ridged cast-iron grill pan—for medium-heat grilling, if you haven't already fired it up for something else. Strip off and discard or compost the darker, wilted outer leaves of the romaine until you are left with a pale green firm heart. Cut in half lengthwise, and swish around in a large bowl or sink full of ice water.

Lift the romaine hearts from the water by the root end and gently shake off as much water as you can without bruising the delicate leaves. Place the hearts cut side down on the hot grill surface and grill for 30 seconds to 1 minute, just until nicely marked with dark grill lines. Transfer to a very large bowl and, with clean hands, toss with the dressing; season with more pepper and scatter the cheese on top. Toss again and place (reverently) on (chilled) plates. Serve.

CENTRAL COAST: Brander Sauvignon Blanc "au Naturel," Santa Ynez Valley
FARTHER AFIELD: A wonderfully bright Sancerre from France

3 large garlic cloves

Fine sea salt and freshly ground black pepper

1 egg yolk

3 oil-packed anchovies, drained

2 tablespoons fresh lemon juice

1 tablespoon Dijon mustard

1 teaspoon red wine vinegar

1 teaspoon Worcestershire sauce

⅓ cup extra-virgin olive oil, grapeseed oil, or canola oil

3 to 6 pale inner hearts of romaine lettuce (depending on size)

⅓ cup grated Parmigiano-Reggiano or Grana Padano

Avocado, Jicama, and Radish Salad with Grapefruit Vinaigrette

Avocado trees don't thrive up in the high levels around Paso Robles, with its violent swings in temperature, but down at the coast near Cambria and Cayucos you'll find the smoothest, greenest, most buttery fruit imaginable. This quintessential California salad stars a colorful array of my state's finest produce: sunny, crunchy, rich—and yet bracingly tart. For one of the most picturesque drives in the West, head west from Paso Robles on Highway 46. Turn right on Santa Rosa Creek Road and wind your way very slowly down to Cambria. Along the way, you'll see scenes of bucolic perfection, mellow cattle, and smoothly rolling hills. By the time you reach the bottom, you'll be in avocado country. Stop at Dos Pasos Farm and pick up a bag of ripe ones. SERVES 6

VINAIGRETTE

1 large pink or white grapefruit

1 medium shallot, minced

2 to 3 tablespoons fresh lemon juice

Fine sea salt and freshly ground black pepper

3 tablespoons grapeseed oil

2 tablespoons extra-virgin olive oil

2 tablespoons mayonnaise

⅛ teaspoon cayenne pepper

10 to 12 ounces jicama (about 1 small), peeled and sliced into ⅛-inch matchsticks

2 bunches white and red radishes, trimmed and thinly sliced

⅓ cup coarsely chopped fresh flat-leaf parsley

3 tablespoons fresh chives, snipped into ½-inch lengths

2 small ripe avocados, preferably Hass

Extra-virgin olive oil, for drizzling

To make the vinaigrette, remove all the peel and pith from the grapefruit with a sharp knife. Working over a large, shallow bowl, cut down on either side of each membrane to release pith-free segments, catching the juices. Squeeze the membrane to release maximum juice; pick out any seeds. Pull the segments into small, rough pieces. Add the shallot, 2 tablespoons lemon juice, and ½ teaspoon each salt and pepper to the bowl with the grapefruit and juice. Whisk in the grapeseed oil and olive oil, then whisk in the mayonnaise and cayenne.

Add the jicama, radishes, parsley, and chives to the bowl and toss thoroughly to be sure all the ingredients are generously coated with vinaigrette. Adjust to taste with salt, pepper, and lemon juice. The vinaigrette should be quite tart. Let stand for 10 to 15 minutes, so the jicama begins to absorb the vinaigrette.

To serve, pit and peel the avocados and slice into thin wedges. Arrange the slices in a single layer on a platter; drizzle with a little olive oil and season with a little salt and pepper. Mound the jicama salad over the avocado (you should be able to see some of the avocado underneath), and serve immediately.

CENTRAL COAST: Verdad Albariño, Sawyer Lindquist Vineyard, Edna Valley
FARTHER AFIELD: Albariño, Rias Baixas, Spain

Windrose Farm

Everywhere you look here, you see people who have fled urban blight to reinvent themselves in a more pastoral form. Yet it still seems improbable that a professional cello player would recast herself as a farmer. But in 1987, cellist Barbara Spencer took stock of her 45 years, and she made two rather sweeping pronouncements. She vowed not to grow old in Burbank. And she vowed to lay down her cello and pick up a hoe.

Barbara tells me that she is only impulsive about 50 percent of the time. That was clearly one of her impulsive moments. She set out to find the perfect place to nurture plants and animals, and narrowed the choice to three possible locations: Sebastopol, the Bonny Doon area behind Santa Cruz, and the northern part of San Luis Obispo County (in other words, Paso Robles). She never intended to make a serious business out of selling her produce. "Maybe apples and herbs at a little folding table at the back of the farmer's market," she says, grinning ruefully.

Then she met Christine Maguire, of Rinconada Dairy, at the Mozart Festival in San Luis Obispo in 1989. Christine was moonlighting as PR director to bring in extra cash to feed her sheep, and they instantly became fast friends (this plot line will return). Within a few months, Barbara took the plunge and bought her first "farm" on the east side of Paso Robles. "It was thin, hardpan soil over bedrock."

One day after arriving to begin her new life, she was "set up" with a local man, Bill Spencer, billed by mutual friends as a "very interesting, really funny guy going through a tough divorce." To Barbara, he sounded like a brown-bag case—there must be something very wrong, right? The two became a couple almost instantly, and within a week gave a party for 30 people. Coming hard on the heels of her new friendship with Christine, it was, perhaps, a karmic message: You have chosen well, grasshopper. Your new life plan is the right one.

But when he quenched his thirst from the old hose, Bill found the sweetest water he'd ever tasted, and he found their farm.

Two decades of almost unimaginably hard work ensued. Meanwhile, the two partners metamorphosed in their own lives—Bill admitted that real estate was not for him; Barbara supported the choice unconditionally. "The land has always been leading us, to where we are now, with no idea where it will lead us next," says Barbara.

Bill put his local expertise to work finding a property where the two really *could* create the farm they both now dreamed of. In 1990, while showing it to a prospective buyer, he first laid eyes on what is now Windrose Farm. It was the middle of July, hotter than hell on the east side of Paso, and the hard dirt seemed completely inhospitable to life. But when he quenched his thirst from the old hose, Bill found the sweetest water he'd ever tasted, and he found their farm. Neither had enough cash, but in another sign of the serendipity that seems to surround these two with a rosy glow, Barbara's 85-year-old father was visiting. Perhaps not too far removed from his New York farming stock, he saw the look in his daughter's eyes and the promise of the land. With his help, these two passionate "kids" laid down roots in the place that's become one of the most prolific and respected sustainable farms south of San Francisco. In Los Angeles, and all across the southern and central part of California, chefs vie for their produce (and, occasionally, lamb) and trumpet "Windrose Farm" on their menus.

Outstanding success in their field has not gone to their heads: "I can never take for granted the amazing experiences we have had since we began farming. It still gives me goose bumps to hear that our produce is being sought out by a wonderful chef to serve in his or her restaurant. Not only here in Southern California, but in New York as well."

IF YOU VISIT:

"Don't bring your dogs, we have plenty," states the Web site. But humans are more than welcome, and the farm is open to visitors Thursday to Saturday from 10 a.m. to 6 p.m. and Sunday from 10 a.m. to 4 p.m.

www.windrosefarm.org

(805) 239-3757

Shaved Artichoke and Pancetta Salad with Lavender

When I was a kid, driving through Castroville—the "artichoke capital of the world"—was the highlight of the long drive between Los Angeles and San Francisco. (We always stopped to load up at the farmstand marked by a huge concrete artichoke.) In my college days, the Castroville Artichoke Festival meant feasting on deep-fried artichokes. In my youth, I prepared artichokes one way only, though: boiled into submission, with a lake of melted butter for dipping.   SERVES 4

4 large globe artichokes

1 lemon, halved

1 tablespoon butter

3 tablespoons extra-virgin olive oil

4 ounces thick-cut pancetta, cut into thin strips

2 tablespoons white balsamic vinegar

5 cups (5 ounces) baby arugula

8 radishes, ends trimmed, thinly sliced

4 scallions, white and green parts, finely chopped

½ cup shelled fresh peas or thawed frozen petits pois

Fine sea salt and freshly ground black pepper

Small bunch fresh chives, snipped

10 fresh lavender flowers (optional; or substitute rosemary flowers)

Working with one artichoke at a time, bend back the dark outer leaves until they snap, leaving the meaty bottom exposed, with the pale, tender green cone of leaves above. Cut off the cone of leaves just above the heart. With a sharp paring knife, carefully trim away the remaining dark green bits from the heart. Scrape out and discard the choke (a melon baller is useful here). Cut each heart into ⅛- to ⅓-inch slices and squeeze some lemon juice over to stop them from browning.

Place a large skillet over medium heat and add the butter and 1 tablespoon of the oil. Sauté the artichoke slices until softened and golden, about 10 minutes. Transfer to a small bowl and add the pancetta to the skillet. Cook until browned and crisp, 7 to 8 minutes, stirring frequently. Drain on absorbent paper, then toss with the artichokes. Discard all but about 1 tablespoon of the fat from the skillet. Add the balsamic vinegar and stir to deglaze the pan and emulsify.

In a large bowl, toss the arugula, radishes, scallions, and peas with the remaining 2 tablespoons olive oil, ½ teaspoon salt, and plenty of pepper. Divide the greens among plates and top with the artichoke-pancetta mixture and the chives. Pull off pieces of the lavender blossoms and scatter over the top.

CENTRAL COAST: Brewer-Clifton Chardonnay, Sweeney Canyon, Santa Rita Hills
FARTHER AFIELD: White Burgundy/Chardonnay, South Africa

Broccoli Rabe and White Beans with Anchovy Dressing

There is nothing more quintessentially Tuscan/Californian than the combination of white beans with one of the most wonderful plants of the brassica family: broccoli rabe. The addition of what I call "rustic salt" (aka anchovies) elevates this quickly prepared dish to rock-star category. I could eat this every night of the week (admittedly, I'd be happiest if I could pair it with a nice fatty pork chop on Monday, a flash-grilled flat-iron steak on Tuesday, smoky sausages on Wednesday . . . well, you get the picture). SERVES 4 TO 6

Bring a large pot of water to a boil and add 1 tablespoon salt and the broccoli rabe. Simmer until almost tender but still bright green, 3 to 4 minutes. Drain in a colander and rinse with cold water to stop the cooking and preserve the color.

Gently squeeze as much water as possible out of the broccoli rabe and chop it coarsely. In a large skillet, warm 2 tablespoons of the olive oil over medium-low heat. Add the smashed garlic and sauté for about 1 minute, then retrieve and discard. Add the anchovies and mash to a paste with a wooden spoon. Add the broccoli rabe, white beans, remaining 2 tablespoons olive oil, ¼ teaspoon salt, and plenty of black pepper. Stir gently and occasionally for about 5 minutes, to meld the flavors. Squeeze the lemon juice over the top and serve.

CENTRAL COAST: Casa Dumetz Viognier "Clementina," Tierra Alta Vineyard, Santa Ynez Valley
FARTHER AFIELD: Viognier, Yalumba Valley, Australia

Kosher salt

2 bunches broccoli rabe, tough stems and outer leaves removed

4 tablespoons extra-virgin olive oil

2 large garlic cloves, smashed with the side of a knife

6 to 8 oil-cured anchovies, soaked in warm water for 5 minutes, patted dry

1 (14.5-ounce) can cannellini beans, well rinsed and thoroughly drained

Freshly ground black pepper

Juice of ½ lemon

Israeli Couscous Salad with Almonds, Blood Oranges, and Greek Olives

This is a hybrid combination of toasted pilaf and couscous that takes advantage of the large, toothsome pearls of Israeli couscous, pairing them with three of the most iconic ingredients of the Central Coast. Paso Robles was once the almond capital of the world, and although many of the almond trees have been pulled out to make way for grapevines—in that constant slow, shifting change that seems to affect all agricultural regions—there are still blossom-covered almonds trees dotting the rolling hills. Rusty Hall, proprietor of Paso Almonds, produces an almond brittle from local almonds that inspires slavish devotion among those who have tasted it. SERVES 4 AS A FIRST COURSE OR SIDE DISH

In a medium nonstick skillet, warm 1 tablespoon of the oil over medium heat. Add the almonds and toast, stirring and shaking, until crisp and golden, 5 to 7 minutes (do not leave unattended, or they are likely to scorch). Set aside.

In a saucepan, warm 1 tablespoon of the olive oil over medium heat and add the onion and garlic. Sauté until softened, stirring occasionally, about 5 minutes. Add the couscous and continue cooking and stirring until the couscous has just begun to brown, about 6 minutes more. Add the vegetable broth, 1 teaspoon salt (or to taste), and plenty of pepper. Bring to a boil over high heat, then reduce the heat, cover the pan, and simmer gently until tender and all the liquid is absorbed, about 8 minutes. Scoop into a large bowl and immediately fold in the remaining ¼ cup olive oil and the mint, fluffing the grains with a fork to separate them.

Add the toasted almonds, diced oranges, olives, lemon juice, and half of the parsley to the bowl of couscous. Toss gently, taste for seasoning, and divide among plates. Scatter each salad with the remaining parsley, and serve slightly warm or at room temperature.

CENTRAL COAST: Tatomer Grüer Veltliner, John Sebastiano Vineyard, Santa Barbara County
FARTHER AFIELD: Grüner Veltliner, Kamptal, Austria

2 tablespoons plus ¼ cup extra-virgin olive oil

¾ cup sliced or slivered raw almonds

1 medium red onion, finely chopped

2 garlic cloves, minced or pushed through a press

1½ cups Israeli couscous (one 8.8-ounce package)

2 cups homemade or store-bought low-sodium vegetable broth

Fine sea salt and freshly ground black pepper

1 tablespoon finely chopped fresh mint (optional)

2 blood oranges, peeled with a knife, cut between the membranes into pith-free segments, and diced

¾ cup brine-cured black olives (such as Kalamata), pitted and diced

2 tablespoons fresh lemon juice

¼ cup coarsely chopped fresh flat-leaf parsley

Cold Avocado Soup with Fried Chickpeas, Lemon, and Dill

Avocado soup may be the first soup I ever made in a blender, right out of high school when cooking was still mystical alchemy to me. Cool, creamy, and mostly make-ahead, it's luscious and bright green colors and flavors are perfect for a California summer. Fried chickpeas add rustic texture, while the lemon and dill lift us into the realm of elegance. Serve in glass bowls for ultimate impact. Or, for a large party, serve in small juice glasses or Moroccan tea glasses. (If you share my lifelong Fear of Frying, the soup is also very good without its rustic garnish.) SERVES 6 TO 12, DEPENDING ON PORTION SIZE

12 ounces English cucumber, peel removed in strips so that some remains

2 tablespoons sherry vinegar

Fine sea salt

1 cup Greek yogurt

2 cups buttermilk

4 tablespoons tiny fresh sprigs dill

Olive oil, for frying

Canola oil (or other vegetable oil), for frying

All-purpose flour, for dredging

Freshly ground black pepper

½ teaspoon smoked paprika

1 (15-ounce) can chickpeas, well rinsed and thoroughly drained

½ lemon, ends trimmed, halved lengthwise, and sliced crosswise into paper-thin pie-shaped wedges

2 ripe Hass avocados, very cold

Halve the cucumber lengthwise and use a small spoon to scoop out and discard the seeds. Very coarsely chop the cucumber and transfer to a bowl. Add the vinegar and 1 tablespoon salt. Toss together and let stand for 30 minutes.

Scoop the cucumbers with all of their liquid into a blender or food processor. Add the yogurt, buttermilk, and 2 tablespoons of the dill to the blender; puree until smooth. Place the covered blender jar in the refrigerator and chill for at least 1 hour and up to 12 hours.

Fill a deep, heavy pot no more than half full with a mixture of half olive oil and half canola oil (or use a deep fryer). Heat the oil to 350°F. Meanwhile, spread about 1 cup of flour in a shallow bowl. Season the flour liberally with salt, pepper, and the smoked paprika.

Throw the chickpeas and lemon slices into the flour; toss well with your hands to make sure they are evenly coated. Transfer to a colander or sieve and shake to get rid of the excess flour. In two batches, fry in the hot oil until golden brown, 2 to 3 minutes. Drain on absorbent paper towels. Just before the second batch is done, throw the remaining 2 tablespoons dill into the fryer; fry for about 10 seconds. Lift everything from the oil and, again, drain briefly on absorbent paper towels.

Pit and peel the avocados. Immediately return the cold blender jar to its base and add the avocados. Blend until smooth; taste for seasoning and adjust with salt, pepper, and/or a drop or two of sherry vinegar. Pour into chilled bowls or wine goblets and scatter with some of the fried chickpea mixture. Serve at once.

CENTRAL COAST: Lone Madrone Chenin Blanc, Paso Robles
FARTHER AFIELD: White wine from the Loire Valley, France

Warm Fingerling Potatoes with Vinegar, White Wine, and Dill

In this simple and delightfully nontraditional potato dish, the wine mixture seeps right into the pores of the delicate fingerlings during cooking, imbuing them with the fragrance and delicate acidity of the wine. The resulting dish, with its buttery shallot "sauce," is light and refreshing yet boasts great depth of flavor. SERVES 6

Prick each potato in two places with a fork. Place the potatoes in a tall, narrow saucepan and add the shallots, wine, vinegar, butter, 1½ teaspoons salt, and a generous grinding of pepper. Cover the pan and place over medium-high heat; bring to a boil, then decrease the heat to very low so the liquid is barely simmering. Cook for 20 to 25 minutes, until the potatoes are tender but not falling apart.

With a slotted spoon, transfer the potatoes to a shallow serving bowl and keep warm in a very low oven while you reduce the sauce.

Return the pan to high heat, uncovered, and simmer briskly until the liquid is the consistency of heavy cream, 5 to 8 minutes. Stir in the dill, drizzle the sauce over the potatoes, and serve.

CENTRAL COAST: Ojai Vineyard Riesling "Kick On Ranch," Los Alamos Valley
FARTHER AFIELD: Riesling Kabinett from Germany

2 pounds fingerling potatoes

4 shallots, very finely chopped

2 cups dry white wine, such as Sauvignon Blanc

⅓ cup white wine vinegar

2½ tablespoons butter

Fine sea salt and freshly ground black pepper

3 tablespoons finely chopped fresh dill or snipped fresh chives

Cirone Farms

Driving down See Canyon Road toward the Pacific, just south of San Luis Obispo, is like entering a time machine: Tidy rows of fruit trees are punctuated with old farming equipment, barrels, and aging artifacts of an agricultural era long past. See Canyon is a geological anomaly in the windy Central Coast. "It's warm in the summer, but not hot, and cool in the winter, yet protected from frosts," explains Mike Cirone, owner of Cirone Farms and See Canyon Apples. The deep, rich, and loamy soil supports a wealth of orchard crops, and the soil is well drained, with plenty of gravel—perfect for large crops like fruit trees, which must have strong, deep roots. Cirone Farms orchards are all dry farmed—no irrigation is used at all. "Dry farming results in incredibly intense fruit. People cannot believe the quality, aroma, and flavor of our fruit. It's something you don't see anymore in commercially grown produce."

"See Canyon has historically been dry farmed because the soils are rich, and there are natural underground aquifers," says Mike. "So we have continued that tradition, and we also grow flavorful, old-fashioned cultivars that produce rich, fragrant, juicy fruit."

Cirone Farms produces a wealth of different apples—including old-time varieties like Esopus Spitzenberg, Bellflower, Smokehouse, and Arkansas Black—plus almost 25 varietals of peaches, Blenheim apricots, avocados, Satsuma mandarin oranges, and white sapote. "I love to watch people take a bite out of a dry-farmed Blenheim apricot—it just doesn't compare to grocery fruit," says Mike. "It blows their minds." In the coastal avocado grove, fruit is allowed to hang for 18 months.

Tidy rows of fruit trees are punctuated with old farming equipment, barrels, and aging artifacts of an agricultural era long past.

"The longer the avocados mature, the more oils they produce," explains Mike. "Typically, our harvest season is in October, but in some years we don't finish until February, which is 22 months. These avocados are completely different than the imported fruits!"

"We don't use cold storage; everything is fresh," says Mike. "The fruit is picked and sold, picked and sold. We often go back to trees five times—we never strip a tree; we selectively pick only the truly ripe fruit." Mike's 14-year-old daughter, Kalena, helps sell fruit at the farmer's markets. "She's been doing it since she was five," says Mike. "A lot of people know her at the markets, and she's become super high-functioning, with poise and skills beyond her age."

Mike knew early in life that he wanted to work with the soil and crops. He majored in botany at Cal Poly and managed the school's peach and plum orchards during his college years. By the age of 24, he was also managing orchards in See Canyon. He leased some land and began planting his own trees shortly thereafter. "See Canyon has a long tradition of fruit stands, and that's how we started," says Mike. "Just a simple roadside stand." Mike credits the booming growth of farmer's markets and public interest in fine food with his success. "It just happened at the right time for me. Farmer's markets have become a very powerful way to reach people who are truly interested in high-quality food. It also gives us a chance to personally connect with people and slice open some fruit to taste."

IF YOU VISIT:
Fruit from Cirone Farms, selling under the banner See Canyon Apples, is only available at farmer's markets. Look for Mike's smiling face at Morro Bay's farmer's market, San Luis Obispo's Thursday night market, and the excellent Saturday Gottschalk's market on Madonna Road in San Luis Obispo (as well as the huge Wednesday Santa Monica market). Check www.cafarmersmarkets.com for times and locations.

Salad of Wine-Braised Baby Artichokes and New Potatoes

This dish tips its hat to a new style of Greek cooking that is fresh and clean, yet marvelously earthy. Think dill is only for fish? This dish will have you wanting to put fresh dill in everything. Trimming artichokes is a bit labor intensive, but oh-so-much better than choosing canned or frozen. In a pinch, use marinated artichoke hearts here, but you can also prep the fresh artichokes several hours ahead of time, then cover and refrigerate. Be sure to return to room temperature before reducing the braising liquid and finishing the recipe.   SERVES 6 AS AN APPETIZER OR SIDE DISH

6 to 8 baby artichokes, 3 to 5 ounces each

1 lemon, halved

½ cup Viognier or other medium-dry white wine (or vermouth)

½ cup extra-virgin olive oil

4 scallions, root ends trimmed, white parts finely chopped and green parts thinly sliced

5 garlic cloves, minced or pushed through a press

Fine sea salt and freshly ground black pepper

12 to 14 small red or white potatoes (preferably straight from the garden or farmer's market)

4 teaspoons fresh lemon juice, plus more as needed

⅓ cup capers, drained

Small handful coarsely chopped fresh dill

Trim off the stem and top half of each artichoke with a sharp knife. Pull off all the tough dark green outer leaves, to reveal the pale green-yellow inner leaves. With a paring knife, trim judiciously around the base just to remove any lingering dark green bits. Don't overdo this, or you'll end up trimming off the best parts. As you work, rub the cut parts with a lemon half to stop them from turning brown. Use a small, sharp spoon (a grapefruit spoon is ideal) to reach into the center and scrape away the choke (if the artichokes are smaller than 3 ounces each, the choke is edible and can be left intact).

In a saucepan large enough to hold all the artichokes in a single layer, nestle them together stem sides down and add enough water to come halfway up the sides. Add the wine, olive oil, scallion whites, garlic, ½ teaspoon salt, and plenty of pepper. Bring the liquid to a boil over high heat, then lower the heat, partially cover, and simmer, spooning the braising liquid over the tops of the artichokes occasionally, until they are tender at the base, 25 to 35 minutes depending on their size. Transfer the artichokes to a large bowl and reduce the liquid in the pan until thick and oily; the time will depend on the size of the pan and how much water you added—you are essentially reducing away all the water, leaving behind the olive oil and the flavor of the Viognier.

Steam the potatoes over simmering water until tender, 10 to 12 minutes. When cool enough to handle, cut in half and add to the artichokes.

Add the reduced braising liquid, lemon juice, scallion greens, capers, and dill; fold together. Taste for seasoning and adjust with salt, pepper, and lemon juice.

CENTRAL COAST: Tessa Marie Wines Vermentino, Camp 4 Vineyard, Santa Barbara County

FARTHER AFIELD: Vermentino or other white from southern Italy

Pinquito Bean and Farro Soup with Arugula and Pancetta

Here is a comforting, rustic, and colorful soup richly endowed with the flavor and homey goodness of beans, cured pork, and greens. Pinquito beans are a specialty of Santa Maria; they look rather like pinto beans, but have a lovely, creamy texture and flavor. Beans from the current year's harvest, generally available in fall and winter, require less soaking and cooking than year-old beans. There's no way to tell, unless your supplier knows. If in doubt, soak for at least 6 hours, and start checking the cooking beans for tenderness at the 1-hour mark. SERVES 6 TO 8

12 ounces pinquito beans, ideally from this year's harvest, or pinto beans from a reputable supplier, such as Ranch Gordo Beans, in Napa Valley

½ cup farro

2 tablespoons extra-virgin olive oil

1 large white or yellow onion, coarsely chopped

1 large carrot, coarsely chopped

1 celery rib, coarsely chopped

3 tablespoons chopped fresh sage

6 stems flat-leaf parsley

4- to 5-inch sprig rosemary

1 fresh bay leaf

1 small ham hock (6 to 8 ounces)

Fine sea salt and freshly ground black pepper

1 tablespoon fresh lemon juice or white wine vinegar

4 ounces pancetta, coarsely chopped

1 cup coarsely chopped arugula

Soak the pinquito beans for at least 2 hours and preferably 6 hours, or overnight.

In a small pot, cover the farro with water by about 4 inches. Bring to a simmer and cook for 25 to 40 minutes, until tender but not mushy. Drain and set aside.

In a large, heavy pot, warm the olive oil over medium-high heat. Add the onion, carrot, celery, and sage and sauté, stirring, until golden. Drain the pinquito beans and add them to the pot along with 10 cups of water, the parsley, rosemary, bay leaf, and ham hock. Bring to a simmer, partially cover, and cook for 1½ to 3 hours, until very tender (depending on the age of the beans); add a little water occasionally, if the level falls below the top of the beans.

Stir in ¾ teaspoon salt, plenty of pepper, and the lemon juice. Discard the bay leaf, parsley, and rosemary. Remove about one-quarter of the beans and puree in a blender or food processor, along with a little of the bean broth, until smooth. Return to the soup pot and add the farro. (If the ham hock is tender enough, you can discard the skin and bones, dice the meat, and return it to the pot. Otherwise, discard the hock or cool, freeze, and use again.) Cover and keep warm over very low heat.

continued on page 60

In a skillet, sizzle the pancetta until it is golden brown and crisp. Remove with a slotted spoon and stir into the warm soup. Stir in the arugula, taste for seasoning, and serve.

CENTRAL COAST: Native 9 Pinot Noir, Rancho Ontiveros Vineyards, Santa Maria Valley
FARTHER AFIELD: Red Burgundy from France

Swiss Chard with Pine Nuts, Golden Raisins, and Brown Butter Vinaigrette

Never, ever, let it be said that chard is boring—please! This is a substantial side dish that is complex and earthy, with that essence-of-butter flavor that can only be provided by browned butter (a favorite secret of chefs, but simple to make at home). It's the perfect partner for a light main course: baked or steamed fish or grilled chicken breasts—and it also makes an excellent "sauce" for pasta: Just fold the finished chard into a large, heated bowl of cooked pasta—perhaps pappardelle—drizzle with the brown butter vinaigrette, and scatter with the pine nuts and a little of your favorite grating cheese. Paired with pasta, this quantity would serve 10 to 12.   SERVES 6 AS A SIDE DISH OR APPETIZER

To make the vinaigrette, in a heatproof measuring jug, combine the shallot, mustard, vinegar, ¼ teaspoon salt, and plenty of pepper. In a small saucepan, cook the butter over medium heat, swirling the pan, until the foam subsides and it starts to turn a nutty caramel brown. Before it can turn black, quickly whisk in the lemon juice (it will sizzle madly). Whisk the hot butter mixture into the shallot mixture, then whisk in the olive oil. Set aside for up to 1 hour (if longer, the butter content may solidify; warm very gently over the lowest heat before serving, just until it flows).

Cover the raisins with the wine and let stand for 5 to 15 minutes to plump up. In a dry skillet, toast the pine nuts until golden, jiggling the pan frequently so they don't scorch. Dump out onto a cutting board and coarsely chop. Set aside.

Slice the chard ribs crosswise about ⅜ inch thick. Pile up the chard leaves and cut them crosswise into ½-inch strips.

Heat the oil in a large heavy skillet over low heat. Add the onion, chopped chard ribs, garlic, and ½ teaspoon salt. Cover and cook for about 10 minutes, stirring occasionally, until tender. Add the chard leaves and (drained) raisins; cover the pan and cook for 5 to 6 minutes, turning over with tongs halfway through. The chard should be tender but not soggy. Turn again gently to mix, taste for seasoning, and transfer to a platter. Drizzle with the vinaigrette and scatter with the pine nuts.

CENTRAL COAST: Alma Rosa Pinot Noir "Vin Gris," El Jabali Vineyard, Santa Rita Hills
FARTHER AFIELD: Rosé from Provence, France

VINAIGRETTE

1 shallot, very finely chopped

1 teaspoon Dijon mustard

3 tablespoons balsamic vinegar

Fine sea salt and freshly ground black pepper

4 tablespoons salted butter, preferably cultured or Irish

1 tablespoon fresh lemon juice

2 tablespoons extra-virgin olive oil

3 tablespoons golden raisins

¼ cup medium-dry white wine, such as Viognier, Chenin Blanc, or Chardonnay

2 tablespoons pine nuts

1½ pounds Swiss chard, leaves cut away from central ribs

1 tablespoon extra-virgin olive oil

About ⅓ cup thinly sliced white or yellow onion

8 garlic cloves, finely chopped

Orecchiette with Fava Beans and Prosciutto

The climate of the Central Coast is very similar to Tuscany, so fava beans thrive beautifully. The season starts early in the spring, when the small, lime green lima bean lookalikes are best eaten raw, peeled with a fingernail and downed with a hunk of sheep's cheese and a drizzle of the best olive oil. As spring turns to summer, the beans and their protective coating toughen slightly, so a cooked presentation, as here, is the better choice. This is a simple and quick weeknight pasta that depends entirely on the high quality of its few ingredients. (I keep Garlic Bread Crumbs in my freezer at all times; throw them into a nonstick pan to re-crisp for just a few moments, and your pasta will achieve virtually effortless excellence.)   SERVES 4

GARLIC BREAD CRUMBS
2 teaspoons extra-virgin olive oil

1 tablespoon minced garlic

Finely grated zest from 1 large
or 2 small scrubbed lemons

½ cup panko (Japanese bread crumbs)

⅓ cup coarsely chopped
fresh flat-leaf parsley

3 pounds fava beans, removed
from their pods (or fresh-
from-the-garden peas)

2 tablespoons extra-virgin olive oil

2 tablespoons butter

5 ounces prosciutto, finely chopped

4 medium garlic cloves, minced
or pushed through a press

Fine sea salt and freshly
ground black pepper

16 large leaves fresh mint,
finely chopped

14 to 16 ounces dried orecchiette

To make the bread crumbs, in a small skillet, combine all the ingredients. Over medium-high heat, toast the mixture, stirring frequently, until golden brown, 3 to 4 minutes. Set aside (this may be done ahead of time).

Over high heat, bring a large pot of generously salted water to a rolling boil, and fill a bowl with ice water. Add the fava beans to the pot and cook for 3 to 5 minutes (more for larger beans, less for smaller). Retrieve the beans with a large skimmer and plunge into the ice water. Turn off the heat under the pot of water and cover it while you skin the favas: After the beans have cooled for a minute or two, drain in a colander. Pinch the eye of each bean and slip off the thin white membrane (it helps to have a friend and a glass of rosé to help with this process).

In a large skillet or sauté pan, warm the olive oil and butter over medium heat. Add the prosciutto and sizzle gently for about 5 minutes, or until slightly golden and crisped. Add the garlic and stir for 1 minute, just until fragrant; stir in the skinned fava beans, ½ teaspoon salt, and plenty of pepper. Cook for 1 to 2 minutes more, just to warm the beans and give them a little color. Stir in the mint and remove from the heat.

Meanwhile, quickly return the pot of hot water to a boil. Add the orec-chiette and simmer until al dente. Drain the pasta well, reserving ½ cup of the cooking water. Immediately add the pasta to the skillet and place it over low heat. Toss with tongs, adding a little—or all—of the reserved pasta water to loosen the mixture and make it juicy. Serve the pasta scattered with the crispy-garlicky bread crumbs.

CENTRAL COAST: Casa Dumetz, "Sonja's Suds" sparkling Syrah rosé, Santa Ynez Valley
FARTHER AFIELD: Cremant d'Alsace Rosé, Alsace, France

L'Aventure Winery

Stephan Asseo has a love-hate relationship with rules. He loves it when Mother Nature bosses him around—not so much when human beings tell him how to make wine. Which is why, 14 years ago, he walked away from his established winery in Bordeaux, uprooting his young family to begin all over again in a land far from home.

Stephan "interviewed" every wine-making region in the world before settling in the hills west of Paso Robles. "I didn't want to make wine as the AVA [American Viticultural Area] dictated—I wanted to start my own story." He went to Argentina, Australia, Chile, and elsewhere in California.

"Even in Argentina, they have a history of how to make the wines; we could not live on a plateau in Chile because we had young children, and the goal was also not to live like wild people." The other requirement was a market that could bear a high per-bottle price, because he always knew the huge amount of work and sacrifice that would be involved in making it *his way*. The terroir in Paso Robles spoke to his soul, there were schools for his children, and there was a potential market for superior wines. Best of all? No rules and very little history.

His wife, Beatrice, a huge hands-on presence at every step of production, remembers the Paso Robles of that time. "There was no fish market, there were no restaurants, there was nothing," she says with a Gallic shrug and a smile. And yet the young family made it work for many years in a mobile home, until the wine started to reach its potential and wine drinkers and reviewers sat up (or rather, jumped up) and took notice. These days, Paso has just about everything Beatrice used to miss (chief among them the excellent fish market).

"I don't make wine for the marketplace. I make the wine I want to drink, that I feel is the best wine that can be made from my terroir,"

Each plant yields only about one bottle . . .

says Stephan, a passionate man with dark, soulful eyes, a mop of unruly salt-and-pepper curls, and laugh lines that hint at a fierce sense of humor behind the strict precision he brings to his wine making. Stephan likes to be in control of every single step, with every single vine, all the way from planting to bottle to glass. It's an intense business, with huge responsibilities (especially because he is considered one of the premier winemakers in the region), but it makes him feel free. In France, the powers that be tried to tell Stephan how to blend his wine. Now, *he* is The Decider. And his way is almost inconceivably tough compared with the techniques of many other winemakers in the region. Each plant yields only about one bottle—it's very high-density, very low-yield viticulture, and the vines are always a little bit stressed. "Not fat and full of sweet juice, like some overly made-up girl attracting all the wrong kind of attention," he says with an infectious grin. The proof is in the glass.

Stephan has been practicing biodynamics for about three years now. It doesn't make things easier, he says, but he feels it fulfills a responsibility to his beloved terroir and sets a good example for other winemakers. It takes three to five years for the natural anti-weed and anti-bug measures to kick in, so in the meantime he spends a lot of time on his tractor, and releases beneficial bugs into the vineyard (hoping they'll stick around and not fly off to the neighbor's place).

L'Aventure produces about 8,000 cases a year, and Stephan has no intention or desire to grow. "If I kept anything from my French culture, it's the importance of the estate above all. At this size, I can still control every step myself. If I'm still around in 10 years, I'll *still* be making 8,000 cases a year from these same 40 blocks." I'll raise a glass to that.

IF YOU VISIT:

The rural tasting room is open Thursdays through Sundays from 11 a.m. to 4 p.m., and at other times by appointment.

2815 Live Oak Road
Paso Robles, CA 93446

(805) 227-1588, ext. 204

www.aventurewine.com

Beans in a Flask in the Embers,
Sort of Like They Do It in Tuscany

In Tuscany, there is a legendary dish that inspires awe in the few who have tasted it and rampant desire in the many bean aficionados who have only heard of it (this includes most denizens of the post-Renaissance era). Sadly, in reality there's a disconnect: *Fagioli nel fiasco*, as it's known, too often results in a true fiasco when attempted by real people with real fireplaces. But it's easy to replicate this lusciously bean-friendly concept in your oven. Low, very slow, and gentle, moist heat results in an unctuous bean that will showcase your best olive oil like a long, slim model shows off a cashmere bathrobe. SERVES 4 TO 6

1 pound dried cannellini or
Great Northern beans

5 to 6 cups homemade or store-bought low-sodium chicken or vegetable broth

6 to 10 garlic cloves, smashed

2 sprigs fresh flat-leaf parsley

1 large sprig fresh rosemary

3 sprigs fresh sage

2 fresh bay leaves or 4 dried

¼ cup extra-virgin olive oil

Fine sea salt

TO FINISH
1 teaspoon Dijon mustard

1½ tablespoons red wine vinegar

4 tablespoons best-quality extra-virgin olive oil, plus more for drizzling

Freshly ground black pepper

2 tablespoons finely chopped
fresh flat-leaf parsley

2 cups cherry tomatoes,
halved or quartered

Cover the beans with 2 inches of water; let soak for 6 hours, or overnight (at room temperature).

Preheat the oven to 300°F. Drain the beans and transfer them to a large covered earthenware or cast-iron pot. Add the broth, garlic, herbs, and olive oil (the liquid should cover the beans by about 1 inch; add a little water, if necessary). Bring to a simmer on the stovetop, then cover and braise for 1½ to 2½ hours, until tender but not falling apart. Stir in ½ teaspoon salt, turn off the oven, and let the beans stand in the cooling oven, uncovered, for 30 minutes more.

With a slotted spoon, transfer the beans to a heavy serving bowl, discarding the remains of the herbs and the bay leaves.

In a small bowl, whisk together the mustard, vinegar, olive oil, ½ teaspoon salt, and plenty of pepper. Fold in the parsley and cherry tomatoes and spoon over the beans. Grind over a little more pepper, and drizzle with a little oil.

CENTRAL COAST: Qupé Roussanne, Bien Nacido Vineyard, Santa Maria Valley
FARTHER AFIELD: White Rhône blend from France

Warm Escarole with Bacon, Almonds, and Sherry Vinegar

This is an incredibly quick side dish with a depth of flavor that seems impossible, given the brief time and effort required of the cook. Like many things in life, its success depends on the quality of bacon selected.   SERVES 6

With a sharp knife, cut the escarole into approximately 1½-inch pieces. Place in a large serving bowl and refrigerate while you cook the bacon.

In a large, heavy skillet, cook the bacon over low heat, stirring occasionally, until most of the fat is rendered and the lardons are slightly crisp. Adjust the heat to medium and add the shallots, almonds, vinegar, sherry, salt, and pepper. Bring to a boil, stir for 20 to 30 seconds, then immediately pour over the escarole leaves, scraping the pan to be sure you get every delicious drop. Quickly toss with tongs; toss for longer than you imagine necessary to thoroughly coat and wilt the leaves and distribute all the ingredients evenly. Serve immediately.

CENTRAL COAST: Casa Dumetz Grenache, Tierra Alta Vineyard, Santa Ynez Valley
FARTHER AFIELD: Light, approachable Rhône blend—ideally a GSM (Grenache, Syrah, and Mourvedre)—from France

2 small heads escarole, cored, dark green outer leaves discarded

8 ounces cured smoked thick-cut bacon, cut crosswise into ⅓-inch strips (lardons)

2 large shallots, minced

1 cup slivered blanched almonds

1½ tablespoons sherry vinegar

1½ tablespoons dry sherry

1 teaspoon fine sea salt

Generous pinch of freshly ground black pepper

Rosé and Lemon Verbena Granita

This crunchy sorbet is as light as a feather and could be served as a palate cleanser between courses, a dessert after a heavy meal, or even as an appetizer on a hot summer day. The alcohol in the wine will proceed intact to the final granita, because it's never cooked off. If you prefer, you may bring the wine to a simmer for 2 minutes in a small saucepan before proceeding; this will cook off some (but not all) of the alcohol. Let cool to room temperature and proceed. Choose a deeply tinted rosé for maximum visual impact. SERVES 4

In a large shallow glass or metal baking dish that will fit in your freezer, combine the wine, grape juice, sugar, and herb. Stir until the sugar is dissolved. Freeze for 4 hours, stirring vigorously with a fork every 20 minutes after the first hour, to keep the granita from freezing into a solid block. Scrape down the sides and make an even mixture of large, flaky crystals. The granita should be served as a chunky ice, not a smooth sorbet. You can quit stirring at the 3-hour mark. Cover and keep frozen until ready to serve, up to 2 weeks. Scoop into a cold bowl or a pretty, chilled wineglass and serve with one or two almond macaroons on the side.

1¾ cups dry rosé wine, preferably a Grenache rosé

½ cup white grape juice (sweetened)

1 tablespoon superfine sugar

2 tablespoons finely chopped fresh lemon verbena, lemon balm, or mint

Almond macaroons or cookies, for serving

CENTRAL COAST: Flying Goat "Goat Bubbles" Sparkling Rosé, Solomon Hills Vineyard, Santa Maria Valley
FARTHER AFIELD: Prosecco from Italy or Cava from Spain

Chardonnay-Grape and Black Monukka Clafoutis

Rotta was one of the first three wineries in the Paso Robles region and beloved of the wine aficionados here long before the world began to recognize Paso's wines. Mike Giubbini remembers working in the vineyards as a kid, before his 30-year career as a fire captain. Now he runs Rotta, still proudly 100 percent family owned and the only producer of this rich, nutty, caramel- and vanilla-scented dessert wine. Black Monukka is made from the rare Black Monukka grape and is reminiscent of an old, really good tawny Port, which may be substituted if you aren't able to lay your hands on a bottle of this nectar. (It's also fantastic with a big hunk of aged cheddar or sheep's cheese.) Clafoutis is a classic French peasant dessert that's easy to make and very tasty. SERVES 6 TO 8

¾ cup Rotta Winery Black Monukka late-harvest dessert wine or tawny Port

2 pounds Chardonnay grapes or seedless red grapes

Unsalted butter (softened), for the baking dish

Granulated sugar, for the baking dish

5 eggs, preferably pasture raised

¾ cups sugar

⅔ cup heavy cream

⅔ cup whole milk

3 tablespoons all-purpose flour

½ teaspoon finely chopped fresh rosemary

Confectioners' sugar, for dusting

Preheat the oven to 425°F.

In a large roasting pan, combine the sweet wine and grapes. Roast the grapes for 25 minutes, shaking once or twice, until slightly shriveled. Remove the pan and lower the oven temperature to 350°F.

Butter an 8 by 12-inch (or similar size) earthenware or porcelain baking dish; dust the inside with granulated sugar, shaking out the excess.

In a blender, combine the eggs, sugar, cream, milk, and flour and blend until smooth. Pour half the batter into the prepared dish, and scatter the grapes (with all their juices) and the rosemary over the top. Pour the remaining batter around the sides of the dish.

Bake for about 1 hour, or until the batter is firm and puffed and the top is golden. Transfer to a rack to cool for at least 10 minutes, then sprinkle with the confectioners' sugar. Cut into squares and serve warm.

CENTRAL COAST: Municipal Winemakers "Fizz," sparkling Shiraz, Santa Barbara County
FARTHER AFIELD: Sparkling Shiraz from Australia

Zinfandel-Poached Pear Tart with Almond Crust and Frangipane

This crowd-pleasing dessert marries what was (once upon a time) virtually my only go-to dessert (pears poached in red wine) with that delicious almond-perfumed French confection called frangipane. You'll need a 12½-inch fluted tart pan with a removable base for this admittedly time-consuming knockout. (Happily, as with almost all of my go-to desserts, most of the work is done in advance.)   SERVES 8

To make the pears, combine the wine, sugar, lemon zest, and lemon juice in a medium saucepan. Bring to a simmer and cook for about 10 minutes. Add the pear halves, cover the pan, and poach at a low simmer for 12 to 15 minutes, until the pears are almost soft but definitely not falling apart (test often; it's better to undercook than overcook). Turn off the heat and let the pears cool to room temperature, uncovered, in their syrup. Ideally, cover and refrigerate overnight, or for up to 3 days. The flavor and color will improve with time.

To make the frangipane, combine the sliced almonds with the sugar in the bowl of a food processor and pulse just until grainy, like cornmeal. Add the eggs, butter, rum, and vanilla and pulse until creamy. Set aside (refrigerate for up to 2 days, if desired).

On a lightly floured surface, roll out the tart dough into a 14-inch circle about ⅛ inch thick. Fit into a 12½-inch tart pan with a removable base, folding the excess back in and pressing firmly to build up the sides. Refrigerate for at least 10 minutes and up to 4 hours before baking.

Preheat the oven to 400°F. Cut a large round of parchment paper and place in the tart shell. Fill with raw rice or pie weights. Bake the shell for 15 minutes, or until the edges of the pastry are barely golden. Remove the parchment and rice and return the crust to the oven for 5 minutes to dry it out. Let cool on a rack for at least 10 minutes and up to 4 hours.

continued on page 74

PEARS

1 bottle good Zinfandel, preferably an old-vine varietal

¾ cup sugar

Finely grated zest of 1 lemon

1½ tablespoons fresh lemon juice

5 almost-ripe Anjou or other small pears, peeled, halved, and cored

FRANGIPANE

4 ounces sliced almonds (just over 1 cup)

½ cup sugar

2 eggs

½ cup (4 ounces) unsalted butter, softened

1½ teaspoons dark rum or bourbon

¼ teaspoon best-quality vanilla extract

Tart Dough (recipe follows)

Red currant jelly or strained apricot jam, for glazing the pears

To finish the tart, preheat the oven to 350°F and place a rack in the lower third of the oven. Pour/spread the frangipane over the base of the tart shell. Slice partway into each pear from the rounded end, in ¼-inch slices, leaving the stem end intact. Distribute the pears rounded side up on top of the frangipane, fanning the slices out slightly. Bake until the frangipane is slightly golden and springy to the touch, 35 to 40 minutes. Let cool on a rack. Just before serving, warm a little jelly in a small pan or the microwave, and use it to brush the pears, just to give them a nice, finished gloss.

Tart Dough

⅓ cup skin-on whole almonds

8 ounces all-purpose flour (about 1⅔ cups, but it's best to weigh)

Pinch of fine sea salt

½ cup plus 1 tablespoon (4½ ounces) very cold unsalted butter, cut into small cubes

3 tablespoons fresh orange juice, cold

2 to 3 tablespoons cold water

Place the almonds in the bowl of a food processor fitted with the metal blade and grind to a fine, grainy powder. Add the flour and salt, pulse to mix, then add the butter and pulse on and off in 2-second bursts, four or five times, just until the mixture resembles large bread crumbs. Remove the cover and drizzle the orange juice and 2 tablespoons of the water evenly over the mixture, then pulse again just until the dough begins to clump together and form a rough, shaggy mass. If it does not begin to clump within 10 to 15 seconds, sprinkle with another tablespoon of water and pulse again; do not overwork.

Bring the dough together into a ball on a lightly floured surface, then form into a 2-inch-thick round disk about 6 inches in diameter. Wrap with plastic wrap and refrigerate for at least 3 hours or overnight. Let stand at room temperature for 20 to 30 minutes before rolling out.

CENTRAL COAST: Tablas Creek Vin de Paille "Quintessence," Paso Robles (Roussanne)
FARTHER AFIELD: Sauternes, France

Potato, Caramelized Onion, and Goat Cheese Gratin

This rustic charmer is the cowboy cousin to the lily-white, refined dish known (and adored) by many as "scalloped potatoes." My version may not win any beauty contests, but you'll be swept right off your feet and holler "More!" To prevent the potato slices from browning, assemble the rest of the ingredients in the baking dish first, before you begin slicing. Don't rinse the sliced potatoes: Their natural starch helps to set this luscious, creamy, and complex gratin. SERVES 6 TO 8

Place a large, heavy skillet over medium-high heat and add the butter and oil. When the foam from the butter has subsided, add the onions and ½ teaspoon salt to the hot fat. Cook, stirring and tossing occasionally, until the onions are golden brown—even a bit charred in places—and tender, about 15 minutes. Transfer to a cutting board, chop coarsely, and set aside. Add the panko to the skillet, stirring to fully blend with the onion-scented fat. Set aside.

Preheat the oven to 400°F. In a large earthenware, ceramic, or glass baking dish (about 10 by 13 by 2 inches), combine the milk, cream, a pinch of nutmeg, ½ teaspoon salt, plenty of pepper, and the garlic.

Slice the potatoes about ⅛ inch thick, preferably in a food processor fitted with the slicing blade or using a mandoline. With clean hands, mix the potatoes thoroughly with the liquid, to be sure the slices are evenly coated. Fold in the caramelized onions, distributing them evenly. Scatter the goat cheese over the top. Cover the dish tightly with aluminum foil. Bake for 1 hour, or until the potatoes are tender when poked with the tip of a sharp knife.

Uncover the dish, scatter the Fontina and panko mixture evenly over the top of the potatoes, and cook for about 25 minutes more, until the top is bubbling and golden brown. Remove from the oven and let stand for 15 to 20 minutes before serving, to firm the "custard" slightly. Reheat for 5 to 10 minutes in a low oven, if desired.

CENTRAL COAST: Kaena Hapa Blanc (Grenache Blanc, Roussanne), Santa Ynez Valley
FARTHER AFIELD: Grenache Blanc, Australia

1 tablespoon butter

1 tablespoon grapeseed or vegetable oil

1 large white or yellow onion, halved lengthwise, then sliced crosswise ½ inch thick

Fine sea salt

½ cup panko (Japanese bread crumbs)

2½ cups whole milk

1¼ cups heavy cream

Ground nutmeg

Freshly ground black pepper

4 garlic cloves, finely chopped or pushed through a press

3 pounds Yukon gold potatoes

4 ounces soft, fresh goat cheese, crumbled

3 ounces Italian Fontina, coarsely grated

Rosemary-Polenta Cake
with Warm Plum Compote

Adding polenta yields a deep yellow, unexpectedly crunchy pound cake with enough structure to stand up to a serious dessert wine. The gentle plum compote tames the masculinity of the pound cake, but you could also top a wedge of this sunny cake with fresh berries, a little sweetened mascarpone, and a drizzle of pure maple syrup.   SERVES 6 TO 8

CAKE

¾ cup (6 ounces) unsalted butter, softened, plus more for the pan

½ cup polenta or coarsely ground yellow cornmeal, plus more for the pan

¾ cup granulated sugar

¼ teaspoon fine sea salt

1 teaspoon best-quality vanilla extract

4 eggs, at room temperature

½ cup all-purpose flour

1 teaspoon baking powder

½ cup polenta or coarsely ground yellow cornmeal

1 tablespoon finely minced fresh rosemary

PLUM COMPOTE

2 tablespoons crème de cassis

2 tablespoons apple juice

1 tablespoon superfine sugar

4 ripe plums, pitted and cut into ⅛-inch slices

2 cups blackberries

LEMON MASCARPONE

1 cup mascarpone

3 teaspoons finely grated lemon zest

2 teaspoons superfine sugar

To make the cake, preheat the oven to 350°F. Generously butter a 5 by 9-inch loaf pan and sprinkle it with polenta, shaking out the excess.

In a stand mixer fitted with the paddle attachment, or with a strong handheld mixer, cream the butter, sugar, and salt together on high speed until light and fluffy, about 7 minutes. Add the vanilla. Lower the mixer speed and add the eggs, one at a time, scraping down the bowl occasionally and completely incorporating each one before adding the next. Sift in the flour and baking powder, then add the polenta and rosemary, and mix until incorporated. Pour the batter into the pan.

Bake until the top springs back when pressed and a skewer inserted in the center comes out clean, about 45 minutes. Let cool in the pan on a rack for 15 minutes. Run a knife around the pan to release the cake and invert it onto the rack. Let cool completely.

To make the compote, combine the crème de cassis, apple juice, and sugar in a medium saucepan. Stir over low heat until the sugar has dissolved. Increase the heat and bring the mixture to a boil. Add the plums and blackberries and reduce the heat to medium. Cover and simmer for 8 to 10 minutes, until the plums are tender. Uncover the pan and simmer for 7 to 10 minutes more, stirring occasionally, until the syrup has reduced to a glaze.

To make the mascarpone, combine the mascarpone with the lemon zest and sugar.

Cut the cake into 1-inch-thick slices and serve with a spoonful of compote and a dollop of mascarpone.

CENTRAL COAST: Palmina Malvasia Bianca "Santita," Santa Ynez Valley
FARTHER AFIELD: Tawny Port from Portugal (or a Port-*style* wine from elsewhere)

CHAPTER 3

From Field and Barnyard

Which came first, the chicken or the egg? There are so many people raising chickens in their backyards these days that I imagine the question has become a pressing part of barnyard discourse. But there's no need to decide. Eggs aren't just for breakfast anymore; they have assumed their rightful role as stars of hors d'oeuvre, salad, and main course. Eggs are an excellent source of protein in a world where we're learning to take full advantage of the sustainable variety. Pasture-raised eggs are to battery-raised eggs as cultured butter is to margarine—not even in the same family. Their color and rich depth of flavor is unparalleled, especially as the days get longer and the chickens get happier. And those chickens? Please search out pasture raised chickens for the dishes in this chapter, if you can. If you're lucky enough to have a grandparent around, he or she is guaranteed to shout, "Aha! This is how chicken is *supposed* to taste!" Don't you want your kids to know the true and honest flavor of chicken? They'll never find out by eating supermarket birds.

In Europe, rabbit is on the menu possibly even more often than chicken (as it was at my wedding, deep in the heart of Tuscany). As we seek lean, clean, responsibly farmed protein in our diets, rabbit is joining the party—and it's *delicious*! Debbie Estrada, of Bella-Sage Rabbitry in Paso Robles, raises her rabbits on natural feed with the addition of sweet meadow hay, without steroids, hormones, or antibiotics. It's a family farm with a passion for doing things right.

Under the lovely green oak trees that dot the rolling hills of the Central Coast, treasure (in the form of mushrooms) can be found whenever there's a little rain followed by some sun. The bounty of chanterelles foraged by our cousin Bob's friend Erin in See Canyon set me off on an extended chanterelle-utilization mode that resulted in some of the recipes in this chapter—such as Soft-Scrambled Eggs with Fresh Chanterelles, and Sautéed Wild Mushrooms with Herb Salad (the ones that shouted "Permanent Keeper!").

While fresh eggs are excellent in almost all dishes, be sure to use eggs that are at least a week old if you plan to hard-cook and peel them. Otherwise, there will be tears. Also, please see the Recipe Note on page xi regarding egg sizes and weights. Eggs from pasture raised hens come in all sizes, so it pays to weigh or measure the yolks and whites!

Wine pairings by Cris Cherry, proprietor of Villa Creek restaurant and Villa Creek Winery

Dandelion Salad with Soft-Boiled Eggs and Crispy Bacon

This rustic and elemental barnyard dish is a fantastic showcase for pasture raised eggs. Serve it for a late brunch on a sunny Sunday and your friends will ooh and aah. The rich, deep yellow color of the yolks is reward enough; add honest, pure flavor and the knowledge that the chickens lived happy lives, and the choice is pretty clear. If dandelion greens are unavailable, substitute the pale inner hearts only of two or three heads of frisée. SERVES 4 TO 6

6 large free-range or organic eggs

6 ounces thick-sliced cured or uncured bacon (about 6 slices)

1 large shallot, minced

Fine sea salt and freshly ground black pepper

1½ teaspoons whole-grain mustard

2 small garlic clove, minced or pushed through a press

2 tablespoons aged red wine vinegar or balsamic vinegar

6 tablespoons extra-virgin olive oil

12 plump, juicy sun-dried tomato halves

6 ounces baby dandelion greens (6 cups; red or green variety)

Place the eggs carefully in a saucepan and cover with cold water. Place over high heat, partially cover, and when the water just begins to simmer, remove from the heat, cover the pan, and let stand for 3 minutes. Drain and immediately cover the eggs with cold water, adding 4 ice cubes to stop the cooking. Let stand for up to 2 hours before serving.

In a heavy skillet, sauté the bacon over medium-low heat until crisp and brown. Drain on paper towels and break apart into large pieces.

In a large mixing bowl, combine the shallot, ¾ teaspoon salt, ½ teaspoon pepper, mustard, garlic, vinegar, and oil. Whisk until smooth and emulsified.

Crack the eggs and scoop them out of their shells, pulling them apart into large chunks with your fingers or a spoon and fork. Distribute the eggs evenly on a platter and scatter the tomatoes over the top. Add the dandelion greens to the mixing bowl and toss to coat the leaves thoroughly. Distribute the dressed greens over the eggs and scatter with the bacon. Serve right away.

CENTRAL COAST: Kinero Chardonnay, Arroyo Grande Valley
FARTHER AFIELD: Chablis from France or Moscato d'Asti from Italy

Soft-Scrambled Eggs
with Fresh Chanterelles

The oaky woods of the Central Coast regularly offer the precious gift of chanterelles, *if* you know where to look for them. If you don't have an inside connection, head for one of the many bountiful farmer's markets in springtime, where you should also be able to pick up some fabulously fresh, deep yellow–yolked eggs from local chickens. This recipe was inspired by one I saw in an Australian travel magazine many years ago. The large, creamy curds are the perfect luxurious canvas for the richness of the chanterelles.   SERVES 4

About 1 pound fresh chanterelles, stem ends trimmed if dry and woody

2 teaspoons extra-virgin olive oil

Fine sea salt and freshly ground white or black pepper

8 eggs, preferably pasture raised and very fresh

1½ cups heavy cream

2 tablespoons butter

2 tablespoons finely snipped fresh chives

Brush the mushrooms clean. Slice them about ⅓ inch thick, then cut into manageable chunks. Warm the olive oil in a large nonstick skillet over medium heat, and cook the mushrooms until they give up their liquid, about 5 minutes, stirring occasionally. Keep cooking until all the liquid is evaporated and the pieces begin to brown. If necessary, add a little more olive oil to keep them from scorching. Season with salt and pepper. Transfer to a plate.

In a bowl, whisk together the eggs, cream, and ¾ teaspoon salt until very smooth. Place the same skillet used to cook the mushrooms over medium heat and add the butter.

When the butter foam has begun to subside, tilt the pan to distribute the butter evenly. Scoop all the egg mixture into the pan and let the eggs cook undisturbed for 2 minutes. Stir gently with a wooden spoon, bringing the partially cooked edges in toward the center. Let stand for 2 minutes more, then add the mushrooms and gently fold them in, keeping the curds nice and large. Remove the pan from the heat and let stand for 1 minute. Spoon onto warm plates and scatter with the chives.

CENTRAL COAST: Villa Creek Roussanne, James Berry Vineyard, Paso Robles
FARTHER AFIELD: Côtes du Roussillon Blanc, France (Roussanne, Carignan Gris, Rolle)

Zucchini and Mint Frittata
with Ricotta Salata

Here's another great candidate for a relaxed wine country–style brunch with friends. So hit the farmer's market and pick up some good eggs and a pound or two of the thick, rustic bacon from Creston Ranch or another local rancher-producer. Frittatas are also great candidates for a bucolic picnic; wrap the wedges individually for ease of serving to picnickers.   SERVES 4

Heat the oil in a small ovenproof nonstick skillet over medium heat. Add the zucchini and shallot and cook for 1 minute, stirring frequently. Cover and lower the heat to medium-low; cook, stirring occasionally, until the zucchini is only just barely tender and still bright green, 2 to 3 minutes. Add a pinch of salt and a grinding of pepper; increase the heat to medium-high and cook, stirring, until dry, about 1 minute.

In a large bowl, whisk the eggs and wine until smooth with another good pinch of salt and grinding of pepper. Fold in the zucchini mixture, half of the mint, and the ricotta salata.

Preheat the broiler.

Wipe out the small skillet and add the butter; place over low heat. Add the frittata mixture and cook, without stirring, until the bottom is light golden, 3 to 5 minutes. As it cooks, occasionally lift the edges and tilt the pan so uncooked egg will flow to the edges.

When the outer 2 inches are set but the center is still jiggly, transfer the pan to the broiler and broil until the top is set and slightly golden. Loosen the edges and slide onto a plate. Cut into wedges and serve, scattered with the remaining mint.

CENTRAL COAST: Ranchero Cellars "Chrome," La Vista Vineyard, Paso Robles (Grenache Blanc, Viognier)
FARTHER AFIELD: Vernaccia from Sardinia or Cassis Blanc from France

2 teaspoons extra-virgin olive oil or grapeseed oil

2 small green or yellow zucchini (or 1 of each), cut into fine julienne

1 large shallot, finely chopped

Fine sea salt and freshly ground black pepper

7 large pasture raised or free-range eggs, beaten until smooth

1 tablespoon medium dry white wine, such as Viognier, Roussanne, or a Rhône blend

1 tablespoon coarsely chopped fresh mint

1½ ounces ricotta salata, crumbled or chopped

1 tablespoon butter

Villa Creek

From my perch on Cris and JoAnn Cherry's sun-drenched deck, way
up Peachy Canyon on Paso Robles's west side, I can see goats, turkeys,
chickens, cats, dogs—and on the slopes opposite, deer and wild turkeys.
"We had some pigs," says Cris, a forty-something mountain biking
aficionado who grew up in a successful restaurant family, "but we're
moving the pens downwind of the house before we get any more."

The land slopes gently upward here, near the top of the canyon, and
the grass-green hills are studded with wizened walnut burls left over from
the first incarnation of this 60-acre property. Soon, there will be vines on
those hills: Spanish clones of Grenache will be both planted and grown
biodynamically. "We're just so inspired by Spanish wines, especially those
from the border areas of France and Spain," JoAnn tells me, as we sit in
barrel-stave wooden chairs, surveying the peaceful pastoral scene.

Everything about this small but immensely passionate operation is
inspired and organic, from its initial conception back in the mid-1990s
to its future cultivation. The Cherrys started visiting the area back in
'96, when they met some of the young winemakers—like Matt Trevisan
and Justin Smith—who were putting Paso Robles on the map. Cris and
JoAnn wanted to raise their young children away from San Diego and
were looking for a place to open a restaurant with his father, Bob Cherry.
Local wine-making pioneers Gary Eberle and Justin Baldwin got wind
of this possibility; longing for a world-class dining establishment in what
was essentially still a cow town, they were full of encouragement. "Open
a restaurant here, please! We'll help make it work for you!" Bob was
skeptical, but when a local agent told them about a dive bar right on the
park, he drove up and took some pictures. Surprisingly, he *loved* the spot.

The locals loved the restaurant, too. Villa Creek quietly opened its
doors in 1998. On a Friday night, old pickup trucks and domestic cars
would fill perhaps half the parking spaces around the park. "Now it's

packed with new pickup trucks and way nicer cars," says Cris.

The Cherrys brought real cheese to Paso. "We'd drive to San Francisco every week to get great cheeses—we even had a cheese course on the menu—revolutionary!" says JoAnn. They also brought a resource arguably crucial to the development of Paso as a world-class wine-making region: a large and varied cellar with wines from the rest of the world. Many winemakers here knew only big Paso wines and had little experience with their own grape varietals as grown in the Rhône valley, or in Spain.

"All truly good winemakers drink globally," says Cris. And now they could—right at home in Paso.

Then, about three years into their success as restaurateurs, they made some wine. And it changed everything. At first the idea was to make a little house wine, but because of their personal connections, they acquired some of the very best grapes in the area: from James Berry and Denner vineyards. It clearly was far more than a house wine. Also clearly, the Cherrys had found their true passion. Armed with long-term contracts for fruit from these renowned vineyards, they brought in an experienced and talented chef from New York, Tom Fundaro, to helm the now renowned Villa Creek's kitchen while the Cherrys passionately pursued their goal: to further develop their estate into a biodynamic farm with vineyards, sheep, cows, pigs, and other edibles.

"We're totally focused on the quality of ingredients and quality of *life*. Integrity is crucial: It's good for you and it's good for the planet. That's why we make the effort to be biodynamic. We're trying to make the best wine possible. I know everybody says that, but we really mean it. It's not about being rich and famous. It's about making a great product that's really amazing, with—and without—food."

At first the idea was to make a little house wine . . .

IF YOU VISIT:

Villa Creek's tasting room is located at 5995 Peachy Canyon Road, in the bucolic hills west of Paso Robles. Open Monday through Thursday by appointment only. Open Friday, Saturday, and Sunday from 11 a.m. to 5 p.m. Appointments recommended; call (805) 238-7145.

www.villacreekwine.com

Shirred Eggs on a Bed of Spinach with Salsa and Smoky Chipotle

This dish really showcases the lovely color of good eggs, and it makes a perfect wine country weekend brunch for two couples (it can also easily be doubled if you have a big gang in the house). Don't skip the bread crumbs here, as they really make the dish. I can't think of too many non-dessert dishes that would not benefit by the addition of crispy bread crumbs. SERVES 4

1¼ pounds spinach leaves

1 tablespoon butter, plus more butter, softened, for the ramekins

1 small shallot, very finely chopped

½ cup heavy cream

Fine sea salt and freshly ground black pepper

4 eggs, preferably pasture raised

About ¼ cup chunky salsa

Chipotle Bread Crumbs (recipe follows) or well-seasoned panko (Japanese bread crumbs)

Bring a large pot of lightly salted water to a boil and add the spinach. Make sure it is fully submerged and cook for 2 minutes. Immediately drain in a colander and run under lots of cold running water until no longer warm. Gather the spinach into 4 or 5 tennis ball–size balls, and squeeze each very firmly to extract as much water as possible (until they are golf ball–size balls). Chop coarsely.

In a large skillet, melt the butter over medium-low heat. Add the shallot and cook for 1 minute, then add the spinach and cook, stirring frequently, until the excess moisture has evaporated, 2 to 4 minutes (the spinach should not brown). Stir in the cream, ½ teaspoon salt, and plenty of black pepper; cook for 4 to 5 minutes more, until thick and quite dry but still bright green. Remove from the heat.

Preheat the oven to 350°F and generously butter four 4- to 5-ounce ramekins. Place them on a baking sheet and divide the spinach among the ramekins, smoothing each top into an even surface. With the back of a spoon, form a rounded 1½-inch well in the top of the spinach in each dish. Break an egg into each well. Carefully transfer the dishes to the oven and bake for 13 to 15 minutes, until the whites of the eggs are set and the yolks are still nice and runny (they will continue to cook a bit after coming out of the oven).

Remove from the oven, mound a spoonful of salsa over each egg, and scatter with some bread crumbs. Serve at once.

Chipotle Bread Crumbs

In a small skillet, melt the butter over medium-low heat. Add the bread crumbs, garlic, and chipotle; season generously with salt and pepper. Stir constantly for 7 to 8 minutes, until crisp. Remove from the heat and set aside. If desired, place in a small, airtight container and keep at room temperature for up to 24 hours before using. Or, you can also freeze them for up to 2 months.

CENTRAL COAST: Villa Creek "Pink," Paso Robles (Grenache, Mourvedre, Carignan)
FARTHER AFIELD: Rosé from Provence, France

2 teaspoons butter or olive oil

¾ cup fresh bread crumbs

1 large garlic clove, minced or pushed through a press (optional)

¼ teaspoon ground chipotle powder, or hot pure chile powder

Fine sea salt and freshly ground black pepper

Sautéed Wild Mushrooms with Herb Salad

When fall brings out the wild mushrooms, it's an ideal time to hark back to the dog days of summer by turning them into a salad with the bright flavors of fresh herbs. I like to add even more earthy-woodsy flavor with some exotic wild mushrooms. If you can't find any cepes/porcini/boletus (very seasonal), dried cepes are usually available and are easily "reconstituted" by soaking in very hot water for about 20 minutes. Be sure to squeeze them to get rid of most of the water, so the water doesn't dilute the dressing.   SERVES 6 AS A SIDE DISH OR APPETIZER

DRESSING

2 tablespoons sherry vinegar

1½ teaspoons Dijon mustard

Fine sea salt and freshly
ground black pepper

6 tablespoons extra-virgin olive oil

1½ pounds mixed wild mushrooms,
such as chanterelles, lobster,
oyster, and/or shiitake

2 tablespoons olive oil

1 tablespoon butter

2 shallots, finely chopped

Fine sea salt and freshly
ground black pepper

4 cloves garlic, minced or
pushed through a press

3 ounces fresh or 1 ounce dried cepes/
porcini/boletus mushrooms (if dried,
reconstituted; optional; see above)

6 cups (about 6 ounces) mixed greens

10 fresh chives, snipped into 2-inch lengths

¼ cup fresh flat-leaf parsley leaves

1 tablespoon coarsely chopped fresh dill
or chervil or 1 teaspoon fresh tarragon

To make the dressing, combine the vinegar, mustard, ½ teaspoon salt, plenty of pepper, and the olive oil in a large bowl. Whisk until smooth and set aside.

Remove any fibrous stems from the wild mushrooms, brush them clean, and slice any larger mushrooms; quarter the smaller varieties.

Heat the olive oil and butter in a large skillet over medium-high heat. As soon as the foam has subsided, add the wild mushrooms and shallots, season generously with salt and pepper, and cook, stirring frequently, until the mushrooms are dry, brown, and slightly crisped, 6 to 8 minutes. Add the garlic and cepes, remove from the heat, and toss for 1 minute more.

Add the greens, chives, parsley, and dill to the bowl with the dressing; toss to combine.

Divide the herb salad among small plates. Top each with a mound of the hot mushrooms and serve.

CENTRAL COAST: Villa Creek "Garnacha," Denner Vineyard, Paso
Robles (Grenache)
FARTHER AFIELD: Gamay from Beaujolais, France, or Garnacha
from Tarragona, Spain

Dubost Ranch Winery

Call Curt Dubost an "old-timer" and his face will light up like the noon sky. His family has been farming and ranching on the west side of Paso Robles, just over the Santa Lucia Mountains from the Hearst Castle and the Pacific Ocean, since the mid-1880s.

Originally from the Cherbourg region of France, the Dubosts— blacksmiths and miners by trade—fled the upheaval of the Franco-Prussian War. The family then settled in South Dakota, where Custer was busy making a last stand. Finding that a bit too crazy as well, they next set up shop in the Sandwich Islands (now Hawaii), briefly pounding iron implements for the royal family. When cinnabar was discovered on the Central Coast, the peripatetic family made its way by clipper ship to Cayucos, and from there inland to the Adelaida area west of Paso Robles, where they *finally* set down roots. They haven't budged since, and if Curt has his way, they never will.

Curt's grandchildren are the sixth generation on the 400-acre ranch, a lyrical arrangement of hills and dales once planted with hard grains such as barley and now home to one of the most engaging grassroots family wine-making operations in the region (as well as a plethora of wild boar and other critters). Unable to make a living dry farming—"This land wouldn't support even one person at today's commodity prices"— Curt was receptive to the passionate plan of his stepson Jacob Raines, who caught the bug working with Ken Volk and other iconic local winemakers. "We'll grow vines and make wine," he told Curt in 2002. Curt saw what was happening in the hills immediately around the ranch: Justin Winery was grabbing worldwide attention, Halter Ranch had just been purchased by a wealthy Swiss businessman, and Tablas Creek was winning awards. Curt saw the wine as a way to keep the land in the family and the family on the land. "You see an ebb and flow here, in the size of these ranches. People keep the land if they can find any possible

way to do so. Many are forced to sell pieces of land to pay estate taxes, or the children lose interest and parcels are broken up."

Curt was in. But there was no money to do things the way the bigger wineries did. "Jacob wore out three pairs of boots planting our vines," says his mother, Kate, a luminous, can-do woman who dresses up like a charm but always has a touch of dirt under her fingernails; her radiance seems to come from loving her family and the land with equally wild abandon.

And so, from barley to grapevines and olive trees, Dubost Ranch made wine and olive oil all from their own estate. They began to attract attention for the quality of Jake's wines and of Kate and Curt's olive oil. Curt often reigned at his heavy iron barbecue, grilling wild boar from the ranch for visitors and enthusiastic wine club members. And then came the summer of 2010—not long before harvest—and an unimaginably tragic accident: Jacob was killed when the ATV he was driving on the ranch rolled over. The family was devastated. Kate still has no idea how they brought in the 2010 harvest. But they owed it to Jake to honor his legacy, and somehow it got done. Jake's younger brother, Zachary, who'd worked under Terry Coulter at Adelaida Cellars for four years, had always hoped to work alongside his brother. But ranching and wine making can make for tough battlefield promotions. Zack stepped into his brother's shoes, and the wines he's now making are every bit as complex and nuanced as they'd been under Jake's helm. "If Zack hadn't been able to step in, the winery would have closed," says Curt. "We had no money to pay a winemaker."

True grit. Verifiably sip-worthy wine. Try the Homestead Red— it really does come from a homestead. And don't miss the olive oil— if there's any left. Or Kate's smile.

Kate's radiance seems to come from loving her family and the land with equally wild abandon.

IF YOU VISIT:

Don't miss the lovely burnt-sienna straw-bale winery, or the vehicular history of the ranch: five hard-working vehicles, from the 1880s spring wagon to the 1955 Ford pickup, housed in a brand-new open shed not far from Curt's grill.

Tasting room hours: Thursday to Monday, 11 a.m. to 5 p.m.
9988 Chimney Rock Road
Paso Robles, CA 93446

(805) 226-8463

www.dubostwine.com

Soft Polenta with Porcini and Mascarpone

The intensity of even a small amount of dried porcini adds plenty of that classic, woodsy, and Tuscan-esque perfume to this cozy dish, but if you can find fresh porcini mushrooms (aka cepes or boletus), by all means substitute a few ounces for the combo of dried porcini and cremini here. You could also substitute shiitake, or any other single fresh mushroom or combination that you can find or forage. I would certainly serve this as a main course, perhaps on a drizzly fall Sunday, accompanied by a beautiful salad of crisp and bitter greens—think radicchio, endive, and walnuts—in which case it would serve fewer people (but it can easily be doubled).

SERVES 4 TO 6 AS AN APPETIZER OR SIDE DISH, OR 2 OR 3 AS A MAIN COURSE

½ ounce dried porcini mushrooms

1 tablespoon extra-virgin olive oil

1 tablespoon butter

2 large shallots, finely chopped

1 teaspoon finely chopped
fresh rosemary

6 ounces cremini or white
mushrooms, woody stems trimmed
away, coarsely chopped

3 garlic cloves, finely chopped

4 cups homemade or store-bought
low-sodium chicken broth

1 teaspoon fine sea salt

1 cup polenta or coarsely
ground yellow cornmeal

Freshly ground black pepper

½ cup grated Italian Fontina

½ cup mascarpone

2 tablespoons finely
snipped fresh chives

Soak the porcini mushrooms in very hot water for 30 minutes. Squeeze dry and chop coarsely.

In a small skillet, warm the olive oil and butter over medium heat. Add the shallot, rosemary, cremini mushrooms, and garlic and sauté, stirring occasionally, for 5 to 6 minutes, until softened. Add the chopped porcini and sauté for 3 minutes more. Remove from the heat.

In a heavy saucepan, bring the chicken broth to a simmer and add the salt. Decrease the heat to low and, when the liquid is gently simmering, sprinkle the polenta over in a very slow, thin stream, whisking constantly until all the grains are incorporated and no lumps remain. Switch to a wooden spoon and stir every 1 or 2 minutes for 25 to 30 minutes, until the mixture pulls away from the sides of the pan and the grains of polenta have softened. Season with plenty of pepper, then stir in the Fontina and remove the pan from the heat.

Return the mushrooms to medium heat, just to warm through. Taste both mixtures for seasoning. Spoon the warm polenta onto individual plates and top with a jumble of mushrooms and a spoonful of mascarpone. Scatter the chives over the top.

CENTRAL COAST: Lone Madrone "Old Hat," Paso Robles (Zinfandel, Petite Sirah)
FARTHER AFIELD: Cornas from France or Nero d'Avola from Sicily, Italy

Coq-au-Viognier

The kind of deep and voluptuous flavors showcased in this riff on the classic French coq-au-vin do not come without effort; it's the careful caramelization in each step that yields such impressive results. I can't think of a better way to spend a chilly Sunday afternoon, when I have no other care in the world than to create a rich and deeply satisfying repast for my loved ones. The result here will be truly, madly, deeply improved if you are able to source a pasture raised chicken. Also note that if you use fresh pearl onions (or small shallots), they will take a bit longer to cook through until tender. Turn down the heat and give them time.   SERVES 4 OR 5

1 (750-ml) bottle Central Coast Viognier or other medium-dry white wine

2 cups homemade or store-bought low-sodium chicken broth

1 (3½ pound) chicken, preferably pasture raised, cut into 8 pieces (2 each: leg, thigh, wing with some of the breast, rest of breast)

Fine sea salt and freshly ground black pepper

6 slices thick-cut bacon, cut crosswise into ¼-inch strips

4 tablespoons salted or unsalted butter

1 large onion, coarsely chopped

1 large leek, white part only, coarsely chopped

3 large garlic cloves, smashed

1 sprig fresh thyme

1 fresh bay leaf or 2 dried

24 frozen pearl onions, thawed (or fresh, peeled; or small shallots, peeled)

12 ounces small white mushrooms, halved (or if large, quartered)

10 plump, juicy sun-dried tomatoes, cut into thick strips

½ teaspoon white wine vinegar

In a large, heavy saucepan, combine the wine and broth; bring to an active simmer, uncovered, to reduce by almost half (to about 3 cups). This will take about 20 minutes. Remove from the heat.

Rinse the chicken pieces with cold water and dry thoroughly. Season generously on all sides, using about 2 teaspoons each of salt and pepper.

In a large Dutch oven or heavy pot, sizzle the bacon over medium-low heat until it's crisp and all the fat has rendered out. With a slotted spoon, transfer the bacon to absorbent paper towels. Add 1 tablespoon of the butter to the bacon fat and sauté the chopped onion, leek, and garlic over medium heat until soft and slightly golden, about 10 minutes. Scoop all the vegetables into a strainer and press to release as much fat as possible back into the pot. Transfer the vegetables to the reduced wine.

Over medium-high heat, warm the fat and add another 1 tablespoon butter. When the butter has foamed, brown the chicken (do this in two batches if the pot isn't large enough to hold all the pieces in one layer without crowding). Turn with tongs to get nice caramelization on all sides and the edges of each piece, 12 to 15 minutes total.

Transfer the chicken to a platter and discard all the fat from the pot. Return the pot to medium-high heat and add the wine-vegetable mixture. Deglaze the pan thoroughly, then add the browned chicken, thyme, and bay leaves. Adjust the heat so the liquid simmers very gently, partially cover, and cook for 45 to 60 minutes, turning the chicken pieces over once, until tender and juicy and infused with flavor.

Meanwhile, in a skillet, melt the remaining 2 tablespoons butter over medium heat. Add the pearl onions and sauté until almost tender and beginning to brown; jiggle the pan and lower the heat if the butter threatens to scorch. Add the mushrooms and cover the pan. Cook until the mushrooms give up their liquid, about 5 minutes. Remove the lid and sauté until the liquid evaporates and the onions and mushrooms are tender. Fold in the bacon and sun-dried tomatoes. Season to taste with salt and pepper.

When the chicken is done, transfer the pieces to a large platter, tent loosely with aluminum foil, and keep warm in a low oven (might as well warm up the dinner plates, too). Strain all the braising juices into a large glass measuring cup, pressing down hard on the solids to extract the maximum juice. Dump the solids from the strainer onto a cutting board and chop very finely (or puree in a food processor). Return the liquid to the pot; if desired, tip it to one side and skim off some of the fat with a large, flat spoon.

Bring the liquid to a brisk simmer and stir in the pureed vegetables. Return the chicken to the pot and add the bacon-onion-mushroom-tomato mixture and the vinegar. Bring to a gentle simmer and cook for about 5 minutes, to warm everything through and thicken slightly. Taste and adjust the seasoning.

CENTRAL COAST: Denner Viognier, Paso Robles
FARTHER AFIELD: Condrieu, Côtes du Rhône, France

Spit-Roasted Lavender Chicken with Fresh Fig Romesco

This dish just shouts summer in California, when it's time to sip and visit around the grill, ideally with a fig-laden tree or two casting some welcome dappled shade over the convivial guests. If you take the time to refrigerate the chickens overnight, uncovered, you will be rewarded with a tremendously crispy skin. Don't worry if the skin discolors a bit in the air of the fridge.
SERVES 5 OR 6

2 small (about 3 pounds each) pasture raised chickens

1 tablespoon fine sea salt

1½ teaspoons freshly ground black pepper

½ teaspoon ground fennel

½ teaspoon dried thyme

½ teaspoon culinary-grade fresh or dried lavender blossoms

Extra-virgin olive oil, for brushing

FIG ROMESCO
3 large, ½-inch-thick slices French, Italian, or sourdough bread, crusts removed (about 2 ounces)

1 cup ice water

⅓ cup sliced or raw almonds

⅓ cup whole pistachio nuts

2 large garlic cloves, minced or pushed through a press

¼ teaspoon fine sea salt

3 tablespoons sherry vinegar

1 tablespoon dry sherry (optional)

1 tablespoon honey

¼ teaspoon best-quality vanilla extract

½ teaspoon sriracha or other bottled hot sauce

¼ cup pistachio oil or extra-virgin olive oil

10 fresh ripe figs, stemmed and cut into eighths lengthwise

Finely grated zest of 1 Meyer lemon or orange

Fleur de sel or fine sea salt, for finishing

Rinse the chickens inside and out with cold water, and shake to remove as much water as possible. Pat thoroughly dry inside and out with absorbent paper towels. In a bowl, combine the salt, pepper, fennel, thyme, and lavender.

Paint the chickens very lightly with olive oil, to help the seasonings adhere. Rub the chickens inside and out with the seasoning mixture, then refrigerate on a rack, uncovered, for at least 4 hours, preferably overnight. Let stand at room temperature for 1 hour, covered with a clean towel or plastic wrap, before you begin cooking.

To make the romesco, toast the bread under a hot broiler or on a grill for 1 to 2 minutes, until golden. Tear into chunks, then combine in a bowl with 1 cup ice water. Let stand for 5 minutes, turning over once or twice. Squeeze to extract most of the water, then place in a food processor. In a small nonstick skillet over medium-low heat, toast the almonds until golden, and add to the processor. Add the pistachio nuts, garlic, salt, vinegar, sherry, honey, vanilla, sriracha, and pistachio oil. Pulse and scrape until nice and chunky, then add the figs and lemon zest and pulse briefly 2 or 3 times. Transfer the chunky sauce to a bowl.

Prepare a charcoal or gas grill for indirect-heat spit roasting (rotisserie) and place a drip pan underneath the place that will be occupied by the two chickens. Mount the chickens on the spit with both legs toward the center and the breasts outermost. Wrap a little twine around the legs and wing tips so they won't flop around as the spit turns. Brush the chickens very lightly all over with olive oil.

Start the motor and spit roast for 50 minutes to 1 hour, until the temperature at the thickest part of the thigh (away from the bone) reaches 158°F and the juices from the thigh joint run clear. Transfer from the spit onto a platter, tent loosely with aluminum foil, and let stand for 5 to 10 minutes. Carve as desired and scatter the pieces with just a touch of fleur de sel (the chicken is well seasoned already). Serve the romesco sauce on the side.

CENTRAL COAST: Villa Creek "High Road," James Berry Vineyard, Paso Robles (Grenache, Syrah, Mourvedre)
FARTHER AFIELD: Châteauneuf-du-Pape, Rhône Valley, France or Priorat, Spain

Talley Vineyards

Before California became the powerhouse of entertainment and lifestyle it is today, it was a rich, fertile breadbasket, blessed by an almost year-round growing season for livestock and produce. The earliest settlers here saw the promise of the land, and those who could began to cultivate that promise. In California, there is ranching royalty, and there is farming royalty. The Talley family falls into the latter category. Oliver Talley grew up in Bradley (Monterey County) and Santa Maria, and began farming in the near-perfect climate of Arroyo Grande in 1948. His son Don took over the family farm in 1980.

Brian Talley remembers thinking in high school how great his dad's job seemed. In those days, the family farmed vegetables, and they still do. Bell peppers, cilantro, brussels sprouts, napa cabbage, lemons, and avocados all left the farm for wholesale distribution across the country. But vegetable farming is an extremely volatile business, and in 1981 Don and Rosemary Talley looked around at the wine grape production in nearby Edna Valley and down south in Santa Barbara. They had a hillside plot that seemed like it might be just about perfect for wine grapes, and so the decision was made—vines were planted and, in 1986, Talley Vineyards was founded. Brian was in college at the time, and the winemaker suggested Brian work in a wine shop, to learn about this new crop. Like many people who get their feet wet in the wine business, Brian was captivated. Now, Brian's two teenage daughters work summers at the winery and farm. Will they follow in his footsteps and become the fourth generation of Talleys farming in Arroyo Grande? "They have varying degrees of interest," says Brian. "For now, as far as I'm concerned, they need summer jobs. As far as they're concerned, they need money. So, we work together on those goals."

To say that this place is idyllic seems, somehow, inadequate.

The climate of Arroyo Grande is extremely moderate—if that makes sense—because of the marine influence. It proved to be the ideal location for cool-climate varietals like Pinot Noir and Chardonnay—grapes that don't normally do well in the hotter climes of Paso Robles. With 200 acres under vine, Talley produces 15,000 cases of estate-grown Pinot Noir and Chardonnay, and also has a second label, Bishop's Peak, which is made from estate-grown grapes and some purchased grapes.

Arroyo Grande has the longest growing season of any world class wine region in the world—it extends gently all the way from the beginning of March to late October. The land is softly rolling, gentle, and green. From the top of the ranch, you can see the ocean. To say that this place is idyllic seems, somehow, inadequate. And there is evident in this family a supreme love of and respect for the land. The Talleys have made an open-space agreement with San Luis Obispo County that permanently protects 4,000 acres of this precious land, yet sets aside a few parcels for very low-impact development, a group of widely spread homes called Las Ventanas at Talley Farms. The sunsets here are intoxicating. And the views from these hills now will be the same for the children and grandchildren of the current inhabitants. The goal is as it has always been: to do the best with and for the land, and yet always preserve its pristine beauty. Ideally, with a glass of Talley's estate-grown Chardonnay in hand, right about sunset.

IF YOU VISIT:
Daily, 10:30 a.m. to 4:30 p.m.

3031 Lopez Drive
Arroyo Grande, CA 93420

(805) 489-0446

www.talleyvineyards.com

Seared and Braised
Feta-Stuffed Chicken Thighs
with White Wine and Green Olives

This gutsy and rustic dish features powerful acidity from the feta, wine, and olives, but the tanginess is tamed slightly by the broth and the natural richness inherent to chicken thighs—one of my favorite bits of the chicken. It's the perfect dish to serve when meat is not on the menu but you plan to serve a good red wine with the main course. SERVES 6

12 boneless, skinless chicken thighs, preferably from a pasture raised chicken

Fine sea salt and freshly ground black pepper

1 (7- to 8-ounce) block feta cheese, cut into 12 small rectangles

2 tablespoons extra-virgin olive oil

2 large shallots, coarsely chopped

Large sprig fresh rosemary

Large sprig fresh thyme

5 garlic cloves, minced or pushed through a press

1¼ cups medium-dry white wine, such as Viognier or a Rhône blend

1 cup homemade or store-bought low-sodium chicken broth

1 lemon slice

1½ cups mild, brine-cured green olives (about 6 ounces), pitted and halved

1 tablespoon coarsely chopped fresh flat-leaf parsley (optional)

Place half the boneless thighs on a work surface with the smaller ends toward you and spread them out flat; season generously with pepper. Place a rectangle of feta in the center of each and roll up to the top. Tie either end with a short piece of thin kitchen twine, to hold in the cheese. Repeat with the remaining thighs and feta. Season generously with salt and just a little pepper.

Preheat the oven to 325°F. Place a large ovenproof skillet over medium-high heat and add the olive oil. When the oil is very hot, add six of the chicken rolls and sear until golden brown on all sides, turning with tongs. Transfer to a platter, let the pan heat up again, and sear the remaining rolls in the same way; transfer to the platter. Pour off all but about 1 tablespoon of the fat from the pan and return it to medium heat. Add the shallots, rosemary, and thyme. Sauté for about 5 minutes, until the shallots are tender, then add the garlic and stir for 1 minute. Add the wine and bring to a brisk simmer; reduce the liquid by about half, 6 to 8 minutes, tipping the pan and skimming the fat occasionally. Return the chicken to the pan and add the broth, lemon slice, ¼ teaspoon salt, and plenty of pepper. Bring to a simmer, cover tightly with aluminum foil and the lid, if there is one, and transfer to the oven. Cook for 20 minutes, then turn the chicken pieces over, add the olives, re-cover, and continue cooking for about 10 minutes more, or until the chicken is very tender.

Transfer the chicken to a warm, clean platter and cover loosely with foil. On the stovetop, place the skillet over high heat and reduce the sauce a little bit to concentrate the juices, stirring, for 5 to 6 minutes. Remove the remains of the herb branches and the lemon slice, return the chicken to the pan for a moment to warm through, and serve, spooning plenty of the chunky sauce over the top and sprinkling with the parsley.

CENTRAL COAST: Villa Creek "Granadina," Paso Robles (Cabernet Sauvignon, Mourvedre)

FARTHER AFIELD: Chinon, Loire Valley, France or Nebbiolo from Italy

Fennel- and Garlic-Crusted Roast Chicken

Wet brining has entered the mainstream of cooking in this country, but dry brining is still more often practiced in restaurant kitchens. Judy Rodgers brought the practice to the home cook's attention with her groundbreaking *Zuni Café Cookbook* back in 2002. It's a technique more home cooks should adopt. The difference is simple, but elemental: Dry-brined birds and roast meats achieve gloriously crisp and brown exterior caramelization that wet-brined protein by definition simply cannot achieve. And that, to me, is what cooking is all about. Using Rodgers's foolproof rule of ¾ teaspoon per pound of weight, a 3½-pound chicken needs 2⅔ teaspoons salt. SERVES 4

1 (3½- to 4-pound) pasture raised chicken

1 tablespoon black peppercorns

1 tablespoon coriander seeds

4 fresh bay leaves, snipped crosswise into julienne

Kosher salt, as needed (¾ teaspoon per 1 pound of the chicken's weight)

3 tablespoons extra-virgin olive oil, plus more for brushing

10 garlic cloves

2 tablespoons fennel seeds

2 teaspoons dried thyme

Zest of 1 lemon

Freshly ground black pepper

Two days before serving: Pull back the chicken skin at the neck and locate the wishbone with your fingers; with a small, sharp knife, carefully score into the flesh along the wishbone on each side, down to the bone. Work your fingers around the bone on one side, and wiggle to release the bone from the flesh; repeat on the other side and pull the entire wishbone out (this operation is optional, but makes the chicken much easier to carve).

Rinse the chicken well inside and out with cold water and pat all surfaces thoroughly dry with absorbent paper towels. To make the dry brine, bruise the peppercorns, coriander seeds, and bay leaves slightly in a mortar and pestle or pulse a few times in a mini prep or standard food processor along with ¾ teaspoon salt per 1 pound of the chicken's weight. Place the chicken on a rack inside a roasting pan and paint very lightly with olive oil, so the dry brine will stick. Rub the spice-salt mixture evenly over all surfaces and inside the cavity, concentrating more on the thicker parts of the thighs. Refrigerate on a rack, uncovered, for 48 hours. Don't worry if the chicken looks slightly shriveled—that's what will give you such a beautifully crispy skin.

About 2½ hours before serving time, remove the chicken from the refrigerator. With a paper towel, blot the skin gently, and wipe inside the cavity to remove any liquid that has risen to the surface; leave most of the dry brine intact. Let stand for 1 hour at room temperature.

Preheat the oven to 450°F. In a mini prep or standard food processor, pulse the garlic until finely chopped. Add the 3 tablespoons olive oil, fennel seeds, thyme, lemon zest, and plenty of pepper. Pulse into a coarse paste. Very gently loosen the chicken's skin at the breast and thighs and spread the flavoring paste underneath the skin and inside the cavity. Be certain the outside of the bird is completely dry.

Transfer the roasting pan to the oven and roast the chicken, breast side down with the legs toward the rear of the oven, for 12 minutes, then turn breast side up and roast for 8 to 10 minutes more, until the skin is actively sizzling and appears golden. Turn the oven down to 300°F and slow roast for about 10 minutes more, until the joints move easily when you jiggle a drumstick and there is only a trace of pink left at the bone. Remove from the oven and tent very loosely with aluminum foil. Allow to rest for 8 to 10 minutes. Use poultry shears to cut into serving pieces, and serve on warm plates.

CENTRAL COAST: Giornata Aglianico, Luna Matta Vineyard, Paso Robles
FARTHER AFIELD: Aglianico, Campania, Italy

Wine-Braised Duck Legs with Dried Cherry–Green Peppercorn Jus

When I lived in London for seven years, duck breasts were my favorite food. Now I prefer the more flavorful, unctuously tender meat of the legs, especially in a long, gentle braise, as here. This sauce is so glossy, so deeply flavored, that your dinner guests will think you have a chef hidden in the kitchen. Some people fear duck because of the fat, but this process removes virtually every ounce of it. Having said that, duck fat is very useful! Reserve it in the fridge or freezer almost indefinitely. Then use it to fry up some lightly steamed and sliced potatoes. Heaven!   SERVES 6

6 whole duck legs (thigh and drumstick section)

Fine sea salt and freshly ground black pepper

3 tablespoons grapeseed or canola oil

1 large yellow onion, coarsely chopped

1 large carrot, coarsely chopped

1 celery rib, coarsely chopped

4 garlic cloves, minced or pushed through a press

1 tablespoon black peppercorns

1 (750-ml) bottle fruity Pinot Noir or Zinfandel

Bouquet garni (2 bay leaves, 3 sprigs fresh parsley, and 3 small sprigs fresh thyme, tied together with kitchen twine)

2 cups homemade or store-bought low-sodium beef broth

½ cup dried sweet cherries

2 or 3 teaspoons green peppercorns

½ cup ruby Port, such as PasoPort

¼ cup crème de cassis

½ teaspoon red wine vinegar

Preheat the oven to 350°F. Pat each duck leg thoroughly dry and season generously on all sides with salt and pepper.

In a large, heavy braising pot or pan, heat the oil over medium-high heat. Add the duck legs and brown thoroughly, turning once or twice, 5 to 10 minutes. Transfer the legs to a platter. Pour off all but about 1 tablespoon of the fat from the pot (reserve the rest of the fat for another use, if desired). Add and sauté the onion, carrot, celery, garlic, and peppercorns, stirring frequently, until softened and slightly golden, about 5 minutes. Add the wine and the bouquet garni, bring to a brisk simmer, and simmer until the wine is reduced by one-third to one-half, 12 to 15 minutes. Return the duck legs to the pan skin side up and pour in the broth. Bring the liquid back to a simmer, then cover the pan and transfer to the oven. Braise for 1½ hours, turning the legs over halfway through, until the meat is very tender but not falling off the bone.

With a slotted spoon, transfer the duck legs carefully to a serving platter; cover with aluminum foil and keep warm in the turned-off oven, with the door open so it doesn't continue to cook. Strain the braising juices into a large heatproof jug, discarding the solids. Allow to settle for 2 minutes, and then remove *all the fat* from the braising liquid (the easiest way to do this is with a bulb baster, inserted through the fat to draw off, bit by bit, all the lovely juices from underneath). You should have about 1½ cups of fat-free liquid.

In a heavy saucepan, combine the defatted braising liquid, cherries, green peppercorns, Port, crème de cassis, vinegar, and ½ teaspoon salt, or to taste. Over high heat, boil the liquid rapidly to reduce by one-third to one-half, until dark and viscous-syrupy. Serve the duck legs with a generous amount of the chunky, glossy sauce.

CENTRAL COAST: Kenneth-Crawford Pinot Noir, Turner Vineyard, Santa Rita Hills
FARTHER AFIELD: Volnay, Burgundy, France

Tuscan-Cowboy Quail
with Red Grape Jus

All good cowboys and cowgirls—Californian or Tuscan—are likely to have two things on hand: rustic bread and salty cured pork (in the form of either bacon or pancetta). When you ride up to the campfire with a brace of plump little quail slung over your saddle, just cut off a few hunks of each and get cooking; the bread turns crispy and golden brown over the hot embers like a great big juicy crouton, while the pancetta helps keep the delicate little birds moist in the skillet. The light but luscious sauce here is a more civilized touch, better suited to preparation in an actual kitchen.   SERVES 6

Needles from 2 large sprigs
fresh rosemary

⅓ cup extra-virgin olive oil

⅓ cup balsamic vinegar

1½ tablespoons honey

Fine sea salt and freshly
ground black pepper

12 whole quail (about 4 ounces each),
ideally with the breastbones removed
(your butcher should be happy to
do this, if it's not already done)

JUS
2 tablespoons extra-virgin olive oil

2 shallots, minced

1 small carrot, minced

3 large garlic cloves, minced
or pushed through a press

1 pound seedless black or
red grapes, halved

½ cup earthy, fruity red
wine, such as Zinfandel

½ teaspoon red wine vinegar

12 (¾-inch-thick) slices rustic bread,
crusts removed (about 2 by 4 inches)

4 slices thick-cut smoked bacon,
cut crosswise into thirds

In a large baking dish, combine the rosemary, olive oil, vinegar, honey, ½ teaspoon salt, and plenty of pepper; add the quail. Turn and massage to evenly coat the birds on all sides. Refrigerate for at least 4 hours and preferably overnight.

To make the jus (up to 2 hours ahead), warm the olive oil in a small, heavy saucepan over medium-low heat. Add the shallots and carrot and cook, stirring occasionally, until softened; add the garlic and cook for 1 minute more. Add the grapes, wine, and vinegar and partially cover the pan. Simmer for 20 to 25 minutes, until just slightly thickened; season lightly with salt and generously with pepper. Remove from the heat, cover, and set aside in a warm place (at the back of the grill, for instance; or, warm through over low heat just before serving).

Lift the quail from the marinade. Add the bread to the same marinade and turn to lightly coat the slices evenly. If there is not enough marinade to coat all the slices, use a light spray of olive oil (otherwise, the bread will scorch). Let the bread stand in the marinade while you preheat the grill.

continued on page 110

Prepare a wood-fired, charcoal, or gas grill for indirect-heat spit roasting (rotisserie) and place a drip pan underneath the place that will be occupied by the quail.

Load the spit as follows: the first holding fork, one quail (the spit should go right through the center of the breast) one piece of bacon, and one piece of bread; repeat until all the ingredients are on the spit and then add the second holding fork. Push the quail and bread snugly but not tightly together, to allow the heat to penetrate. Don't worry about the little legs sticking out—yes, they will get very crispy: delicious!

When the fire has burned down to very hot coals, mount the spit and start the rotisserie motor. Spit roast for 35 to 40 minutes, just until the quail are cooked through (about 160°F) and the bread is golden and crisp-juicy. (Stop the rotisserie and pinch a quail breast hard: If it's firm, the quail are done.)

Divide the quail, croutons, and bacon among plates and spoon some of the warm grape jus alongside.

NOTE: Ideally, mince the shallots, carrot, and garlic in a small food processor, to be sure they are very finely chopped.

CENTRAL COAST: Villa Creek "Avenger," Paso Robles (Syrah, Mourvedre, Grenache)
FARTHER AFIELD: Mencia, Bierzo, Spain

Chicken Braised in Aged Red Wine Vinegar

Traditionally this dish is made with all the parts of a chicken, but I like to use legs and thighs because their flavor is deep, rich, and complex, especially when compared with breasts. If you'd like to fully utilize a whole chicken instead, cut each breast in half on the diagonal through the cartilage into roughly equal triangles. Add the breast pieces about 5 minutes after you begin browning the legs. Ideally, use cultured butter for finishing the sauce at the end; it has a subtle tang that works beautifully with the mellowed-out vinegar.   SERVES 4 OR 5

Rinse all the chicken pieces with cold water and pat dry thoroughly with absorbent paper towels. Season all sides of each piece generously with salt and pepper.

In a wide, heavy casserole or braising pot, warm the oil over medium-high heat.

When the oil is very hot, add the chicken pieces; brown all sides well, turning with tongs, for at least 10 minutes, adding the carrots about halfway through the cooking time. (The more time and attention you give to this process, the better the flavor of the final dish.) Transfer the chicken pieces to a platter. Tip the pot and spoon off all but about 1 tablespoon of the fat, add the shallot and cook, stirring all the time, for 1 minute. Gradually add the vinegar (be careful, as it will splatter), scraping up the tasty browned bits. Add the bay leaf and honey, return the chicken to the pot, and simmer partially covered until the liquid is reduced by about half, 8 to 10 minutes. Turn the pieces once or twice during cooking.

Add the broth, tomatoes, ½ teaspoon salt, and plenty of pepper. Lower the heat so the liquid barely simmers, and cover the pan. Cook for 25 minutes more, or until the chicken is tender.

Remove the pot from the heat, lift out the chicken pieces, and discard the bay leaf. Whisk the butter into the sauce just until it's glossy and smooth. Taste and adjust the seasoning with salt and pepper; return the chicken to the pot and serve with plenty of chunky pan juices. Scatter a little dill on top of each serving.

CENTRAL COAST: Tablas Creek Mourvedre, Paso Robles
FARTHER AFIELD: Bandol, Provence, France, or Jumilla (Mourvedre), Murcia, Spain

3½ to 4 pounds whole, pasture raised chicken legs, separated at the thigh joint into thighs and drumsticks

Fine sea salt and freshly ground black pepper

2 tablespoons extra-virgin olive oil

2 carrots, peeled, halved lengthwise, and cut crosswise into ¼-inch half-moons

1 large shallot, finely chopped

1 cup aged red wine vinegar

1 fresh bay leaf or 2 dried

1 tablespoon honey

½ cup homemade or store-bought low-sodium chicken broth

1 cup diced San Marzano or other Italian tomatoes, well drained

2 tablespoons very cold butter, cut into 4 pieces

2 tablespoons coarsely chopped fresh dill or flat-leaf parsley

Penne with Wine-Braised Chicken Sausage, Pancetta, Kale, and Carrot Sugo

This is a rustic, wine-infused dish that's full of bold, take-no-prisoners flavor. If your market or butcher shop makes its own fresh sausage, use it here (keep in mind that fresh sausage will absorb more wine than precooked). Otherwise, there are many precooked sausages to choose from, and you can change the flavor profile of the dish based on the style of sausage chosen (chicken-apple is probably not a good choice here, though). SERVES 4 TO 6

4 links (about 1 pound total) fresh or precooked chicken or pork sausages

3½ cups earthy red wine, such as Syrah or Zinfandel

1 tablespoon extra-virgin olive oil

2 ounces pancetta, coarsely chopped

2 large shallots or ½ small onion, coarsely chopped

3 large carrots, peeled, sliced thickly crosswise, and then criss-cross-cut into almond-size chunks

2 garlic cloves, minced or pushed through a press

1½ tablespoons tomato paste

Fine sea salt and freshly ground black pepper

2 tablespoons finely chopped fresh sage

1 pound penne

1 (14-ounce can) chopped Italian plum tomatoes, with their juice

1 cup coarsely chopped kale leaves

½ teaspoon red wine vinegar

1 cup grated Parmigiano-Reggiano or Grana Padano

Slice the sausages into ⅓-inch-thick slices, then halve the sausage slices crosswise. In a heavy saucepan, combine the sausage and 2 cups of the wine. Bring to a simmer and cook, uncovered, for 15 minutes, stirring occasionally, until the chunks are lusciously plumped up with wine. Remove from the heat.

In a large skillet, warm the olive oil over medium heat and sauté the pancetta for 2 minutes, or until just beginning to crisp. Add the shallots and carrots and sauté, stirring occasionally until everything is golden, about 10 minutes. Add the garlic and cook for about 1 minute more, then add the sausage with the remaining wine from the pan, the tomato paste, ¾ teaspoon salt, and plenty of pepper. Adjust the heat so the mixture simmers actively. Stir frequently so it does not stick to the pan, and reduce the liquid until most of the wine has evaporated. Add the sage and the remaining 1½ cups wine; partially cover the pan and cook over medium-low heat for about 12 minutes more, or until thick and saucy. At this point you could cover the sauce and set it aside for up to 1 hour; if so, gently reheat before continuing with the recipe.

While the sauce cooks, bring a generous amount of water to a boil in a large saucepan and add 1 tablespoon salt. Add the penne to the boiling water and at the same time add the tomatoes, kale, and vinegar to the sauce. Cook the pasta until al dente, according to the package instructions. Stir the gently simmering sauce while the pasta cooks and taste for seasoning. Drain the pasta and add it to the skillet with the sauce. Add about ½ cup of the cheese, and toss to coat the pasta evenly. Serve in large shallow bowls and pass the remaining cheese at the table.

CENTRAL COAST: McPrice Myers "Beautiful Earth," Paso Robles
(Syrah, Grenache, Mourvedre)
FARTHER AFIELD: Corbières Rouge, Languedoc-Roussillon, France

Soused Rabbit
with Picholine Olives

Throughout the countries of the Mediterranean, rabbit is a common sight on menus and tables, from haute to humble. Even served without skin, as it always is, rabbit is often much tastier and meatier than chicken. In recent years, rabbit has begun to grow in popularity in the U.S., as we look for sustainable sources of protein. Although this bright and wine-rich dish achieves a profound depth of flavor from the wine and all the yummy aromatics, it's still very light—perfect for a summer evening with a table set among the vines.   SERVES 6

2 cleaned rabbits (about 3½ pounds each), each cut into 8 pieces

2 yellow medium onions, chopped

12 ounces young carrots, cut into ¼-inch chunks (don't use the ones in the bag!)

8 garlic cloves, minced or pushed through a press

Bouquet garni (2 bay leaves, 3 sprigs fresh flat-leaf parsley, 2 sprigs fresh rosemary, and 5 small sprigs fresh thyme, tied together with kitchen twine)

Fine sea salt and freshly ground black pepper

1 (750-ml) bottle medium-dry white wine, such as Viognier, Chenin Blanc, or a white Rhône blend

½ cup extra-virgin olive oil

1 (15-ounce) can diced Italian plum tomatoes, with their juice

¾ cup Picholine or Lucques olives, pitted and halved

1 tablespoon herbes de Provence

2 cups homemade or store-bought low-sodium chicken broth

¼ to ⅓ cup cold unsalted butter, cut into 8 pieces

¼ cup packed fresh flat-leaf parsley leaves, finely chopped

The day before serving: Place all the rabbit pieces in a shallow dish large enough to hold them in a single layer. Add the onions, carrots, garlic, and bouquet garni. Season with salt and pepper and pour the wine over everything until the rabbit is fully submerged in the wine. Cover the dish with plastic wrap and refrigerate overnight.

Preheat the oven to 375°F. Lift the rabbit pieces from the marinade, reserving it. Pat each piece dry with a clean kitchen towel or paper towels. Place a roasting pan over medium-high heat and add the olive oil. Add the rabbit pieces and brown thoroughly on all sides, 8 to 10 minutes. Transfer the rabbit to a platter and pour off about half the oil. Strain the marinade into the pan, reserving the vegetables, and increase the heat to high. Skim off the foam and simmer the liquid to reduce it by half, about 10 minutes. Return the rabbit to the pan and add the tomatoes, olives, herbes de Provence, and reserved vegetables plus bouquet garni. Pour in the broth, cover the pan, and braise in the oven for 1½ hours, turning the rabbit pieces over halfway through.

With tongs and a slotted spoon, carefully transfer the rabbit to a serving platter and cover with aluminum foil, or keep warm in the turned-off oven. Set the braising pan over high heat and simmer to reduce the liquid by about half. Discard the bouquet garni. Whisk in the butter until it's absorbed and the juices are glossy. Taste and adjust the seasoning with salt and pepper. Bring up to just under the simmering point and add the parsley. Serve the rabbit in wide, shallow bowls, with plenty of the chunky sauce spooned over the top.

CENTRAL COAST: Villa Creek Syrah, Bassetti Vineyard, Cambria
FARTHER AFIELD: Côte-Rôtie, Rhône Valley, France

Tablas Creek Vineyard

The air is truly rarefied at Tablas Creek's blending table. The annual sacred ritual takes place in the springtime—it's the yin to the harvest's yang. Wine samples are "thieved" from the hundred or so barrels representing each Rhône grape variety grown at Tablas Creek, by clone, by vineyard location, and by date of harvest. (Often, varieties in certain sections are picked two or three times during the fall harvesting season so that specific clusters of grapes can be hand-selected for their own individual purpose.) Each batch is then fermented separately to best represent the nuances of the season. The crew, which includes the owners, winemaker, and cellar assistants, begin their blending trials by tasting and rating each of these samples—think 20 lots of Grenache, 15 lots of Syrah, and so on—before they begin to experiment with blending percentages for each of the 14 to 18 different blends that will become the Tablas Creek Vineyard lineup for that vintage. Not surprisingly, this is the crew's favorite time of year.

This blending model came about from a unique partnership started in the 1960s between Robert Haas, a wine importer for his company, Vineyard Brands, and the Perrin family, owners of the storied Château de Beaucastel in Châteauneuf-du-Pape. At Beaucastel, the family farms all 13 Rhône grape varieties, and blending is king. Haas was the exclusive U.S. importer for Beaucastel, and the Perrin family made many visits here over the years. They expressed to Haas their amazement that Rhône varieties were not more commonly planted in California. Thus began a new phase in their relationship, and Tablas Creek Vineyard was the result.

After searching up and down the coast of California for a number of years, looking for a location that best emulated the climate, limestone soils, and rainfall of Châteauneuf-du-Pape, in 1989 the partners chose a 120-acre parcel west of Paso Robles. Vine cuttings from Beaucastel were imported, quarantined, and then planted. The goal was to impeccably farm organically grown grapes and thus create wines exuding finesse and

> *Vine cuttings from Beaucastel were imported, quarantined, and then planted.*

balance—and a supreme expression of their location. As winemaker and vineyard manager Neil Collins says, "To me, the farming of these grapes is the soul of what we end up with in our glass. While our model is Beaucastel, our goal is to make wines that shine as an expression of *this* estate." The location has proved itself so promising that an additional 150 acres was recently purchased right next door.

Even though Beaucastel wines are celebrated and acclaimed around the world, the Tablas Creek model was, initially, not an easy sell to the American market. "We realized that we would have to explain why we grow grapes no one has ever heard of—like Picpoul Blanc and Counoise—and why we believe in blending them together," says partner Jason Haas, son of Robert and general manager of Tablas Creek since 2002. The winery had to build its reputation one consumer at a time. Haas says the direct connection to the end user was not part of the original Tablas Creek plan, and it's been a steep uphill learning curve. Clearly he's mastered the process quite successfully— Tablas Creek is one of the best-known and critically acclaimed wineries in the country, a flagship for the region. Jason is the principal author of the popular and informative Tablas Creek blog, which has an avid following and has garnered several awards. Haas invites readers into every aspect of the work in the vineyard and the cellar, from dealing with rainfall and frost damage to sheep grazing behavior and harvest decisions.

"The blog is a way of continuing the education process, and it's taken on a life of its own," Haas says. "It is our way of personalizing the business, making sure people become invested in the choices and stories that make us who we are. We feel it is important to take them through the process—to understand what it takes to make wine, from soil to grape to glass—so they can truly connect with the end result."

IF YOU VISIT:

Daily, 10 a.m. to 5 p.m. Bring a picnic to enjoy with the wines on their expansive patio, overlooking the vineyard. (That is, if you can remove yourself from the beautiful tasting room and knowledgeable staff—all overlooked by the massive, awe-inspiring 1,200-gallon foudres [superlarge barrels].)

9339 Adelaida Road
Paso Robles, CA 93446

(805) 237-1231

www.tablascreek.com

Muscat Zabaglione over Fresh Berries

Yes, I have gone a little overboard with eggs in this chapter. But eggs are so *good!* And pastured, happy chickens produce such incredible eggs—eggs that are to battery-raised chicken's eggs as freshly squeezed orange juice is to Sunny Delight. Zabaglione is a heady, decadent, old-fashioned Italian favorite that envelops the berries like a fine cashmere blanket.

SERVES 4 (MAKES 2 TO 3 CUPS SAUCE)

Place a large saucepan containing about 2 inches of water over medium-high heat and bring to a boil. Lower the heat so the water is just barely simmering. Place the egg yolks and sugar in a large copper or stainless-steel bowl that will not touch the surface of the water when it is set atop the saucepan. Begin beating the yolks and sugar with an electric mixer set to low. Increase the speed to high and beat for about 1 minute, or until the mixture is thickened, pale, and fluffy. Add the wine and brandy and place the bowl over the simmering water. Beat at medium speed for 2 minutes, checking the water frequently to be sure it does not boil. Increase the speed to high and beat for about 3 minutes more, continuing to check the water, until the foam has tripled in bulk and shows the circular trail of the beaters. It should look beaten egg whites about 30 seconds before they reach the soft-peak stage. Remove the bowl from the saucepan and whisk for 30 seconds more, to stabilize the foam.

Divide the berries among dessert bowls and spoon the foamy zabaglione over the top. Serve immediately.

CENTRAL COAST: Adelaida Cellars Ice Wine, Paso Robles (Muscat, Viognier)

FARTHER AFIELD: Vin de Paille from France

ZABAGLIONE

3 egg yolks, preferably pasture raised

¼ cup superfine sugar

⅔ cup Muscat (sometimes labeled Moscato)

1 teaspoon brandy or Cognac

2 pints fresh ripe raspberries, blackberries, blueberries, boysenberries, or a mixture of as many berries as possible

Lemon Curd and Chocolate-Chip Tart with an Almond Crust

This stunning blend of golden lemon custard and chocolate chips can be made entirely ahead of time, then assembled just before serving. Unless the lemons come from your own tree or a local farmer's market, scrub them under warm water to remove the wax that's often applied by large citrus growers to protect them during shipment. You'll need a 12½-inch fluted tart pan with a removable base for this showstopper. SERVES 8 TO 10

Tart Dough (page 74)

FILLING
6 eggs, preferably pasture
raised or free range

6 egg yolks, preferably pasture
raised or free range

Zest of 4 lemons, preferably
removed with a Microplane grater

1¼ cups fresh lemon juice

⅔ cup water

1 cup sugar

½ cup (4 ounces) unsalted
butter, cut into 6 pieces

1 cup semisweet chocolate chips

On a lightly floured surface, roll the tart dough out into a 14-inch circle about ⅛ inch thick. Fit into a 12½-inch tart pan with a removable base, folding the excess back in and pressing firmly to build up the sides. Refrigerate for at least 10 minutes and up to 4 hours before baking.

Preheat the oven to 400°F. Cut a large round of parchment paper and place in the tart shell. Fill with raw rice or pie weights. Bake for 15 minutes, or until the edges of the pastry are barely golden. Remove the parchment and rice and return the crust to the oven for 5 minutes to dry it out. Cool on a rack for at least 10 minutes and up to 4 hours.

Beat the eggs and egg yolks together well in a bowl. In the top of a double boiler set over medium heat, combine the lemon zest, lemon juice, water, sugar, and butter and stir until the sugar has dissolved and the butter has melted. Remove from the heat and let cool for 5 minutes. Whisk about ⅓ cup of the lemon mixture into the beaten eggs, and then pour the egg mixture into the top of the double boiler. Cook over medium-low heat for about 10 minutes, stirring quite frequently, until the mixture is very thick.

Remove from the heat and let cool for 6 to 8 minutes. Scatter the chocolate chips over the top, then let stand for 1 minute. Fold the chips gently into the lemon mixture, only just enough to create pretty swirls. Scoop the filling into the tart shell and smooth the top. Serve immediately, or refrigerate for up to 1 hour (any longer and the pastry will begin to get soggy).

CENTRAL COAST: Sculpterra Late Harvest Primitivo, Paso Robles
FARTHER AFIELD: Demi-Sec Champagne, or Vouvray, Loire Valley, France

Ginger Flan with Ripe Apricots

Some years ago, I was hired to test the entire ice cream chapter for *The New All-Purpose Joy of Cooking*, and one of the benefits of testing so many ice creams (besides the obvious) was my discovery of the loving relationship between fresh ginger and dairy products, especially cream. I've always been a huge fan of the hot-bright flavor of ginger, but I was more likely to put it into a cocktail (preferably with aged dark rum) than into food. Ginger is not a native crop to California, but there is a substantial organic ginger industry in the Central Valley, just over the Gabilan mountain range from my home. This creamy dessert starts off with a definite kick, then soothes the palate with smooth, ripe apricots.   SERVES 4 TO 6

Preheat the oven to 325°F. Butter a 1-quart gratin or soufflé dish. In a saucepan, combine the milk, cream, star anise, and orange zest. Over medium-high heat, bring up to just below the boiling point, then remove from the heat and let stand, covered, for 20 minutes to infuse the flavor of the aromatics into the liquid. Strain the liquid into a bowl and discard the solids.

Put a kettle of water on to boil for the bain marie (water bath). In a bowl, whisk the eggs for 1 minute, until frothy. Then, whisking all the time, drizzle the infused milk mixture into the eggs. Stir in the fresh ginger, ground ginger, vanilla, and sugar, whisking until the sugar has dissolved. Pour the custard into the prepared baking dish and place in a roasting pan a little larger than the dish. Pour boiling water into the outer pan to come about halfway up the sides of the inner dish, and cover the pan with aluminum foil. Bake for 40 to 45 minutes, until the custard is just set through to the center (it will still jiggle slightly).

Remove the gratin dish from the bain marie and let cool to warm room temperature. If desired, serve right away, or chill for up to 6 hours, covered. (If refrigerated, remove the custard from the refrigerator 15 minutes before serving.) Spoon the custard straight from the dish into serving bowls, and top with the sliced apricots. Scatter each serving with a tiny pinch of cinnamon and some crystallized ginger.

CENTRAL COAST: Alta Colina Late Harvest Viognier, Paso Robles
FARTHER AFIELD: Tokaji from Hungary

Softened butter, for the baking dish

1¼ cups whole milk

⅔ cup heavy cream

4 pods star anise, or 1 tablespoon broken pieces

Grated zest of 1 orange

3 eggs

2 tablespoons grated fresh ginger

1 teaspoon ground ginger

¾ teaspoon best-quality vanilla extract

2 tablespoons sugar

2 ripe apricots, pitted and thinly sliced

Ground cinnamon, for serving

3 tablespoons crystallized ginger, chopped

CHAPTER 4

From
the Sea

When I was a little kid spending holidays on the Hollister Ranch just north of Gaviota, we picked bright orange mussels from the craggy tide-pool rocks and simmered them with Inglenook Chardonnay and sweet butter, and I wolfed down creamy crab concoctions served in scallop shells. Although Dungeness crab did come back after many years of scarcity (my mother declared a week of celebration), in today's world we can no longer take the bounty of the Pacific Ocean for granted.

Since there are no easy answers to this crucially important issue of sustainability, the diner will have to do some homework. Start with your responsible fishmonger (like Pier 46, in Templeton). First, ask what method was used to catch a fish or shellfish. Gill nets are bad, longlines are good. Check with Monterey Bay Aquarium's Seafood Watch (www.montereybayaquarium.org), NOAA's www.fishcatch.com, and/or www.cleanfish.com.

Many responsible diners believe that all farmed fish is a no-no, but the reality is far more complex. In my opinion, at least for now, farmed salmon from the Pacific isn't a good choice, but New Zealand and Scotland are both farming fish cleanly and sustainably, and their salmon is firm and delicious.

The water in the Morro Bay estuary changes completely every 28 hours. Morro Bay Oysters founder, marine biologist Neil Maloney, tells me oysters are filter feeders, so they thrive on the fast-changing water. That's why the oysters farmed in the estuary have such an amazingly pure taste. I like to drive down and buy the small, sweet Pacific Gold oysters right after they've been pulled out of the water, then serve them on the half-shell. Medium oysters are great for soups, salads, and pizza. The large local Hispanic farming population happily snaps up the bigger, meatier oysters, which they grill up fresh.

Here is a collection of recipes that celebrate the ocean's bounty, pairing it with the fruits of the sun, soil, and vine to evoke the earthy sensibility of California's wine-centric lifestyle.

Wine pairings by Stephan Asseo of L'Aventure Winery, Paso Robles

Oysters on the Grill with Papaya and Avocado Salsa

The cool, jewel-like salsa makes such an appealing, bright contrast to the warm brininess and slightly smoky flavor of the barely cooked oysters. You could also forgo the grill and serve your shellfish raw. Many good fishmongers in coastal California—and anywhere with a large oyster-loving population, like New Orleans and Florida—will shuck the oysters for you (with a little advance notice), and provide them on the half-shell. Or, find a willing oyster shucker and be sure he or she wears a protective glove on the hand that is *not* wielding the oyster knife.   MAKES 24 OYSTERS

SALSA
1 small ripe avocado, pitted, peeled, and cut into ¼-inch dice

About ½ cup finely diced ripe papaya (¼-inch dice)

2 teaspoons minced shallot

1 tablespoon minced red bell pepper (optional, but pretty)

½ teaspoon fine sea salt

2 tablespoons fresh lime juice

1 tablespoon finely chopped fresh cilantro

24 small or medium oysters on the half-shell

To make the salsa, in a small bowl, fold together all the ingredients. Refrigerate, covered, for up to 30 minutes.

Shuck the oysters, if you have not already done so. Place them on a large, heatproof platter, keeping them upright so you don't lose too much of the oyster liquor.

Prepare a charcoal or gas grill for medium-high-heat grilling. Grill the oysters in their shells, with the grill lid closed, until the oyster liquor starts to bubble and the edges of the oysters just begin to curl, 3 to 4 minutes.

With tongs or leather gloves, transfer the hot oysters in their shells back to the platter. Spoon a little of the cool salsa over each oyster, and serve.

CENTRAL COAST: Jack Creek Cellars Chardonnay, Paso Robles
FARTHER AFIELD: Riesling "Hugel," Alsace, France

Red Wine Risotto with Scallops and Bacon

I've been a risotto lover ever since Los Angeles chef Joachim Splichal patiently schooled me in how to make the perfect risotto. I can now reveal that it's not at all brain surgery: Just make sure the time expended between adding the first ladleful of hot broth and being ready to serve is 18 minutes (do this by regulating the heat). And it doesn't hurt that the savvy cook can easily expand a risotto to serve unexpected diners. Since I am committed in this book to include wine in as many dishes as possible, it was unlikely that this classic from Tuscany would fail to make my short list of the most delicious wine-country dishes on earth.   SERVES 6

Add the broth to a saucepan and bring to a simmer over medium heat; maintain a low simmer.

In a large skillet, warm the bacon with 1 tablespoon of the olive oil over medium heat until the fat begins to render. Add the red onion and stir for 2 to 3 minutes, until softened. Add the scallops and cover the pan. Let steam for 5 minutes, then season lightly with salt and pepper. With a slotted spoon, transfer the bacon and scallops to a plate and set aside (leave most of the onion and fat behind in the pan).

Add the rice and stir constantly for 2 to 3 minutes, until the kernels look slightly translucent. Add 1 teaspoon salt and the wine; cook until it is absorbed. Start adding the hot stock a ladleful at a time, stirring all the time and adding more stock as each batch is absorbed. It should take about 18 minutes to add all the stock and achieve a creamy consistency and slightly al dente rice. Stir in the bacon-scallop mixture, cheese, and arugula; warm through for about 1 minute, then remove from the heat. Grind fresh pepper over the top and check the seasoning; adjust with salt, if necessary. If desired, place an egg yolk, in half an eggshell, on top of each serving; diners may stir it into the risotto for added richness.

CENTRAL COAST: L'Aventure "Côte à Côte," Paso Robles (Grenache, Syrah, Mourvedre)
FARTHER AFIELD: Domaine de la Janasse, Châteauneuf-du-Pape, Rhône Valley, France

3½ cups homemade or store-bought low-sodium chicken or vegetable broth

4 ounces thick-sliced smoked bacon, cut into matchstick strips

2 tablespoons extra-virgin olive oil

½ large red onion, finely chopped

8 ounces small bay scallops, patted dry

Fine sea salt and freshly ground black pepper

2¼ cups (1 pound) Arborio or Carnaroli rice

2 cups dry red wine

1¼ cups grated Parmigiano-Reggiano or Grana Padano

¼ cup coarsely chopped baby arugula leaves

6 small pasture raised or free-range egg yolks (optional; reserve the shells)

Grilled Lobster with Syrah Butter and Orange Sea Salt

This off-the-charts dish was inspired by a New Year's Eve wine pairing by Stephan Asseo of L'Aventure winery: I served a rich lobster bisque, and Stephan chose one of his estimable estate Syrah wines as accompaniment. The resulting taste-bud revelation set me to thinking how I could further extend the partnership of Syrah and lobster onto the plate and palate. The result is this truly extraordinary dish, an edible ode to the outside-the-box thinking that characterizes our Central Coast wine region. SERVES 4

In a small saucepan, simmer the wine and shallot until almost all the wine is gone; the shallots should still be slightly juicy. Remove from the heat and add the butter and pepper to taste; mash with a fork to blend evenly.

Bring a large pot of water to a boil, add ¼ cup salt, and plunge the lobsters into it headfirst (you may need to cook them in batches). Cover the pot and let the lobsters par-cook for 2 minutes. Drain and cool, shell side up, on a cutting board. Place with the head facing you and, with a large heavy knife, cut down through the head at the conveniently located dent. Rotate 180 degrees and cut down to the tail (use kitchen shears if the shell will not yield to your knife). Pull out and discard the round, whitish gravel sac near the head section of each half. With a small sharp knife, detach and discard the long, dark green intestinal vein, if it is visible. Crack the claws with a heavy mallet. Brush the exposed tail meat and the cracks in the claws with the melted butter; season very lightly with salt and pepper.

Melt the Syrah butter over very low heat just until liquid, stirring constantly; *immediately* remove from the heat and divide among four small ramekins.

Prepare a charcoal or gas grill for very hot grilling, and grill the halved lobsters with the meat sides down for 2 minutes. Turn over and grill for 2 to 3 minutes more, until the shells are completely pink and the meat is firm but not tough. Scatter with a pinch each of chives and orange sea salt, and serve immediately, with lobster picks or small forks. Place the ramekins of lovely wine-dark butter on the side, for dipping.

CENTRAL COAST: Terry Hoage Vineyards Syrah, Paso Robles
FARTHER AFIELD: Château Beaucastel Blanc, Rhône Valley, France

1½ cups Syrah

1 large shallot, minced

¾ cup (6 ounces) salted butter (preferably cultured), softened, for the Syrah butter

Freshly ground black pepper

Coarse sea or kosher salt

4 (1½- to 2-pound) live lobsters

3 tablespoons salted butter, melted, for brushing the lobster

2 teaspoons snipped fresh chives

¾ teaspoon Hawaiian Alaea (orange) sea salt

Toasted Angel Hair "Paella" with Chorizo and Shrimp

Once the prep work is done, this is a marvelously simple and interactive dish to create on your grill with a gang of people gathered around to ooh and aah. Whenever lobster is on the menu, I save the shells in a big zip-top bag in the freezer. They can be easily roasted along with the poultry parts and aromatic vegetables to make the incredibly rich and flavorful concoction here. Or, use purchased shell-on shrimp. When it comes to making broth, 95 percent of the flavor of shellfish is in the shells, and it's easily released into the simmering broth. The broth is what *makes* this dish—which is far less costly than the usual paella, by the way—so it's worth the effort to build the flavor. SERVES 8 TO 10

BROTH

1½ pounds turkey or chicken parts (thighs, wings, necks/backs)

1 large white or yellow onion, cut into chunks

4 carrots, cut into chunks

1 head garlic, loose papery bits pulled off, cut into quarters

2 fresh bay leaves or 3 dried

Small bunch fresh thyme sprigs

2 or 3 empty lobster shells/legs/tails, or 4 to 6 ounces shell-on shrimp, coarsely chopped

49 ounces homemade or low-sodium chicken broth

1½ cups wine (any varietal or color; a great use for leftover bottles!)

4 cups water

1 tablespoon black peppercorns

1 (28-ounce) can crushed San Marzano or other Italian plum tomatoes, with the juice

1½ pounds capellini or fideo

Extra-virgin olive oil, as needed (about ½ cup)

1¼ pounds shell-on shrimp, legs removed

1 tablespoon butter, melted

½ head young, firm garlic, finely chopped

1½ teaspoons smoked paprika (pimentón)

Fine sea salt and freshly ground pepper

12 ounces soft chorizo, removed from the casing, if necessary

3 large shallots, finely chopped

Preheat the oven to 450°F. To make the broth, in a large heavy roasting pan, combine the turkey pieces, onion, carrots, garlic, bay leaves, and thyme. Roast in the hot oven for 30 minutes, or until golden brown and aromatic. Add the lobster shells (or shrimp) and roast for 15 minutes more. Remove from the oven and cool for 5 to 10 minutes, then transfer the large pieces to a large soup pot and add the chicken broth. Deglaze the roasting pan with the wine, scraping up all the caramelized bits on the base and sides of the pan, and transfer this mixture to the soup pot. Add the water and peppercorns. Bring to a simmer, partially cover, and simmer gently for at least 2 and up to 4 hours. Let stand for 15 to 20 minutes, then pour the broth through a colander into a large bowl to remove the larger solids. Return to the original pot, add the crushed tomatoes, and bring to a simmer. Remove from the heat. Ideally, you should have about 3 quarts of broth.

Again, preheat the oven to 450°F. Break up the capellini: Working in a deep bowl to avoid scattering noodle pieces everywhere, break them into approximately 1-inch lengths. Transfer the pasta to a large roasting pan and drizzle *generously* with olive oil; toss with tongs until evenly coated.

Roast the noodles in the oven for 8 minutes, or until the top layer turns deep toasty brown (be careful not to scorch); turn carefully with tongs to bring the untoasted noodles up from the bottom; roast for 5 minutes more.

In a bowl, toss the shrimp with the butter, garlic, smoked paprika, and a big pinch each of salt and pepper.

Prepare a charcoal or gas grill for medium-high-heat grilling. Assemble all your ingredients and equipment at the grill, and place an 18- or 19-inch paella pan on the grill. Add 3 tablespoons of olive oil and, when it is very hot, dump in the shrimp and toast, turning occasionally, for 3 to 4 minutes, until bright pink and firm. Quickly, with a slotted spoon, transfer the shrimp to a platter. Add the chorizo and shallots to the paella pan and stir frequently, breaking up the chorizo, until the fat has rendered and the chorizo has cooked through. Add the toasted noodles and spread into an even layer. Ladle all the chunky broth over the top, cover the grill, and cook for 5 minutes. Remove the cover and begin to turn and stir occasionally for about 8 minutes more, or until the noodles are tender and coated with a rich, reduced sauce.

Distribute the cooked shrimp over the noodles, cover the grill again, and cook for 1 minute more, just to warm the shrimp through. Serve straight from the pan.

CENTRAL COAST: Epoch Winery Tempranillo, Paso Robles
FARTHER AFIELD: Tempranillo from Spain

Head-On Spot Prawns
in Orange-Pernod Vinaigrette

Available in spring and summer, these huge, sweet-and-buttery shrimp tend to be quite pricy, unless you are lucky enough to be near picturesque Avila Pier just south of San Luis Obispo, where there's an excellent fish market. They're pricy because only 30 fishermen are legally allowed to fish for them in the whole state of California, but they're also available all along the western seaboard up to Alaska. (British Columbia has a Spot Prawn Festival every May.) With spot prawns, most of the deliciousness is in the heads. If you're too squeamish to suck the sweet shrimp nectar out of the heads, you're probably better off choosing another dish.   SERVES 4

ORANGE-PERNOD VINAIGRETTE
Fine sea salt and freshly ground pepper

1 tablespoon Dijon mustard

2 large garlic cloves, minced or pushed through a press

Finely grated zest of 1 large orange or 2 small blood oranges

Finely diced flesh of the above orange(s), all pith, seeds, and membranes removed

1 medium shallot, minced

2 tablespoons Pernod or Ricard

1 tablespoon white wine vinegar

½ cup extra-virgin olive oil

12 large, head-on, live Santa Barbara or California spot prawns (see Note)

Extra-virgin olive oil, for brushing

Fine sea salt and freshly ground black pepper

Rich mashed potatoes, for serving (such as Goat-Cheesy Tarragon Mashed Potatoes, page 227; optional)

Small handful coarsely chopped fresh chervil or snipped chives

To make the vinaigrette, combine ½ teaspoon salt, a little pepper, the mustard, garlic, orange zest, orange flesh, shallot, Pernod, vinegar, and olive oil in a bowl. Whisk together until smooth and set aside.

Snip off the long, sharp "unicorn horn" coming from the head of each prawn; snip through the head from its base up to the tip, between the eyes. Snip down through the shell from the base of the head to the tip of the tail. Don't remove the shell! If the prawns are wet, dry them gently with paper towels or a clean kitchen towel. (If wet, they won't sear well.)

Prepare a charcoal or gas grill for high-heat grilling.

Very lightly brush the prawns on both sides with olive oil and season
sparingly with salt and pepper. Grill over direct heat for 2 to 2½ minutes
per side, until bright pink, firm, and opaque where the head joins the tail.
Divide the prawns among individual plates, placing them atop a mound
of your favorite mashed potatoes, if desired. Spoon lots of the chunky
vinaigrette over the prawns, scatter with the chervil, and serve immediately. (Provide napkins: There's no way to eat these crustaceans with a
knife and fork.)

NOTE: Yes, the prawns will be alive when you snip through the head shells.

CENTRAL COAST: James Berry Vineyard Chardonnay "Broadside,"
Paso Robles
FARTHER AFIELD: Cloudy Bay Sauvignon Blanc, Marlborough,
New Zealand

Abalone Farm

The rays of the setting sun are blinding as my car summits the last hill separating me from the Pacific, between the small charming towns of Cayucos and Cambria. As my eyes adjust, it looks as though I've been magically transported back to Big Sur's Esalen Institute in the 1960s, when (I gather) bathers enjoyed the nourishing hot water in old bathtubs, instead of the stylish stone and concrete vessels of today.

Only instead of naked people, these long bathtubs by the sea are full of abalone. Abalone in every size known to mankind, from microscopic to dinner-plate-size huge. The shepherd of these shellfish is Brad Buckley, a grinning, blue-eyed southern boy in high-tops who started working at the abalone farm in 1987 as a temporary gig while he searched for the kind of government job he'd trained for back at Mississippi State. At the time, his only knowledge of abalone came from *National Geographic*: Abalone was a shellfish, he knew, but was it edible? Raised around catfish farms, Brad was familiar with aquaculture but certainly never imagined these prehistoric-looking creatures could be farmed.

Landowner John Alexander started raising abalone on this site in the '60s, bringing to bear his expertise in prefab concrete, pumping, and water reclamation. In the early years, 80 to 90 percent of the abalone went live on the shell to Asia, though a local restaurant had a small standing order for tenderized steaks. Then came Japan's lost decade: In the mid to late 1990s, demand from Asia began to drop. Simultaneously, the U.S. food industry began to talk about sustainability and clean farming practices for fish and shellfish. Abalone is by its very nature organic: It's a low excreter—as opposed to finfish, which bring up ammonia nitrate levels in the water. In fact, abalone are so incredibly sensitive to chemicals that the larvae are used to test water quality. So abalone farming was termed "good aquaculture." By 1996, when sport harvesting of abalone was severely regulated by the Department of Fish

Brad was familiar with aquaculture but certainly never imagined these prehistoric-looking creatures could be farmed.

and Game, it became clear that the domestic market would take all the abalone that had once gone to Asia—and more.

All this excitement brings us inevitably to a piece of conventional wisdom that's prevailed for generations among people not familiar with the mollusk: Abalone is tough. Okay, if you've chewed your way through an incorrectly prepared piece of abalone, you too may have lost interest. But just think: Who was the first person who ventured to eat an artichoke? Thank goodness he or she did. Preparation of abalone requires a little practice and instruction, but if the difficult and sometimes dangerous process of opening oysters has become mainstream in America's kitchens, so too can tenderizing abalone.

Brad, now an owner-manager after almost 25 years at the farm, is working to expand the market beyond the pre-tenderized steaks that are sold by local purveyors and from the company's Web site. Demand for live, on-the-shell abalone is growing and so too is distribution. And abject fear of pounding is truly unnecessary: on the Web site, and on page 144, are all the instructions you need to make this ancient shellfish a part of your culinary repertoire.

When I was a kid visiting the Hollister Ranch years ago, we collected the huge shells for ashtrays and pan-fried the big steaks in cracker crumbs and butter (after my dad had pounded them on a big, flat rock). The abalone you're likely to find now are younger, far smaller in size, much easier to tenderize, subtly briny, and delicious. Some chefs, thinking their customers will want their steaks perfectly white, trim the edges, thereby removing a huge amount of flavor. But you shouldn't trim: Leave the dark marbling around the edges.

How exciting that this old-California shellfish, a valuable part of my home state's culinary heritage and now barely available in the wild, can come to our tables once again.

IF YOU VISIT:

The Abalone Farm, although not open to the public, offers limited educational tours during the summer months of June to August. Call, e-mail, or check the summer tour schedule online at the farm's Facebook page.

(805) 995-2495

www.abalonefarm.com

www.facebook.com/theabalonefarm

Bacon-Wrapped Shrimp on the Grill with Green Goddess Dressing

This dish is unapologetically, enthusiastically retro. And why shouldn't we wrap already delicious foods in bacon? (At least, once in a while.) Green Goddess dressing is quintessential old California, invented in the Garden Room of San Francisco's iconic Palace Hotel in honor of a renowned actor, then appearing in a play called (natch) *The Green Goddess*. If serving as an appetizer, put one shrimp near the tip of each skewer (easy to nibble). For a main course, skewer four or five.

SERVES ABOUT 10 AS AN APPETIZER, OR 4 OR 5 AS A MAIN COURSE

GREEN GODDESS DRESSING

3 anchovies, minced

1 scallion, white and green parts, minced

2 tablespoons finely chopped fresh flat-leaf parsley

1 tablespoon finely chopped fresh tarragon

1 cup homemade or store-bought mayonnaise

2 tablespoons white wine vinegar

2 tablespoons finely snipped fresh chives

⅛ teaspoon fine sea salt, or to taste

¼ teaspoon freshly ground white pepper (optional)

6 slices thin-sliced bacon (about 4 ounces), cut into thirds crosswise

20 large shrimp (about U16), peeled, deveined, if necessary

Fine sea salt and freshly ground black pepper

To make the dressing, whisk all the dressing ingredients together in a small bowl. Cover with plastic wrap and chill for at least 1 hour and up to 3 hours.

If serving this dish as an appetizer, soak 20 skewers in water for about 30 minutes. If serving as a main course, soak 4 or 5 skewers.

Meanwhile, cook the bacon pieces in a large skillet over medium-high heat until some of the fat is rendered out but the pieces are still pliable, about 2 minutes on each side. Drain on paper towels. (This may be done up to 1 hour in advance.)

Season the shrimps very lightly all over with salt and pepper. Wrap a piece of bacon around the middle of each shrimp. Thread one shrimp onto the tip of each bamboo skewer (for appetizers), skewering through the point where the bacon ends overlap to keep it from unraveling. Or, thread 4 or 5 shrimp onto each skewer (for a main course).

Prepare a charcoal or gas grill or broiler for medium-high-heat cooking. Grill or broil the shrimp for 5 to 8 minutes, turning occasionally with tongs to crisp and cook evenly. The shrimp should be pink and firm, the bacon crisped. If flare-ups occur over hot coals, move the shrimp to a cooler part of the grill. Serve with a small pot of the dressing on the side for dipping.

CENTRAL COAST: Clos Solene "La Rosé," Paso Robles (Grenaches, Syrah, Mourvedre)

FARTHER AFIELD: Verdejo, Spain

Steamed Mussels
with Goat Butter

This dish is an homage to the south coast (or, really, any region) of France, where *moules* are ubiquitous any-night fare on menus and dinner tables. Goat butter—in France, used interchangeably with cow butter—is available in well-stocked markets and in regions where goats roam. Don't let the very pale color make you think it's bland: The flavor is pure and clean, yet pleasantly earthy and slightly tangy. *Goaty.* Cultured cow's butter or Irish butter would make a good substitute.

SERVES 6 AS AN APPETIZER, OR 4 AS A MAIN COURSE

Heat 1½ tablespoons of the olive oil in a large, heavy saucepan over medium-high heat, and add half the onions, plus ½ teaspoon each of salt and pepper. Sauté the onions, stirring frequently, until slightly golden, 7 to 9 minutes. Add the garlic and cook for 1 minute more, then add the wine, increase the heat to medium-high, and simmer to reduce the liquid by about half, 6 to 8 minutes. Add the fish stock, tomato juice, thyme, and saffron and bring to a boil; reduce the heat to low and simmer for 10 minutes. Pour through a sieve into a large, heatproof jug. Discard the solids and reserve the broth.

Place a large sauté pan or skillet that will hold all the mussels in a single layer over medium-high heat and add the remaining 1½ tablespoons olive oil; add the remaining onion. Sauté briefly, stirring occasionally, until just beginning to brown, 4 to 5 minutes. Add the mussels to the pan, distributing them in an even layer, and sauté for 2 minutes. Add all the broth and bring to a boil, then immediately reduce the heat to low, cover the pan, and simmer gently for 3 to 5 minutes, until all the mussels are opened (discard any mussels that have not opened after 8 minutes).

With a slotted spoon, transfer the mussels to wide soup bowls, then quickly toss the butter and parsley into the broth and swirl the pan until the butter emulsifies into the broth, which will become smooth and glossy. Spoon some broth over each bowl of mussels and serve immediately, with plenty of crusty bread on the side.

CENTRAL COAST: Lone Madrone Chenin Blanc, Paso Robles
FARTHER AFIELD: Muscadet Sur Lie Loire Valley, France

3 tablespoons extra-virgin olive oil

2 medium white or yellow onions, slivered lengthwise

Fine sea salt and freshly ground black pepper

4 garlic cloves, thinly sliced

1½ cups medium-dry white wine, such as Viognier or Riesling

2½ cups best-quality fish stock

1 cup tomato juice

1 sprig fresh thyme

Pinch of saffron

3 pounds small black mussels, scrubbed and debearded

½ cup (4 ounces) cold goat's milk butter, cut into 8 chunks

Handful of fresh flat-leaf parsley leaves, coarsely chopped

Hunks of crusty bread, for serving

Fennel and Garlicky Bread Crumb–Stuffed Squid Braised in Malbec

This Mediterranean-centric dish may sound like an all-day project, but it's super simple and the result is unexpected and sophisticated enough for really special guests. I like to serve the toothsome tubes with soft polenta, rice, or couscous to soak up the winey sauce. If your squid don't come with their tentacles, double the amount of fennel and increase the bread crumbs to 3 cups.   SERVES 6

6 tablespoons extra-virgin olive oil

½ small fennel bulb, quartered, cored, and finely chopped

2 cups fresh bread crumbs

4 garlic cloves, minced or pushed through a press

16 large, cleaned squid bodies, with their tentacles, rinsed and patted dry (3 to 4 pounds)

2 tablespoons coarsely chopped fresh flat-leaf parsley

¾ cup grated Parmigiano-Reggiano or Grana Padano

Fine sea salt and freshly ground black pepper

1¼ cups Malbec or other full-bodied red wine with soft tannins, plus more as needed

2 teaspoons balsamic vinegar, plus more as needed

¾ cup tomato puree

1 pint cherry tomatoes, halved

Heat 2 tablespoons of the olive oil in a small skillet over medium-high heat. Add the fennel and cook, stirring, until slightly softened, about 5 minutes. Add the bread crumbs and garlic and cook, stirring constantly, until the bread crumbs are slightly toasted, about 2 minutes more; don't let the garlic burn. Scoop into a large bowl.

Chop the tentacles of the squid finely and add to the bowl; stir in 2 tablespoons of the olive oil, 1 tablespoon of the parsley, the cheese, ½ teaspoon salt, and plenty of pepper. Blend thoroughly with a fork.

Use your fingers to stuff the calamari bodies: Pick up a pinch of stuffing at a time and gently work it into each opening at the top. Don't completely fill the bodies—the squid will shrink as they cook—and be careful, as they can tear easily. Skewer the top of each with a toothpick to seal, threading it through both sides twice, like a sewing needle; set aside.

Heat the remaining 2 tablespoons olive oil in a large, heavy braising pan over medium-high heat.

Working in two batches, place the squid in the hot pan in a single layer. Cook for 2 to 3 minutes, until just slightly golden; turn with tongs and sear the other sides, about 2 minutes more. When you have browned both batches, return the first batch of squid to the pan and add the wine and vinegar; bring to a simmer. Add the tomato puree and cherry tomatoes, decrease the heat to very low, and cover the pan. Cook the squid for 15 minutes, then turn each one over; cook for 15 to 20 minutes more, until the squid is tender (poke with a small, sharp knife to check). Add a splash of wine if the sauce seems too thick. Taste for seasoning and adjust with salt, pepper, and a tiny splash of vinegar, if necessary.

Transfer the squid to a warm serving platter or plates and pull out the toothpicks. If desired, reduce the sauce over high heat to thicken and concentrate slightly. Snip the squid in half across the center with kitchen shears, and return to the sauce to warm through, or spoon the hot sauce over the top. Scatter with the remaining 1 tablespoon parsley and serve immediately.

CENTRAL COAST: Lone Madrone Malbec, Paso Robles
FARTHER AFIELD: Achával Ferrer Malbec, Mendoza, Argentina

Charred Squid, Artichoke Heart, and Chorizo Salad

My affection for combining spicy sausage with seafood is certainly the result of spending three years living on the south coast of Spain (the Costa del Sol). There was no shortage of either commodity in Estepona, and I discovered many festive ways to join them together. As a California native (lonely for my home state much of the time), I jumped at the chance to add my favorite thistle to this hearty party dish. If you can't find frozen or canned artichoke hearts, use marinated artichoke hearts from a jar, but be sure to drain them really well (the marinating mixture has a tendency to taste of preservatives). SERVES 4 AS A MAIN COURSE, OR 6 AS AN APPETIZER

1 pound cleaned squid (thoroughly thawed frozen is fine)

3 tablespoons plus ½ cup extra-virgin olive oil

Fine sea salt and freshly ground black pepper

2 or 3 garlic cloves, finely chopped or pushed through a press

½ cup coarsely chopped fresh flat-leaf parsley leaves

Zest and juice of 1 large lemon, preferably Meyer (about ¼ cup juice)

1½ teaspoons paprika, preferably smoked

Cayenne pepper

8 to 10 ounces fully thawed frozen artichoke hearts (or canned, drained weight), halved lengthwise

3 ounces dry-cured chorizo, casing removed, thickly sliced, slices quartered crosswise

1 large fennel bulb, trimmed, cored, quartered, and slivered crosswise

1 small head radicchio, cored and slivered crosswise

Cut the body section of the squid into ⅓-inch rings and pat thoroughly dry with a clean kitchen towel or absorbent paper towels. Leave the tentacles intact but make sure all are well dried.

In a bowl, toss the squid with 3 tablespoons of the olive oil, ½ teaspoon salt, and a little pepper.

In a large bowl, whisk together the garlic, parsley, lemon juice, ½ teaspoon salt, paprika, a pinch of cayenne, and the remaining ½ cup olive oil. Add the artichoke hearts, chorizo, fennel, and radicchio and fold together until combined. Transfer the salad mixture to a large platter.

Prepare a charcoal or gas grill or a well-seasoned cast-iron griddle pan for medium-high-heat cooking. When the grilling surface is really, really hot, mop it with a rag coated lightly with oil, to create a nonstick grilling surface.

In two batches, grill the squid pieces for 1 to 1½ minutes on each side (just until firm); as the squid pieces are done, transfer them to the platter, over the top of the salad mixture. Finish grilling the second batch of squid, transfer to the platter, and shower the lemon zest over the top. Serve while the squid are still warm, or at room temperature.

CENTRAL COAST: L'Aventure Roussanne, Paso Robles
FARTHER AFIELD: Muscadet Sur Lie, Loire Valley, France

The Fishing French Family

"Fishermen don't retire," says Jeff French, who has fished out of Morro Bay since he was knee-high to his dad, fisherman Al French. Jeff just laughed when I asked him what he saw himself doing in five years. "Maybe I'll be fishing a little *less*, since I'll be over 60," he allowed.

Making a living as a fisherman/woman in California gets harder every year. Fish and politics is not an intuitive pairing, but it's also not fun to realize that our children's children may never get to taste the ocean's bounty we Californians grew up taking for granted: salmon, abalone, and Dungeness crab. These independent-minded people chafe under restrictive regulations that change constantly. Hey—*they* know sustainable fishing is the right thing to do—commercial fishermen created many of the rules because they knew that without them, there would *be* no next year's catch. The problem is, there are no easy answers. Even the Seafood Watch cards that all responsible fish lovers carry in their wallets can't accurately tell the whole story.

Lori and Jeff French met at Cal Poly in the early 1980s, and they married in 1984. Jeff took off for the salmon season as soon as school let out, and she didn't see him again until September. The 2010 salmon season in California lasted only eight days. The 2008 and 2009 total season closures may have paid off, though: The Klamath and Sacramento River catches look set to make a strong comeback. Jeff and his brother and partner, John, have two boats, meaning one can be in dock being reoutfitted for the next season while the other is out on the waves. The Frenches have trapped crab in the winter and spring for two generations, and when the summer salmon (and black cod) season comes, it takes a month to swap out the traps, either for salmon gear or black cod longlines. To say that every member of the family pitches in would be an understatement.

Our children's children may never get to taste the ocean's bounty we Californians grew up taking for granted . . .

With a ganion and hook every three feet on the longline, Lori ties ganions at home, at meetings for the volunteer work she does (for Morro Bay Chamber of Commerce and the Harbor Festival board), at family gatherings, and practically in her sleep.

Will Jeff's two sons follow in his footsteps, as he followed in his father's? Lorrin French studied architecture—he'll work on the boat this summer *only* if he can't get a job in his chosen field. Younger son Drew studies computer information science at Chico State. Sure, he fishes when he's home on school breaks. (He's been known to break out his laptop for some programming on the boat, after a full day of work on the ocean.) As a career? "We'll see." John's son Ryan has just been accepted to the Maritime Academy. The family is very proud—but he won't be a fisherman. (They hope he'll get a gig on a cruise ship, so they can have a vacation.)

"We don't do 9 to 5," says Lori, who works full time (that's where the health insurance comes from) and volunteers as Education Co-ordinator for Central Coast Women for Fisheries, in Morro Bay. She also founded Faces of California Fishing, which helps people "get to know their fisherman" (and their fish).

Does she worry? For every family that's fished for more than a generation there is a boat that didn't come home—sometimes, with more than one family member on board. Lori tells Drew, "Don't ever get in between the dock and the boat, wake someone up if you go out on deck at night to pee, keep your feet free from the ropes. . . ."

This is a fiercely resilient group of people, but the weather is the final decider in the French family. It dictates everything from family time to vacations, and it rules the checkbook with an iron hand.

IF YOU VISIT:

I can't encourage you enough to investigate the people who supply your family with fish by browsing around www.facesofcaliforniafishing.com (there's also great info on where to buy the freshest fish and how to decipher all the different names and species).

If you can, get yourself to Morro Bay, where you can shop for fresh-from-the-boat fish at Giovanni's Fish Market, or to the Olde Port Fisheries at Avila Beach/Port San Luis. Also check out www.eatalbacore.com, from a husband-and-wife team who have been catching one fish at a time out of Morro Bay since they built their boat in 1979.

Flash-Grilled Abalone Steaks with Lemon-Soy Tartar Sauce

You want live or recently alive abalone for this dish, which showcases this most beloved of California's shellfish bounty at its very best. For further images and instructions on shucking, see www.abalonefarm.com/shucking_abalone. Remember, do not trim off the delicate dark marbling at the edges of the abalone—it's full of flavor. When pounding, you want to achieve an even amount of pliability throughout, yet not pound so much that the muscle tears. Even pliability is more important than even thickness—though, in a perfect world, you will achieve even thickness *and* even pliability. (Some parts will require a little more pounding, some a little less.) The flavor of the tartar sauce is best if made ahead and allowed to rest for 24 hours before serving.

SERVES 4 AS AN APPETIZER

About 8 live or recently alive abalone, in the shell or just shucked by your fishmonger (see above)

Grapeseed or other flavorless oil, for brushing

Fine sea salt

½ lemon

Lemon-Soy Tartar Sauce (recipe follows)

If necessary, shuck the abalone, gently scraping the foot muscle from the shell with an old spoon; the resulting disk will be very solid and stiff. Place an abalone between two sheets of plastic wrap, as you would a veal scallop or a chicken breast. Begin pounding gently in the center, working gently outward to the edge and rotating as you work, aiming for an approximate thickness of ⅓ inch (see above).

Prepare a charcoal grill or ridged cast-iron griddle pan for high-heat cooking, until screaming hot (most gas grills cannot achieve this level of heat). Gently brush each side of each abalone with oil and season very lightly with sea salt. Place the abalone on the hot grill surface and sear without moving for 1½ to 2 minutes, until, when lifting slightly to peek, you can see that the undersides are just beginning to brown. Flip over and hit with a little squeeze of lemon juice, then give it just 30 seconds more. Remove from the grill and serve immediately, with the tartar sauce on the side.

Lemon-Soy Tartar Sauce

MAKES ABOUT 2 CUPS

Push the garlic through a press and scrape into a food processor or blender; add the whole egg, egg yolk, salt, pepper, soy sauce, and wasabi. Process until evenly blended. With the motor running, drizzle in the olive and grapeseed oils very slowly at first, adding at a just slightly faster rate after the first ⅓ cup or so has been emulsified. Add the lemon juice and pulse two or three times more. Transfer to a bowl and fold in the pickled ginger, lemon zest, and chives.

The tartar sauce will improve and mellow if allowed to rest for 24 hours; cover and refrigerate, then return to cool room temperature before serving. It will keep for up to 5 days in the refrigerator; leftover sauce makes a great sandwich spread.

NOTE: Abalone come in many sizes, but you are most likely to find very small shellfish. Count on a shelled meat weight of about 30 percent of the original, in-the-shell weight.

CENTRAL COAST: Booker "White," Paso Robles (Roussanc, Viognier)
FARTHER AFIELD: Domaine Baumard Cuvée Clos de Papillon, Loire Valley, France

1 small, firm garlic clove, peeled

1 egg, at room temperature

1 egg yolk, at room temperature

Scant ½ teaspoon fine sea salt

¼ teaspoon freshly ground white or black pepper

1 tablespoon tamari or best-quality soy sauce

1 teaspoon wasabi paste or hot mustard

¾ cup extra-virgin olive oil

¾ cup grapeseed or canola oil

2 tablespoons juice and the finely grated zest from 1 lemon

¼ cup finely chopped pickled red ginger (available in many markets and wherever sushi is sold to go)

1 tablespoon finely snipped fresh chives

Petrale Sole with Pinot Noir Butter Sauce

As you browse through this chapter, it becomes clear that I am not one of those people who believes fish should be served only with white wine. Pinot noir has a lovely refined elegance that blankets the delicate white flesh of the sole with a complex and heady perfume, aided by the touch of pastis and brought together in the classic French way: with great butter.

Everything depends on working quickly so that a subtle golden crust can be achieved with a light coating of flour and butter just on the verge of browning. This recipe is not viable for more than two people unless you have two very large nonstick skillets and an extra pair of hands.   SERVES 2

PINOT NOIR BUTTER SAUCE

1 large shallot, very finely chopped

1 cup Central Coast Pinot Noir

1 teaspoon ouzo, Pernod, or anisette

¼ teaspoon Pinot Noir salt or fine sea salt

6 tablespoons salted butter (preferably cultured), softened

1½ teaspoons coarsely chopped fresh flat-leaf parsley

½ cup all-purpose flour

1 teaspoon ground fennel (optional)

½ teaspoon fine sea salt

¼ teaspoon mild or hot chili powder

12 ounces petrale, Dover, or rex sole or flounder fillets, patted dry

2 tablespoons butter

To make the sauce, in a small saucepan, simmer the shallot, wine, ouzo, and salt until almost all of the wine has evaporated but the mixture is still slightly juicy, 20 to 25 minutes. Let cool for 10 minutes. In a small food processor, combine the wine mixture, butter, and parsley. Process until smooth. If desired, refrigerate for up to 12 hours; return to room temperature before proceeding.

Blend the flour, fennel, salt, and chili powder on a plate. In a large, nonstick skillet, warm the butter over medium-high heat. When the butter foam has subsided and is about to turn brown, dredge the sole fillets thoroughly in the flour mixture, shaking off the excess. Slide the fillets carefully into the pan and sauté for 1½ to 2 minutes on each side, turning gently once, until golden brown. Immediately transfer to warm plates and top with a few spoonfuls of the softened, deep purple-red butter sauce. Serve at once.

CENTRAL COAST: Windward Vineyard Pinot Noir "Barrel Select Gold," Paso Robles
FARTHER AFIELD: Meursault, Burgundy, France

Herb-Roasted Whole Fish with Heirloom Tomatoes and Meyer Lemons

Save this dish for a day when you can score some perfectly fresh, small, whole fish. Some people like their whole fish served with the head on, while others find it unappealing; head-on fish certainly make for a rather rustic, messier presentation. If your guests don't seem too adventurous, remove the heads in the kitchen and gently lift the fillets away from the bones, then serve each person two of the delicate fillets with a spoonful of the tomatoes and lemons on the side. Be sure to warm your plates in a low oven before serving, so the fillets aren't cold by serving time.   SERVES 4

Preheat the oven to 450°F and line two large, rimmed baking sheets with aluminum foil. Pat each fish dry with absorbent paper towels and paint with olive oil inside and out. Generously season the outside and inside the cavity of each fish with fine sea salt and pepper.

Arrange the sliced lemons on the baking sheets to act as a base for each fish, then transfer two fish to each prepared baking sheet over the lemon slices (it's okay if the tails overhang the edges). Divide the tomatoes, garlic, rosemary, thyme, and mint equally among each fish cavity. Scatter the bay leaves over the tops of the fish. Bake until the flesh is just opaque and flakes when pressed gently with a fork, 15 to 20 minutes. Let the fish rest for 5 minutes, then drizzle with a little more olive oil and scatter with a little coarse sea salt.

CENTRAL COAST: Tablas Creek "Esprit de Beaucastel Blanc," Paso Robles (Rousanne, Grenache Blanc, Picpoul Blanc)
FARTHER AFIELD: Châteauneuf-du-Pape Blanc, Rhône Valley, France

4 whole fish, such as sea bass, striped bass, or black bass (1 to 1½ pounds each), cleaned and scaled

3 tablespoons flavorful extra-virgin olive oil, for both brushing and drizzling

Fine sea salt and freshly ground black pepper

2 medium Meyer or standard (Eureka) lemons, thinly sliced

3 medium ripe heirloom tomatoes, cored and sliced ¼ inch thick

3 garlic cloves, thinly sliced

4 small sprigs fresh rosemary

4 small sprigs fresh thyme

4 small sprigs fresh mint

2 to 4 fresh bay leaves

½ to 1 teaspoon coarse sea salt

Qupé Wine Cellars

Sandwich day at the Clendenen Lindquist Winery in the Santa Maria Valley means Bob Lindquist is cooking. Or, rather, not cooking. "I enjoy cooking, but it would take me hours to cook a meal for the 10 to 15 people at the winery, so when it's my turn, I bring sandwich fixings," says Lindquist, owner and winemaker of Qupé. The daily communal lunch break began when Lindquist and his business partner and longtime friend Jim Clendenen, owner and winemaker of Au Bon Climat, joined together in 1989 to open a winery at Bien Nacido vineyards. This renowned vineyard has been the primary source of fruit for both winemakers since the start of their winemaking careers in the early 1980s. But the remote location of the winery made it difficult to run out and grab a quick lunch. So everyone sits together at one table, and various folks on the staff take turns preparing a meal, which always includes conversation and sharing of wines. Based on the European winery tradition that Lindquist deeply respects, the lunches emphasize the conviviality he loves about the wine business. "Wine is meant to be shared," he says. "Normally, you enjoy wine during a meal with family and friends, and this is the best opportunity to come together." (The lunches are famous throughout the Central Coast wine world.)

As a young man in the early 1970s, he fell in love with a particularly splendid $10 bottle of wine acquired via a work trade (a departure from the usual $2 bottles—all he could afford at the time). "That bottle blew me away—it was a defining point. I had to find out how that wine could have been so good," he said. He became a fixture at a local wine retailer near his home in Costa Mesa, Hi-Time Cellars (it's still there). He attended regular wine tastings and read every book he could get his hands on. And then he decided to forgo his degree at the University of California, Irvine, for the world of winemaking. Bob spent the next several years working at various wineries, tasting rooms, and retailers on the Central Coast before landing in the cellar of Zaca Mesa winery, in the Santa Ynez Valley. At the time, Zaca

Mesa was fertile ground for the next generation of winemakers—this was still early days for the Santa Barbara wine industry. The winemaker was Ken Brown (today of Ken Brown Wines), the assistant winemaker Jim Clendenen—who later became Lindquist's mentor and winery partner—and the enologist Adam Tolmach (today, of Ojai Vineyards, and former partner with Clendenen at Au Bon Climat). The energy must have been palpable in the quaint and quiet valley. Lindquist, through hard work and tenacity, was able to contract the best grapes possible, trading labor for wine-making space, until he and Clendenden forged their own path with the Bien Nacido winery.

I had to find out how that wine could have been so good.

From the start, Lindquist focused Qupé wines on Rhône varietals from cooler-climate vineyards; the wines immediately gained critical acclaim. The standard so many up-and-coming winemakers strive toward today is the one set by Lindquist from the start. And Lindquist has continued the generosity shown to him by mentoring many other winemakers now making their own names on the Central Coast. His wife, Louisa Sawyer Lindquist, and two sons, Ethan and Luke, have also benefited from Lindquist's nurturing hand. He allows them plenty of space to make independent decisions. Louisa focuses on Spanish varietals, making wine for her own label, Verdad, while Ethan makes Ethan Wines and is also the national sales representative for Qupé and Verdad. Luke is the winemaker for Tres Hermanas.

After 30 years, Lindquist continues to focus on the future of Qupé. "As I have evolved as a winemaker, I have realized more and more the importance of the quality of grapes," Lindquist says. "Which isn't anything new, but when I started it was all about the wine making. We are going to keep doing what we're doing to make better wines as our own vineyard develops and matures," he says. "The best wines from this vineyard are yet to come."

IF YOU VISIT:

The Qupé tasting room also offers Verdad and Ethan wines. Daily, 11 a.m. to 5 p.m.

2963 Grand Avenue
Los Olivos, CA 93441

(805) 686-4200

www.qupe.com

Crispy Pan-Fried Rex Sole
with Quick Orange-Dill Aioli

In the heady days of Sinatra and James Beard, sand dabs graced just about every good California menu. Sadly, these delightfully retro little fish are almost impossible to find today. Rex sole, however, is an amazingly delicate small fish, very similar in flavor and texture to sand dabs, and wild caught in the Pacific (you could also use Dover or petrale sole or Pacific flounder). This recipe is designed for only two people because lots of pan real estate is necessary to sauté the fish. If you have two large pans and a helper, go ahead and double the recipe. I am indebted to the talented chef Antonio, of Pier 46, in Templeton, for personally schooling me in how to achieve moist, crisp perfection with these very delicate fish. Scales on the thin-skinned rex sole are almost nonexistent, so there's no need to remove them (which would certainly destroy the skin). One side of the sole is white and called the "belly." This is where the fish rests in the sand while trying to escape the notice of passing predators. The other side, pale gray, acts as camouflage. The gray side—slightly less delicate—always goes down first when cooking.   SERVES 2

QUICK ORANGE-DILL AIOLI
½ cup store-bought mayonnaise, preferably made with olive oil

1 teaspoon minced or grated orange zest

2 teaspoons fresh orange juice

1½ tablespoons finely chopped fresh dill

1 cup panko (Japanese bread crumbs)

1 tablespoon all-purpose flour

Fine sea salt and freshly ground black pepper

2 tablespoons grapeseed or extra-virgin olive oil

3 or 4 whole, skin-on rex sole (about 1½ pounds), cleaned

2 tablespoons butter, melted

1 tablespoon white wine (any varietal)

Lemon wedges, for serving

To make the aioli, whisk together the mayonnaise, orange zest and juice, and dill in a small bowl until smooth. If desired, transfer to a squeeze bottle. If making more than 30 minutes before serving time, refrigerate until ready to use.

Pulse the panko in a food processor briefly, to break them down to a more powdery texture so that they'll adhere to the fish.

Warm two plates in a low oven. On a large plate, combine the panko and flour and season generously with salt and pepper. Place a very large skillet over medium heat and add the oil (or, use two skillets, to avoid overcrowding). When the oil is hot, dredge the sole in the panko mixture, patting to help the crumbs adhere. Place the fish in the pan with the belly (white) side up and sizzle *without moving* for about 1½ minutes, or until the skin is crisp and golden. Drizzle the melted butter over the tops of the fish and then, with a long, slotted metal spatula, carefully turn the fish over. Continue cooking until opaque through and only just firm to the touch, 3 to 3½ minutes more. Splash the wine into the pan, and then transfer the fish to the warm plates and add a wedge of lemon. Serve the aioli on the side or drizzle a little on top of each.

To eat, run a knife along the faint line that runs down the center from top to tail, then peel away the fillet toward the edge, to avoid getting hung up on the ends of the bones. Repeat to remove the other fillet, then insert the knife between the bones and the bottom fillets and gently lift away the skeleton, up toward the top. There are no pin bones, so you're done.

CENTRAL COAST: Denner Viognier, Paso Robles
FARTHER AFIELD: Domaine D'Ott Blanc, Provence, France

Capellini with Oysters, Wine, Spicy Sausage, and Watercress

The divine marriage of ranch, sea, garden, and dairy in this perky yet sensual dish epitomizes my goal of eating all across the spectrum of California's lush bounty. Be sure to plan the final assembly carefully, since there is nothing worse than an overcooked oyster! If you have all your ducks in a row, this dish is very quick to assemble yet still elegant and eminently suitable for company.   SERVES 6

12 ounces precooked spicy pork sausage, sliced ½ inch thick

1 tablespoon coarse sea salt

1 tablespoon salted butter

2 large shallots, finely chopped

1½ cups homemade or store-bought low-sodium chicken broth

1 sprig fresh thyme

1 pound capellini

⅔ cup heavy cream

1 pint small shucked oysters, with their liquor (halve or quarter larger Pacific oysters)

¼ to ½ teaspoon freshly ground white pepper

1 small bunch watercress, tender leaves and stems only, coarsely chopped

Preheat a cast-iron grill pan or cast-iron skillet until hot. Sizzle the sausage slices for 2 minutes, turning over halfway through, until brown and crisp. Drain on absorbent paper towels and cut in half, so they are about the size of the oysters. Set aside.

Bring a large pot of water to a boil and add the salt. Warm six wide bowls in a low oven. When the water is about to boil, melt the butter in a very large sauté pan over medium-low heat. Add the shallots to the butter and sauté, stirring, for about 5 minutes, or until they are softened. Add the broth and thyme to the sauté pan and increase the heat to medium-high. When the broth in the sauté pan is simmering, add the capellini to the boiling water and, at the same time, stir the cream, oysters with their liquor, and white pepper into the broth. Cook both the sauce and the pasta for about 3 minutes, then quickly but thoroughly drain the pasta and add it to the sauce along with the reserved sausage and the watercress. Decrease the heat to low and toss the mixture with tongs just until the pasta is evenly coated and heated through; do not overcook or the oysters will be tough. Remove the thyme sprig and serve in the warmed bowls immediately.

CENTRAL COAST: Epoch "Zinfandel Blend," Paso Robles (Zinfandel, Syrah, Tempranillo)
FARTHER AFIELD: Domaine Tempier Rosé, Bandol, Provence, France

Warm Potato and Smoked Fish Salad with Lemon and Chives

I like to serve this salad warm, to really awaken the complex flavors, but it's also great at room temperature, as a picnic dish. In the summer, Lone Madrone Winery on Route 46 west of Paso Robles holds occasional outdoor concerts in their beautiful garden. It's a great spot to bring your dog, spread out a blanket, and sip some fantastic wines while munching on a sophisticated al fresco repast under a shade tree. Lone Madrone's co-owner Neil Collins (with his sister Jackie Meisinger) is also the winemaker at highly respected Tablas Creek—the wines are truly top-notch. SERVES 6 AS A LIGHT MAIN COURSE, LUNCH, OR BRUNCH DISH

Fine sea salt and freshly ground black pepper

1½ pounds Yukon gold potatoes

¼ large red onion, finely chopped

2 tablespoons finely snipped fresh chives, plus more for garnish

2 tablespoons finely chopped fresh flat-leaf parsley

2 tablespoons drained capers, plus a few more for garnish

⅓ cup mayonnaise

Finely grated zest of 1 large lemon

2 tablespoons fresh lemon juice

7 ounces smoked trout or sturgeon, flaked into ½-inch chunks

5 cups loosely packed mixed baby salad greens (about 5 ounces)

6 tablespoons best-quality extra-virgin olive oil

Bring a large saucepan of water to a boil for cooking the potatoes; add a generous pinch of salt. Cut the potatoes into ½-inch chunks.

In a large, heatproof bowl, combine the red onion, chives, parsley, capers, mayonnaise, lemon zest, 1 tablespoon of the lemon juice, and a little pepper.

Assemble the remaining ingredients and necessary equipment near the stove, and warm six plates in a low oven.

Add the potatoes to the boiling water, and adjust the heat so the water simmers gently. Cook the potatoes for 5 to 6 minutes, until tender but not falling apart. Drain thoroughly in a colander, and immediately add to the bowl with the mayonnaise mixture. Combine thoroughly, then add and gently fold in the flaked trout. In another large bowl, quickly toss the salad greens with the olive oil, remaining 1 tablespoon lemon juice, and just a tiny bit of salt and pepper (the fish and capers are already quite salty).

Divide the greens among the warm plates, spreading them out in an even layer; make a well in the center. Spoon some of the potato salad into the center well, and scatter with a few capers and chives.

CENTRAL COAST: L'Aventure "Estate Rosé," Paso Robles (Syrah, Mourvedre, Grenache)
FARTHER AFIELD: Côtes de Provence Rosé, Provence, France

Pan-Seared Halibut
with Wine-Braised Leeks

Leeks are perhaps the most refined member of the larger onion family. Their potentially pungent flavor is tempered by a low-and-slow bath in the floral perfume of Viognier. The resulting velvety leek bed for your nice piece of halibut is made richer by the sublime marriage of wine, thyme, and a tiny touch of butter. What could be better?

Cast iron gives a lovely caramelization to the halibut without drying it out, but heavy-gauge stainless steel works well, too. If you don't have a large pan, use two pans to avoid crowding the fish; if so, you will need 1 tablespoon of butter and 1 teaspoon of oil per pan.   SERVES 4

Trim and discard (or compost) the dark green tops from the leeks, leaving about 2 inches of light green attached. Cut into 2½-inch lengths, then cut each piece in half lengthwise. Cut each half lengthwise into ¼-inch strips. In a colander, rinse the leek julienne thoroughly, and shake dry. In a large skillet, combine the leeks, wine, broth, vinegar, 1 tablespoon of the butter, parsley, thyme, ½ teaspoon salt, a little pepper, and bay leaf. Bring to a very slow simmer, then place a piece of aluminum foil over the top and the pan's lid on top of that. Braise very gently for about 30 minutes, or until the leeks are lovely and tender.

Warm four plates in a low oven. Pat the halibut dry and season both sides lightly with salt and pepper. Place a large cast-iron skillet over medium-high heat and add the remaining 1 tablespoon butter and the oil. When the butter foam has subsided and is just beginning to brown, swirl the pan to coat it evenly, and quickly add the fillets. Cook without moving for about 3 minutes, or until the edges have begun to turn opaque. Gently turn over and cook for 1½ to 2 minutes more, until only just firm to the touch. With tongs or a slotted spoon, lift the leeks from the pan juices and divide among the warm plates. Carefully transfer a fillet atop the leeks, and add a spoonful of the leek juices. Scatter each with chives and serve immediately.

3 large or 6 small leeks, root ends trimmed

½ cup medium-dry white wine, such as Viognier

1 cup homemade or store-bought low-sodium chicken broth

1½ teaspoons white wine vinegar

2 tablespoons butter

3 sprigs fresh flat-leaf parsley

1 sprig fresh thyme

Fine sea salt and freshly ground black pepper

1 fresh or dried bay leaf

4 (6- to 7-ounce) halibut fillets or other white-fleshed, saltwater fish, about 1 inch thick

1 teaspoon grapeseed or canola oil

2 tablespoons finely snipped fresh chives (optional)

CENTRAL COAST: Lone Madrone Viognier, Paso Robles
FARTHER AFIELD: Meursault Blanc, Burgundy, France

Macaroni with Garlicky Shrimp, Tomatoes, and Feta

Iconic Côte d'Azur chef Roger Verge may have been the first, arguably, to make a lobster mac and cheese (though it had a far fancier name). This gutsier, less refined take on the cheese-a-licious marriage of noodle and shellfish tips its hat to the sunny islands of Greece. It's the perfect centerpiece for a poolside buffet, with no last-minute attention required. Keep in mind that Greek feta is stronger and saltier than French, so choose your cheese based on your personal taste.

SERVES 6 TO 8

6 tablespoons unsalted butter, plus more for the baking dish

1 bunch scallions, white and green parts separated, both thinly sliced

5 tablespoons all-purpose flour

4 garlic cloves, finely chopped or pushed through a press

3 cups whole milk

1 fresh bay leaf or 2 dried

1 sprig fresh thyme

Fine sea salt and freshly ground black pepper

8 ounces Greek or French feta, crumbled

4 ounces Parmigiano-Reggiano or Grana Padano, grated

Kosher salt

1 pound macaroni

8 ounces cooked and shelled baby (61/70) or medium (41/50) shrimp (coarsely chop the medium shrimp, if using)

2 cups cherry tomatoes, quartered and seeded

About 30 fresh mint leaves, coarsely chopped

1½ cups Garlic Bread Crumbs (recipe follows)

Thoroughly butter a 9 by 13-inch (or similar-size) earthenware, ceramic, or glass baking dish. Put a very large pot of water on to boil for the pasta, and preheat the oven to 375°F.

In a large saucepan, melt the butter over medium-low heat and add the scallion whites. Cook until softened, stirring occasionally, about 5 minutes. Sprinkle the flour evenly over the scallions and stir constantly for 2 minutes, but do not allow the flour to brown.

Stir in the garlic, then start adding the milk a little at a time at first, stirring constantly, until you have added about 1 cup. Stir until smooth, then add the bay leaf, thyme and the remaining 2 cups milk. Increase the heat to medium-high and keep stirring frequently until the liquid reaches a boil (watch carefully so that it does not boil over). Boil for 1 minute, then lower the heat so the milk barely simmers and continue to cook, stirring frequently, for 10 minutes more.

Remove from the heat and let stand for 5 minutes; transfer to a very large bowl. Immediately stir in 1½ teaspoons sea salt, about 1 teaspoon pepper, and both of the cheeses, stirring until the cheese is just melted (the feta will remain a little lumpy).

Add 1 tablespoon kosher salt and the macaroni to the boiling water, and stir a few times, just until it returns to a boil. Cook until just al dente, according to the package directions. Drain the pasta in a colander, shaking well.

Stir the drained macaroni into the sauce, and add the shrimp, cherry tomatoes, scallion greens, and mint. Toss thoroughly until all the ingredients are evenly distributed. Spoon the mixture into the prepared baking dish, smooth the top, and scatter with the bread crumbs.

Bake for 25 minutes, then turn the oven to broil and brown the dish for 1 to 3 minutes (watching carefully), until the bread crumbs are golden. Let stand for 5 minutes before serving.

Garlic Bread Crumbs

MAKES 1½ CUPS

Remove the crusts from the bread and cut into large chunks. In a food processor, pulse the bread, garlic, ¼ teaspoon salt, a pinch of pepper, and the olive oil into coarse bread crumbs.

CENTRAL COAST: Terry Hoage Vineyards Picpoul Blanc, Paso Robles
FARTHER AFIELD: Albariño, Spain

3 ounces country-style white bread (about 2 thick slices)

2 small garlic cloves, finely chopped or pushed through a press

Fine sea salt and freshly ground black pepper

1½ tablespoons extra-virgin olive oil

Wild Salmon with Chanterelles and Roasted Kale

Born out of a windfall of chanterelles foraged by my husband, Casey, one January in See Canyon, south of San Luis Obispo, this deceptively simple dish can travel effortlessly from white-linen dinner to raucous, rough-hewn wooden tabletop repast. Once, central California gave us everything we would need to create this riot of flavors and textures, from its superb and precious wild salmon to the deep green kale and gutsy garlic. Depending on the now-unpredictable nature of the California salmon season, you may instead find wild-caught salmon from Oregon, Washington, or Alaska. All are great choices, as is, in a pinch, farmed salmon from New Zealand or Scotland. Farmed salmon from the United States? Not so much.   SERVES 4

Preheat the oven to 375°F. On a large, rimmed baking sheet, drizzle the kale with some olive oil and sprinkle with salt. Toss and massage with your fingertips until each piece is coated with a thin layer of salty oil. Bake for 15 minutes, then toss with tongs and roast for 5 to 6 minutes more. The kale should be deep, dark green with the occasional brown edge.

Meanwhile, slice the mushrooms about ⅓ inch thick, then cut into manageable chunks. Warm a little olive oil in a sauté pan and cook the mushrooms until they give up their liquid. Keep cooking until all the liquid is evaporated and the pieces begin to brown. Add a little more olive oil to keep them from scorching. Season with salt and pepper, then stir in the garlic and vinegar; cook for 1 minute more.

Line another baking sheet with baking parchment and place the salmon on it, skin side down. Season lightly with salt and pepper. Remove the kale and let rest while the salmon goes into the oven for 10 to 12 minutes per inch of thickness. Divide the salmon among plates and top with a jumble of chanterelles and kale.

CENTRAL COAST: Windward Vineyard Estate Pinot Noir, Paso Robles
FARTHER AFIELD: Volnay, Burgundy, France

1 bunch kale, leaves pulled from stems in bite-size pieces

Extra-virgin olive oil, for drizzling and sautéing

Fine sea salt

About 1 pound fresh chanterelles, stem ends trimmed if dry and woody

Freshly ground black pepper

5 or 6 garlic cloves, minced or pushed through a press

½ teaspoon balsamic vinegar

1½ pounds wild-caught salmon fillets

Eberle Winery

"I didn't even drink wine until I was 25," says Gary Eberle—often referred to as the father of the Paso Robles wine industry—as he gazes out over his 63-acre estate, now producing 25,000 cases of wine a year.

Gary was just two semesters shy of achieving a doctorate in genetics from Charity Hospital in New Orleans when he walked away, his future a complete unknown. One of Gary's professors there had succeeded (perhaps a little too well) in convincing him to trade up from his chosen wine—Mateus rosé—to Chateau Latour and Beaucaillou. Tasting these wines provoked a life-altering epiphany.

Pioneers are, by definition, takers of risk. You only hear about the ones who succeed. Gary flew to San Francisco, rented a car, and drove to Davis to meet with Professor Harold "Hod" Berg, then head of the Davis viticulture program. Hod told him, "You've already got the biochemistry prerequisites. If you're crazy enough to do this—if you *really* want to make wine—then I'll accept you into my program without an exam, and you'll study under me."

It was July of 1972. That September, Gary drove into California with $800, a seven-year-old Pontiac, and a U-Haul full of hand-me-down furniture. Soon, he was digging for soil samples on the east side of Paso Robles, assisting the most revered viticulturist in the United States, Doctor Harold Olmo. Olmo enthused, "This is the next great red wine-growing region in California." With its poor soil, abundant sunshine, dry conditions, and virtual absence of insects, it was much like the Rhône Valley and Tuscany.

Gary was listening. When he returned with his PhD in hand, it was as the winemaker and vineyard manager of Estrella River Winery (later Meridian). Gary's job: Grow the winery. He grew it past the point where it held any pleasure for him. "I liked it at about 50,000 cases a year. But under duress, I took it up to 300,000, with 1,000 acres under vine and new plantings of Syrah which no one had yet planted in California. By 1981, I knew I wanted to strike out on my own." Gary took out his sweat equity (less than 2 percent) in wine—he bought wines he'd made himself for $18 a case and sold them wholesale for $60. And that was the seed money for today's highly respected Eberle Winery.

The appellation then was San Luis Obispo County—there was no Paso Robles appellation. "We started it," he says. "A group of us went to the Bureau of Alcohol, Tobacco, and Firearms (BATF). I did the geology and weather, and drew the boundaries. We created the sixth viticultural appellation in California."

"I've done two things in my life: go to school and make wine. I didn't back into wine making as a second career. We sell 50 percent of our wine out of our tasting room—last year, 50,000 people came through. And we always sell out. But I'm not interested in growing this winery. I'm 68 years old and, as you can see, I'm not missing any meals." Gary pats his substantial girth with an infectious grin. "Nature willing, I'll be around for another 15 or 20 years. I wouldn't change a single thing."

Gary Eberle is big in many ways, but mostly he has a big heart. His stature in the community is huge, his contribution to the wine-making region he chose 40-plus years ago, indelible.

Pioneers are, by definition, takers of risk.

IF YOU VISIT:

Daily, 10 a.m. to 5 p.m. from October through March; 10 a.m. to 6 p.m. April through September

VIP tours (including the fabulous, clubby tasting room in the center of the underground cave): $25

Picnic lunches may be ordered 48 hours in advance and enjoyed on the spectacular deck overlooking Estrella Vineyard

3810 Highway 46 East
Paso Robles, CA 93446

(805) 238-9607 or www.eberlewinery.com for details of regular grilling events and parties

Salt-Baked Snapper

Save this classic interactive dish from Spain for a day when you score an impeccably fresh fish, ideally right at the dockside from a returning fisherman. When I helped the talented Greek-American chef Michael Psilakis write his cookbook, he taught me the perfect way to gauge doneness in fish: Poke a thin skewer into the center and leave it there for a few seconds. Remove and immediately press against your lower lip. If the skewer is hot, the fish is done. Below, I've suggested a digital thermometer, in case you're not comfortable with the skewer method. SERVES 3 OR 4

1 (3-pound) whole red snapper
or sea bass, sea bream, or porgy
(gutted but not scaled)

Freshly ground black pepper

2 long strips orange zest (removed
with a vegetable peeler)

4 small sprigs fresh thyme

4 to 5 pounds kosher salt

Best-quality extra-virgin
olive oil, for serving

1 small lemon, cut into wedges

Preheat the oven to 400°F. Rinse the whole fish and pat it dry with absorbent paper towels. Season inside the cavity with pepper, and place the orange zest and thyme inside. In a heavy roasting pan or earthenware casserole large enough to hold the fish and all the salt, make a 1½ -inch layer of salt. Make a shallow, fish-shaped impression in the salt and lay the fish on top. Distribute the remaining salt around and over the fish so it's completely covered. Pat the salt down gently. Bake, uncovered, for about 45 minutes. After 35 minutes, poke an instant-read digital thermometer through the salt into where you think the thickest part of the fish will be; the temperature should reach 135°F.

Tap the salt firmly to crack (it will have formed an armorlike crust). Break the crust and pull off as much of the salt as possible. Peel away and discard the skin, then gently lift away the top fillet using spatulas, transferring it to a warm platter. Now, lift the skeleton away by pulling it up gently by the tail. (The head is attached; it will lift away also.) Discard the zest and thyme. The lower fillet will be exposed; lift it and peel away the skin (easy peasy). Use a pastry brush to flick away any bits of salt still adhering to the tender flesh. Pull the fillets gently apart into four portions and transfer to warm plates. Season with a little more black pepper, drizzle with a generous amount of exquisite olive oil, and serve immediately with lemon wedges.

CENTRAL COAST: L'Aventure Roussanne, Paso Robles
FARTHER AFIELD: Sancerre, Loire Valley, France

Pancetta-Wrapped Salmon with Pistachio–Brown Butter Vinaigrette

This outrageous, in-your-face dish screams "Flavor!" with all the subtlety of a cowgirl rounding up the herd. It ain't your grandma's Friday night fish dish. For low-impact last-minute effort, assemble the salmon packages up to 6 hours before serving time, if desired. If using store-bought tapenade, taste it for saltiness; add a few finely chopped ripe black olives to cut the salt, if necessary.   SERVES 6

Season the salmon on both sides with pepper and spread a pinch of lemon zest on the top. Wrap a slice of pancetta around each piece of salmon. Place on a platter and, if desired, cover with plastic wrap and refrigerate for up to 6 hours. (Or cook immediately.)

Place a baking sheet on the center rack of the oven and preheat the oven to 425°F.

Let the salmon stand at room temperature for 10 minutes if it was just removed from the refrigerator. Transfer the salmon packets to the very hot baking sheet. Roast for 5 minutes, then reduce the oven heat to 325°F and cook for 10 to 12 minutes more, until firm to the touch.

A few minutes before the salmon will be done: Place a small, heavy saucepan over medium heat and add the 6 tablespoons unsalted butter. As it melts, watch—and listen—carefully. The butter will bubble and sizzle, then suddenly go silent and still and begin to turn brown. As soon as the butter turns a dark, nutty brown, remove the pan from the heat, stand back, and add the pistachios and vinegar (be careful, as it will splatter madly). Now add the 4 pieces of cold butter and the parsley and immediately swirl the pan just until the butter melts and thickens the sauce slightly. Spoon alongside or over the salmon and serve at once.

CENTRAL COAST: RN Estate Pinot Noir, Paso Robles
FARTHER AFIELD: Chardonnay from Sonoma Valley, California

6 (6- to 7-ounce) center-cut pieces skinless wild-caught salmon

Freshly ground black pepper

Finely grated zest of 1 lemon

6 very thin slices pancetta

6 tablespoons best-quality unsalted butter (ideally, cultured butter)

¾ cup roasted salted pistachios, coarsely chopped

1½ tablespoons white wine vinegar

2 tablespoons very cold butter, cut into 4 pieces

1 tablespoon finely chopped fresh flat-leaf parsley (optional)

Wood-Grilled Bass with Heirloom Tomato Fondue

This is one of those elemental dishes—basically, very simple in execution—that depends entirely on the quality of the ingredients. Be sure to check one of the online resources at the beginning of this chapter (see page 123) before purchasing the small fish, to be sure you make a responsible choice. Good fishmongers, such as the estimable Pier 46 in Templeton, are also a great source of information about sustainable fish choices.

The simple key to no-tears, no-stick grilling of fish is a very hot grill and a very cold fish. Also, please use self-restraint and resist the urge to move the fish around once it hits the hot grill. The fondue can be made up to 4 hours ahead.   SERVES 6

TOMATO FONDUE
1½ pounds ripe heirloom tomatoes

3 tablespoons best-quality extra-virgin olive oil

1 small red onion, finely chopped

2 teaspoons fresh lemon juice

¼ teaspoon sriracha or other hot sauce

Fine sea salt and freshly ground black pepper

1 large sprig fresh basil

Grapeseed or vegetable oil, for the grill

3 whole fish (about 1½ pounds each), such as striped bass, gutted and scaled, kept chilled until just before grilling time

1 small lemon, thinly sliced

3 garlic cloves, thinly sliced

4 sprigs fresh thyme

4 sprigs fresh flat-leaf parsley

Extra-virgin olive oil, for brushing

4 tablespoons very cold goat's milk butter or cultured cow's milk butter

To make the fondue, bring a large saucepan of water to a boil and fill a medium bowl with ice water. Cut a shallow X in the base of each tomato and blanch for 30 seconds. Transfer to the ice water to stop the cooking. Slip off and discard the skins and core the tomatoes. Cut in half crosswise through the center and squeeze out the seeds into a sieve set over a bowl to capture the juices (or remove the seeds with a small spoon). Cut the tomatoes into large dice.

In a medium saucepan (ideally, one that you don't mind warming later on the grill), warm the olive oil over medium-high heat. Add the red onion and stir occasionally until softened, about 4 minutes. Add the chopped tomatoes, reserved juices, lemon juice, sriracha, 1 teaspoon salt, and plenty of pepper. Decrease the heat to medium-low and cook, stirring occasionally, until the tomatoes begin to break down, about 6 minutes, depending on their ripeness. Add the basil sprig and remove from the heat.

Using oak, almond, or another hardwood, prepare a hot fire in a charcoal grill. Let the fire burn down until the coals are glowing brightly and slightly covered with a thin layer of ash, then rake into an even bed of *very hot* coals. If possible, position the grill grate within about 6 inches of the coals. Scrape the grill grate clean with a wire brush, then dip a clean rag into a little grapeseed or vegetable oil and mop it lightly over the grate. Cover the grill to reheat (or, if using an uncovered grill, cover the cooking area with the lid of a wok or a disposable aluminum roasting pan, so the surface will be as hot as possible).

Stuff the cavity of each fish with the sliced lemons, garlic, and herbs, and brush both sides with just a little bit of olive oil; season lightly with salt and pepper. Bring the stuffed cold fish, sauce, and plates to the grill station.

Just before you are ready to grill, cut a few slashes in the thickest part of the fish on both sides (to help them cook evenly). Grill the fish for 4 to 5 minutes on each side, turning only once, until nicely charred on both sides and done through to the center. The time will depend on the thickness of the fish: To test for doneness, insert a metal skewer near the backbone for a few moments, then hold the tip of the skewer against your lower lip. If the skewer is warm, the fish is done. Or, test with an instant-read thermometer; the temperature at the center should reach 135°F. Transfer to a large platter.

Warm the tomato fondue on the grill just until steaming, discard the basil, and whisk in the butter just until emulsified. Remove from the heat. Carve the fish as desired and serve with a spoonful of the slightly warm fondue.

CENTRAL COAST: Linne Calodo "Contrarian White," Paso Robles (Viognier, Roussanne, Grenache Blanc, Picpoul Blanc)
FARTHER AFIELD: Weingut Knoll Riesling Smaragd, Austria

CHAPTER 5

From
the Ranch

Here on the Central Coast, we are lucky enough to have an abundance of livestock raised mostly on a diet of grass, rather than grain. Grain feeding of meat livestock is a relatively new custom, started only in the past century, when our demand for protein on the hoof outstripped our availability of grazing lands. Animals thrive on grass, needing no antibiotics to keep them "healthy," as grain-fed livestock do. If grass-fed meat is available where you live, I urge you to seek it out. A grass diet is better for the animals, and the resulting meat is better for you! The flavor is cleaner, the texture firmer, and it's far less fatty than grain-fed meat.

Here, I present dishes that showcase the amazing variety of protein available in this fertile region—beef, pork, lamb, boar, and goat—most of them taking advantage of the bewitching effects of wine and time.

A NOTE ON COOKING TIMES AND TEMPERATURES: Because of its lean-ness, cooking times and temperatures for grass-fed meat should be adjusted slightly downward to prevent the delicate meat from drying out. In this book, I've given times and temperatures based on grain-fed meat because unfortunately it's still the kind of meat most cooks will be able to find. But that is changing, gradually. As a general guide, when cooking grass-fed meat you should reduce both the cooking time and the oven/fire temperature by 10 to 15 percent. This is especially true when cooking on the grill, as that fierce, dry heat can quickly suck all the moisture out of the lean, delicate meat. As always, let your senses be the final guide to when it is done, and keep track of your results in the margins with a sticky note or two.

Wine pairings by Wes Hagen, vineyard manager-winemaker at Clos Pepe

Rhône Wine- and Fig-Braised Pork Chops

I am frequently motivated to unite pig and fig in a recipe—it's an urge I never question. If you make this rustic, unctuous, and wine-dark dish during fig season, quarter a few fresh figs and scatter them over and around the chops just before serving.

Don't attempt to move the chops until they have been in the hot oil for at least 1 minute, to allow the fatty flavor paste to bond with the meat. Use a flat-ended metal spatula to turn the chops. If your dried figs are very hard, soak them in hot water for 15 minutes before mincing. SERVES 6

6 nicely marbled pork chops, about ¾ inch thick, preferably from a heritage-breed pig

MARINADE/SAUCE BASE
1¼ cups Rhône-style red wine, such as Syrah

¼ cup balsamic vinegar

Finely grated zest and juice of 1 large orange

1 large shallot, minced

8 dried figs, stemmed and very finely diced (about 4 ounces)

⅓ teaspoon *each* fine sea salt and freshly ground black pepper

2 tablespoons extra-virgin olive oil

3 garlic cloves, minced or pushed through a press

2 teaspoons minced fresh rosemary

1 teaspoon all-purpose flour

Fine sea salt and freshly ground black pepper

2 tablespoons olive oil

2 tablespoons cold butter, cut into 4 pieces

Trim off most of the visible exterior fat from the chops, and reserve it, chilled.

In a large baking dish, combine all the ingredients for the marinade/sauce base. Immerse the chops in the liquid and turn to coat all sides. Cover and refrigerate for 4 to 6 hours, turning over halfway through.

Cut the reserved pork fat into ¼-inch bits and combine in a small food processor (or a mortar and pestle) with the garlic, rosemary, flour, and a pinch each of salt and pepper. Process or pound to a smooth paste.

Lift the chops from the marinade, scraping off all the solids; reserve the marinade. Pat both sides of each chop thoroughly dry. Spread a little of the pork-fat paste on each side of each chop, spreading it thin, flat, and very smooth.

In a very large skillet (or in two batches), heat the olive oil over medium-high heat until very hot. Sear the chops on both sides until golden brown, about 2½ minutes per side, using a metal spatula to carefully turn the chops in order to preserve the flavor paste. Return the first batch of chops to the skillet, if necessary, and add all the reserved marinade. Bring to a simmer, then lower the heat and simmer very gently, half-covered, until the chops are done (firm to the touch, or 142°F), 5 to 6 minutes, turning the chops over once.

continued on page 172

Transfer the chops to a platter and keep warm in a low oven. Reduce the chunky marinade over high heat until slightly syrupy. Remove from the heat and swirl in the cold butter until it's emulsified and the sauce is glossy. Spoon a generous amount of the chunky sauce over the top of each chop and serve.

NOTE: If using grass-fed pork, reduce both the cooking time and cooking temperature by 10 to 15 percent (that is, cook on medium heat instead of medium-high heat).

CENTRAL COAST: Jaffurs Grenache, Thompson Vineyard, Santa Barbara County
FARTHER AFIELD: Jaboulet or Perrin Côtes du Rhône, Rhône Valley, France

Rustic Bread, Pork, and Bacon Skewers with a Mustardy Salad

Long ago, I discovered a recipe in an old Time-Life book for grilling bread on a skewer (along with other tasty ingredients), and I have incorporated the technique into several recipes in this book, and other dishes throughout my career. This is a truly winning technique—who doesn't love a nice, crisp, and juicy crouton? SERVES 6

To make the vinaigrette, in a large glass or ceramic bowl, combine and whisk together all the ingredients for the vinaigrette. Set aside.

In a large mixing bowl, combine the pork chunks, bacon, olive oil, cumin, oregano, 1 teaspoon salt, and plenty of pepper. Toss together and let stand at room temperature for 15 minutes (or refrigerate for up to 2 hours; return to room temperature for 10 to 15 minutes before grilling). Add the bread to the bowl, and fold together; the bread should be well coated with the marinade. Toss again if the bread doesn't seem evenly coated.

Prepare a hardwood or charcoal grill or a gas grill for medium-high-heat grilling, or heat a cast-iron griddle pan over high heat.

Thread the ingredients onto six long bamboo skewers or twelve shorter skewers, alternating the pork, bacon, and bread. Wrap the blunt end of each skewer with aluminum foil to stop it from catching fire. Grill the skewers for 3 to 4 minutes on each of all four sides, until the pork is firm and just slightly golden and the bread cubes are golden brown. Add the lettuce to the bowl with the dressing and toss until thoroughly and evenly coated with the dressing; divide among plates. Top each salad with a skewer (or two), removing the foil, and serve at once.

NOTE: If using grass-fed pork, reduce both the cooking time and cooking temperature by 10 to 15 percent (that is, grill over medium heat instead of medium-high heat).

CENTRAL COAST: Cold Heaven Viognier, Sanford and Benedict Vineyard, Santa Rita Hills
FARTHER AFIELD: Riesling from Columbia Valley, Washington

VINAIGRETTE
1 tablespoon Dijon mustard

2 small garlic cloves, minced or pushed through a press

½ teaspoon fine sea salt

¼ teaspoon freshly ground black pepper

2 tablespoons white wine vinegar

6 tablespoons extra-virgin olive oil

1½ pounds pork tenderloin, cut into 1-inch cubes (about thirty 1-ounce chunks)

30 pieces ¾-inch square smoked or unsmoked bacon (about 6 slices)

¼ cup extra-virgin olive oil

¾ teaspoon ground cumin

¾ teaspoon dried oregano

30 cubes country bread, cut about 25 percent smaller than the pork cubes

1 small head iceberg lettuce, wilted outer leaves discarded, thinly sliced

Three-Hour, Bone-In Berkshire Pork Shoulder with Brandy and Black Pepper Apples

I've certainly been one of the first mainstream cookbook authors to bring the concept of residual-heat cooking out of the restaurant kitchen and into the home. Chefs have been doing this for generations, but in my classes on residual-heat cooking, the students literally mob me at the end of the session. This unconventional method yields a deeply caramelized, barklike crust and a tender and juicy interior that is hard to come by with today's supermarket pork—often overly lean. Do make every effort to source a nice, fatty pork shoulder from a heritage breed, such as Duroc or Berkshire. Having said that, trim away any large pockets of fat visible on the surface of the meat before brining.   SERVES 8

1 cup medium-dry white wine, such as Riesling or Viognier

Kosher salt, as needed

6 pounds boneless pork shoulder (Boston butt or picnic)

Sugar, as needed

5 garlic cloves, smashed with the side of a knife

3 fresh bay leaves or 5 dried, crumbled

1 tablespoon juniper berries, lightly crushed

5 sprigs fresh thyme

Freshly ground black pepper (coarsely ground)

1½ tablespoons grapeseed or vegetable oil

6 tablespoons salted butter

4 Pink Lady or other apples, quartered, cored, and cut into ¼-inch slices

⅓ cup Calvados or brandy

1 cup medium-dry white wine, such as Riesling or Viognier

Warm the wine in a small saucepan and add ¼ cup of salt. Stir until the salt has dissolved, then let cool to room temperature. Transfer to a tall nonreactive container or crock (glass or plastic) that will snugly hold the pork while allowing the liquid to completely cover it, and fit in the refrigerator (large food service containers are ideal). Place the pork in the container, and then make up enough water-based brine to completely cover the meat, using the following ratio: ¼ cup salt and 1 tablespoon sugar stirred into each quart (4 cups) of water until dissolved. Add the garlic, bay leaves, juniper berries, and thyme. Cover with plastic wrap and refrigerate for about 48 hours (be sure the pork is completely submerged in the liquid).

About 3½ hours before you plan to serve the pork, remove it from the brine. Pat thoroughly dry all over with absorbent paper towels, then let stand for 1½ hours, to come to room temperature.

In a small bowl, combine plenty of pepper and 1 tablespoon of the oil. Rub this paste all over the pork, working it into any nooks and crannies.

Place a rack in the center position and preheat the oven to 450°F. Place the pork fattier side down in a large, heavy roasting pan. Roast for 25 minutes, then turn fat side up, decrease the oven temperature to 325°F, and poke a heatproof meat thermometer into the thickest part of the meat. Return the pork to the oven with the thermometer facing the glass door (or, ideally, use a probe thermometer on a cable). Roast for 40 minutes more. Now, turn off the oven but *DO NOT OPEN THE DOOR*. Leave the pork in the turned-off oven for 1 to 1½ hours more; do not let anyone open the door during this time! Watch the temperature through the glass door front or on the monitor; it should reach 150°F to 155°F. (The timing will depend on your oven and how long you let the pork stand before beginning to cook.)

When the pork has reached about 145°F, make the apples. In a large, heavy skillet, melt the butter over medium heat. Add the apples, season very lightly with salt, and sprinkle with 1 teaspoon sugar. Cook, turning over occasionally, for 8 to 10 minutes, until the apples are tender but not falling apart. Add the Calvados, jiggle the pan, and set the liquor alight. Jiggle the pan until the flame dies away, and season generously with pepper. Set aside.

About 25 minutes before serving time, turn the oven back on to 450°F and roast the pork for 15 minutes (this serves to warm up and crisp the exterior; the internal temperature will not change). Remove from the oven and transfer to a warm serving platter. Cover loosely with aluminum foil and let rest for about 10 minutes. Tip the roasting pan to the side and spoon off most of the fat from the corner. Add the wine and place the pan over medium-high heat. Simmer for 4 to 5 minutes to deglaze, stirring and scraping the pan to dislodge all the tasty bits from the side. (Because of the brine, you will probably not need to season these pan juices.)

Carve the pork across the grain about ¼ inch thick and serve at once with a jumble of apples, spooning a little of the pan juices over each serving.

NOTE: If using grass-fed pork, reduce both the cooking time and cooking temperature by 10 to 15 percent (that is, cook at 425°F instead of 450°F).

CENTRAL COAST: Cold Heaven Viognier, Sanford and Benedict Vineyard, Santa Rita Hills
FARTHER AFIELD: Riesling, Columbia Valley, Washington

Hearst Ranch Beef

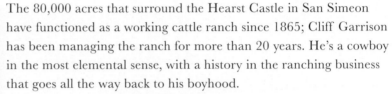

The 80,000 acres that surround the Hearst Castle in San Simeon have functioned as a working cattle ranch since 1865; Cliff Garrison has been managing the ranch for more than 20 years. He's a cowboy in the most elemental sense, with a history in the ranching business that goes all the way back to his boyhood.

Cliff wholly embraces grass-fed beef simply because of the flavor. "When you eat a lot of quality grass-fed beef, and then go back to corn-fed, you can taste the waxy-greasy flavor. If you really want to see the difference, eat a piece of each, cold, out of the fridge. The grass-fed has a clean flavor, the other—it's like eating Crisco. That tells you something. Nature designed the cow as the perfect machine for converting low-quality forage into protein using solar power—they've got four stomachs to help them do it." Then man got involved and messed it up. "Man created intra-muscular marbling— not nature."

Hearst Ranch did it like everybody else until 2003: The cattle were raised on grass until weaning age, at 500 to 600 pounds, then shipped off to Kansas to be fattened—up to 1,200 pounds or so—on grain. There wasn't much choice, because the grass ran out. The Midwest feedlot system was created to take up the slack when grass stopped growing in the summer. There were two choices: Move them north or to Colorado, where there was still rain and grass—a costly choice; or, ship them east and start the corn diet.

"I wasn't spending enough time being a cowboy," he says. "All I did was look at the bottom line, and I didn't like what happened to my cattle when they left here." The simplicity of an all-grass diet appealed to him. "I like things simple and right. I'd seen wild cattle— they look great and they're healthy, and man has no hands on their management. Of course, they're wilder than hell."

Nature designed the cow as the perfect machine for converting low-quality forage into protein using solar power . . .

Cliff calls himself a grass farmer. "There *is* enough feed here to take them all the way to market size, but you have to manage it well. If the grass isn't "disturbed" by the process of grazing, it grows too high and gets knocked down by wind and rain into an impenetrable covering that stops moisture and sunlight from getting through. It dies. A cow's hoof is cloven, that is, split. That cloven hoof helps break up the crust on the ground to allow seeds to germinate and moisture to penetrate, and the cycle continues. "You can't mess with nature," Cliff says. "If you don't have grass, you don't have beef."

The old cows were too big for grass, so a big part of Hearst's program involves cross-breeding for a smaller, less blocky animal. "We *had* the right cow, and then they went to taller and longer European breeds. We're bringing back the breeds that haven't been changed since the '50s, mostly Angus but crossing in some Hereford, Devon, and Shorthorn."

Cliff nudged his horse gently and rode off, literally, into the sunset: a man doing what he loves and creating something good for the cows, good for the planet, and damned good to eat. *Yeeee-ha.*

IF YOU VISIT:

You can't visit the cattle on Hearst Ranch (although you can see them from the iconic California Route 1 near the entrance to the Hearst Castle), but you can taste Hearst Ranch beef, in one of the best-tasting beef burgers this side of the Mississippi. Just visit the Hearst Ranch Winery tasting room, in "downtown" old San Simeon, one of the sweetest slices of old California I've ever seen (and I look for such things). Bonus: Sip one (or more) of Hearst's excellent wines at the same time. The tasting room is in the old Sebastian's general store, which operated for almost 100 years.

442 San Luis Obispo–San Simeon Road
San Simeon, CA 93452

Daily, 11 a.m. to 5 p.m.

www.hearstranchwinery.com

Brined Pork Porterhouse with Smoky Lentils and Vineyard-Dried Tomatoes

This is one of the more time-consuming and involved recipes in this book, so reserve it for an event when you really want to wow your guests. Most of the work can be done in advance, so the final assembly is fairly painless (something of a signature for me because at the last minute I prefer to be on the patio with a glass of wine than in the kitchen). It will be even easier if you have a master griller in the family, one who will not be alarmed at the hugeness of these chops. Speaking of master grillers, I bravely served this dish to Paso Robles's Grill-King, Gary Eberle, and his adorable wife, Marcy; Gary was guardedly pleased.

Sourcing such a large, thick pork porterhouse may take longer than prepping the dish: Ask your local farmer or butcher for help. SERVES 6

8 cups water

½ cup kosher salt

2 tablespoons sugar

½ cup white wine

2 dried bay leaves, crumbled

2 tablespoons black peppercorns

3 bone-in pork porterhouse chops, each about 2 pounds and 2 inches thick, preferably from a pastured, heritage-breed pig

Freshly ground black pepper, for seasoning

DRESSING FOR LENTILS

1 garlic clove, sliced

1 shallot, sliced

3 tablespoons sherry vinegar

1 tablespoon capers

2 teaspoons Dijon mustard

Fine sea salt and freshly ground black pepper

½ cup extra-virgin olive oil

LENTILS

1 tablespoon extra-virgin olive oil

2 medium shallots, finely chopped

2 slices smoked bacon, minced

1 celery rib, finely chopped

1 large carrot, finely chopped

2 garlic cloves, finely chopped

1½ cups small French green lentils

2 cups low-sodium or homemade chicken broth

Fine sea salt and freshly ground black pepper

2 teaspoons smoked paprika

2 teaspoons finely snipped fresh chives

Vineyard-Dried Tomatoes, for serving (optional; recipe follows)

In a tall, narrow, nonmetal container that will fit in your fridge (such as a ceramic crock or plastic bulk food container), combine the water, kosher salt, sugar, wine, bay leaves, and peppercorns; stir until the salt and sugar are fully dissolved. Submerge the chops in the brine (if you want to serve more than 3 chops and there is not enough brine to completely cover them, make up half the amount of brine above, maintaining the same ratio of salt, sugar, and wine to water). Refrigerate the pork overnight.

To make the dressing for the lentils, combine the garlic, shallot, vinegar, capers, mustard, ½ teaspoon sea salt, a little pepper, and the olive oil in a blender. Blend until smooth. Cover and refrigerate until it's time to dress the lentils (up to 2 days).

To make the lentils, place a large, heavy saucepan over medium-low heat and add the oil. Sauté the shallots and bacon for about 4 minutes, or until the shallots are softened. Add the celery and carrot. Stir for 3 to 4 minutes, until wilted, then add the garlic. Stir for 1 minute more, and add the lentils. Stir to coat them with the oil, then add the broth and enough water to cover the lentils by about ¼ inch. Bring to a boil, then reduce the heat, partially cover the pan, and simmer very gently for 25 minutes, or until the lentils are tender but still have a nice bite to them. Taste and adjust the seasoning with sea salt and pepper. Remove from the heat and let stand, covered, for 5 minutes. If there is a lot of excess liquid, drain the lentils in a colander. While still nice and hot, combine them with a generous amount of the dressing; fold in the paprika and chives. Let stand for about 1 hour at room temperature, to allow the flavors to blend.

Lift the chops from the brine and pat both sides thoroughly dry with absorbent paper towels. Place on a rack and let stand at room temperature, loosely covered, for 1 hour before cooking.

Prepare a grill (preferably charcoal) for direct and indirect grilling (very hot on one side and medium on the other). Brush both sides of each chop lightly with olive oil, and season generously with pepper. Grill the chops over direct heat for 2½ minutes without moving, then turn over and cook for 2½ minutes more. Move the chops to the indirect side of the grill with the fatty edge facing the fire, and cover the grill. Continue grilling the chops gently for 35 to 45 minutes more, allowing the fire to die down naturally and turning the chops every 8 to 10 minutes, until the temperature at the thickest point, away from the bone, reaches 135°F to 140°F. Transfer to a cutting board and cover with aluminum foil. Let rest for about 5 minutes (the internal temperature will climb to 145°F to 150°F).

Carve the whole sirloin and whole tenderloin away from the bone on either side of each chop; slice each piece of meat crosswise about ¼ inch thick. Divide the slices among warm plates, and serve with a large spoonful of lentils on the side and some juicy tomatoes on top.

NOTE: If using grass-fed pork, reduce both the cooking time and cooking temperature by 10 to 15 percent (that is, grill at medium-high heat instead of very high heat).

Vineyard-Dried Tomatoes

⅓ cup extra-virgin olive oil

Fine sea salt and freshly
ground black pepper

2 pounds ripe cherry tomatoes, halved

Sprigs fresh thyme

Coat a large baking sheet with about half of the olive oil, and season the pan generously with salt and pepper. Place the tomatoes cut side down on the oil and drizzle the remaining oil over the top. Season again with salt and pepper and scatter with the thyme. Place the baking sheet on a sunny deck overlooking a vineyard and let the sun dry the tomatoes naturally, until they are dehydrated but still a little juicy (protect with a screen if bugs are a problem). During the summer, the tomatoes will dry faster, but the best results will be achieved on a cloudless, low-humidity day, when the air is crisp and clean and you can see the mountains from miles away. (The process will take from 1 to 3 days, and is a matter of taste.) Refrigerate, covered, until needed. You may make these up to 3 days in advance.

NOTE: For those without a deck overlooking a vineyard, bake the tomatoes cut sides down in a 350°F oven for about 45 minutes, or until shriveled but still quite juicy. These are completely unlike commercial sun-dried tomatoes, and instead should be similar in consistency to a dried apricot that has been soaked in very hot water for half an hour.

CENTRAL COAST: Loring Wine Company Pinot Noir, Rancho la Vina, Santa Rita Hills
FARTHER AFIELD: Pinot Noir from anywhere in California

Spicy Sausage on a
Bed of Braised Red and Green Grapes

Deceptively simple, elemental, and rustic—all the hallmarks of great wine country cuisine—this dish requires little attention and no great culinary skill. And yet it rewards the cook and his or her friends and family with a full-bodied and delightful repast that requires nothing more than crusty bread and, perhaps, a simple butter lettuce salad with a mustardy dressing. Some of the grapes break down as they braise, creating their own ambrosial sauce. Cheers! SERVES 6

Combine the oil and sausages in a very large skillet and set over medium-low heat. Cook the sausages, turning occasionally, for about 10 minutes, or until they are browned on all sides. (If using fresh sausages, prick each sausage in a few places, and cook for 5 minutes more, or until done through.)

Transfer the sausages to a platter and keep warm in a low oven. If more than a tablespoon or two of fat remains in the pan, discard some of it. Add the grapes and shallot, and increase the heat to medium-high. Cook, stirring occasionally, until some of the grapes collapse. Stir in the vinegar and season lightly with salt and generously with pepper. Simmer for a few minutes more. Spoon the grapes and pan juices onto the platter and serve the sausages atop the grapes.

CENTRAL COAST: Axis Mundi Grenache/Syrah, Ballard Canyon, Santa Ynez Valley
FARTHER AFIELD: Tavel rosé, Provence, France

2 teaspoons grapeseed or extra-virgin olive oil

2 pounds fresh or precooked spicy sausage (pork, chicken, turkey, or lamb)

4 to 5 cups seedless grapes (about 1 pound), preferably a mixture of green, black, and red—maybe even champagne grapes

1 large shallot, minced

2 tablespoons good-quality balsamic vinegar, ideally aged

Fine sea salt and freshly ground black pepper

Justin Vineyards & Winery

In 1981, Justin Baldwin purchased 160 acres of raw land in the remote Adelaida region west of Paso Robles, and shortly afterward began construction of a winery. At the time, Justin was an international investment banker, more comfortable in pinstripes than overalls. In the spring of 1982, he planted a 72-acre vineyard and surrounded it with two miles of electrified fence to keep out the deer, boars, and wild turkey, which virtually outnumber the local human population.

"When we started, there were less than 10 wineries in the entire area," recalls Justin. These days, Justin Vineyards & Winery has expanded into an opulent, four-star destination far from downtown's many tasting rooms and the summertime hustle and bustle of Route 46 and Vineyard Drive. Now, there are wineries and vineyards all the way out Chimney Rock Road.

A love of French Bordeaux led to plantings of the three classic red Bordeaux grape varieties: Cabernet Sauvignon, Merlot, and Cabernet Franc. These original plantings have been supplemented with several other grape varieties, with a special concentration on Syrah.

The 1987 harvest was also the beginning of commercial production of the individual varietals Cabernet Sauvignon, Cabernet Franc, Merlot, and a small amount of Chardonnay—plus a Bordeaux blend originally called Reserve and now renowned (and acclaimed) as Isoceles. By the following year, production was up to 4,000 cases and construction of a French auberge-style tasting room and visitor's center had begun.

In 1997, local history was made when the 1994 Isosceles won the *Pichon Longueville Comtesse de Lalande* trophy for "World's Best Blended

At the time, Justin was . . . more comfortable in pinstripes than overalls.

Red Wine" at the London International Wine Competition. More accolades followed, and Justin remained in the *Wine Spectator* Top Ten Wines of the World for several years. Critics and wine writers began to eye the once sleepy appellation of Paso Robles, and Justin wines were suddenly in high demand.

"I loved working at Justin," recalls Mary Baker, the winery's business manager in the mid-1990s. "The level of activity and energy was amazing. Business came in faster than we could expand and we were bursting at the seams. The innkeeper and tasting-room manager had to share the same space with a temperamental chef. Some days, pots and dishes went flying!"

The winery had begun as a small outbuilding and outdoor crush pad attached to the original two-suite inn, one suite of which was the Baldwins's home for many years. Tastings and winery dinners were held in the same downstairs room, simply by rearranging furniture as needed. As the winery's reputation grew, so did its girth, with the addition of a new, larger winery building, which includes offices and conference rooms, expansive wine caves, and an event center. The winery also boasts a cozy kitchen. Across from the main entrance is a bermed cave—a small stucco room used for entertaining distributors and other visiting VIPs. The cave also has an outdoor pizza oven built into the wall, perfect for entertaining guests on the private patio.

Each vintage of Justin single-varietal releases features a different artist's painting of the property; a full horizontal collection of Justin bottles is also a portrait of its dynamic history.

IF YOU VISIT:

Linger over a luscious, wine-country lunch at The Restaurant, the only fine-dining venue contained within a winery in the Paso Robles area. Ideally, stay over for a romantic weekend at the ochre- and burnt-sienna-tinted Provençal auberge-style inn, the JUST Inn. In the expansive yet comfortable tasting room, taste your way from the crisp and minerally Sauvignon Blanc all the way through decadent, bittersweet-chocolate-perfumed Obtuse.

Daily, 11 a.m. to 4:30 p.m.

11680 Chimney Rock Road
Paso Robles, CA 93446

(805) 238-6932

www.justinwine.com

Maple-Glazed Berkshire Pork Belly with Frisée and Garlicky Dressing

This luxurious winter warmer takes some time but is *so* worth it. Braise the pork belly the day before and refrigerate it in the liquid. Save the strained braising liquid for a soup, ideally with some leafy greens. Pork belly is most often sold without the skin, and that's what you want here. But if you *can* get the pork belly with the skin on, choose another recipe, one where that skin will crisp up beautifully. The skin will not crisp with this treatment and would end up rubbery. Here, the belly resembles pork Jell-O by the time it's done. Pork Jell-O, that is, with delicately crispy fat on top. SERVES 6

⅓ cup granulated sugar

⅓ cup kosher salt

2 tablespoons black peppercorns, lightly crushed

2 tablespoons allspice berries, lightly crushed

2 tablespoons fennel seeds, lightly crushed

1 (2-pound) slab boneless, skinless pork belly

1 large white or yellow onion, halved and thinly sliced

4 to 5 cups homemade or store-bought low-sodium chicken broth

2 tablespoons butter

2 tablespoons dark brown sugar

1 tablespoon maple syrup

Fine sea salt

SALAD

Pale inner hearts of 3 heads frisée, cut into bite-size pieces

2 heads red-leaf lettuce, cut into bite-size pieces

2 medium shallots, minced

Caesar Dressing (page 43)

Freshly ground black pepper

3 tablespoons finely snipped fresh chives

In a roasting pan just large enough to hold the pork belly with an inch or so of clearance all around, combine the sugar, kosher salt, black peppercorns, allspice berries, fennel seeds, and ½ gallon of water. Stir until the salt and sugar have dissolved. Add the belly fat side up, make sure it is fully submerged, and refrigerate for 24 hours.

Preheat the oven to 300°F. Lift the pork from the brine. Strain and discard the brine, reserving the spices. In the roasting pan you used for brining, combine the onion with the spices and spread into an even layer. Place the pork belly on top, fat side up, and pour in enough broth to come halfway up the sides of the pork. Cover the pan with a large sheet of baking parchment and a sheet of aluminum foil, crimping the edges. Braise in the warm oven until a meat thermometer inserted into the

center reads 160°F, 1½ to 2 hours. Let cool completely in the broth. Cut lengthwise in 2-inch strips, then crosswise into 2-inch rectangles.

When ready to serve, preheat the oven to 375°F. Put the belly pieces on a rimmed baking sheet. In a small saucepan, warm the butter, brown sugar, maple syrup, ½ cup of the braising liquid, and ¼ teaspoon sea salt. Pour the liquid over the pork and heat in the oven, basting occasionally, until warmed through, about 15 minutes. Transfer to, or turn on, the broiler. Broil about 6 inches from the heat source, watching all the time, until the tops are golden brown and slightly crisped, 1½ to 3 minutes.

Meanwhile, to make the salad, in a large bowl combine the frisée, red leaf lettuce, shallots, dressing, and plenty of pepper; toss until evenly combined. Serve the salad as a bed for the hot pork-belly "croutons" and scatter some chives over all.

CENTRAL COAST: Clos Pepe Estate Pinot Noir, Santa Rita Hills
FARTHER AFIELD: Pinot Noir from Oregon

Tuscan Cowboy Pork and "Beans"

In the lexicon of my two recent meat books, this process would be called a reverse-sear. Grill and barbecue geeks are very familiar with this technique and know that it yields incredibly juicy and flavorful results. In the summer, finish crisping the ribs on a hot grill while the chickpeas are baking. The goal is a rich, brown, and crusty exterior; the inside will be already cooked at that point. This is a very flexible dish; the timing is completely up to you. You can brown the ribs right after the initial cooking, or wait for up to 4 hours. SERVES 6

PORK

4 large garlic cloves, thinly sliced

¼ cup loosely packed fresh rosemary needles

2 teaspoons extra-virgin olive oil

Fine sea salt and freshly ground black pepper

3½ pounds country-style pork ribs (preferably, heritage breed and/or pasture raised), cut about 1 inch thick

BEANS

1 tablespoon rendered bacon fat or olive oil

2 medium white or yellow onions, coarsely chopped

3 garlic cloves, minced or pushed through a press

1 large carrot, coarsely chopped

1 cup chopped canned plum tomatoes, with their juice

1 (15-ounce) can beef, chicken, pork, or turkey broth (or use homemade)

2 (15-ounce) cans best-quality chickpeas, rinsed and drained

⅓ cup coarsely chopped fresh flat-leaf parsley

½ teaspoon dried thyme

Fine sea salt and freshly ground black pepper

⅓ cup fine, dry bread crumbs

½ cup coarsely grated Parmesan or other robust salty cheese, such as ricotta salata

To make the pork, mince the garlic and rosemary together using a sharp knife. Then mix into a paste with the olive oil, ¾ teaspoon salt, and plenty of pepper. Place the ribs in a shallow baking dish, rub all over with the paste, then cover and refrigerate for at least 6 hours, preferably overnight.

In the late morning or afternoon before you plan to serve, preheat the oven to 325°F. Line a large, rimmed baking sheet with aluminum foil and place the ribs bone side down on the foil without touching. Roast on the middle rack of the oven for 30 to 40 minutes, until the temperature in a thick part of the meat reaches 150°F to 155°F. Immediately remove from the oven. Let stand at room temperature for up to

30 minutes, then continue with the beans and the browning phase immediately (see below), or cover loosely and refrigerate until 30 minutes before serving time (up to 4 hours).

To make the beans, preheat the oven to 400°F. In a flameproof and ovenproof braising pan, warm the fat or oil over medium heat. Add the onions, garlic, and carrot and sauté, stirring occasionally, until glossy and starting to soften, about 8 minutes. Stir in the tomatoes, broth, chickpeas, parsley, thyme, ½ teaspoon salt, and plenty of pepper. Bring to a simmer, then transfer to the oven and bake uncovered for about 25 minutes, or until most of the liquid has been absorbed. Scatter evenly with the bread crumbs and cheese and cook for 15 to 20 minutes more, until the top is golden. Remove from the oven, cover, and let stand while you finish the ribs.

Turn the oven to broil, and place the pan of ribs 7 to 8 inches from the heat source. Brown the ribs, turning with long tongs every 5 minutes or so, until all sides are deeply browned, crusty, and sizzling, 15 to 20 minutes. Serve the ribs with a scoop of "beans" on the side.

CENTRAL COAST: Alma Rosa Pinot Blanc, La Encantada Vineyard, Santa Rita Hills
FARTHER AFIELD: Riesling, Grüner Veltliner, or other white wine from Germany or Austria

Passoulet

I don't claim authenticity for this much simpler take on the hearty and revered French countryside classic, but then it doesn't take three days to prepare, either. The very first Passoulet was cooked in the tiny, very basic kitchen of a rental house on Oak Street, back when I was interviewing Paso Robles as a potential home. I'd gone boar hunting on Dubost Ranch with Mary Baker and master hunter Matt Tupen, and we immediately turned some of "Our Boar" (as Mary and I liked to call him) into a rich and crusty bean dish: Passoulet!

If you prefer to cook your beans from scratch, I take my hat off to you. Just reserve 1 cup of the cooking water for the braise. SERVES 8 TO 10

2 pounds boneless shoulder of wild boar or locally sourced, heritage-breed pork, cut into ¾-inch cubes

Fine sea salt and freshly ground black pepper

5 tablespoons grapeseed or vegetable oil

1 pound fresh garlicky pork sausage

1 pound fresh fruit-flavored poultry sausage

1 pound fresh andouille-style or hot Italian sausage

1 medium white or yellow onion, coarsely chopped

2 celery ribs, thinly sliced

¼ cup tomato paste

1½ cups medium-dry white wine (such as a Rhône blend)

½ cup water

10 medium garlic cloves, finely chopped

1 tablespoon chopped fresh thyme or 1 teaspoon dried

Five (15-ounce) cans cannellini or Great Northern beans, well rinsed and drained

1½ cups homemade or store-bought low-sodium chicken or beef broth or water

2 cups dry bread crumbs

½ cup finely chopped fresh flat-leaf parsley

Season the boar cubes generously with salt and pepper. Place a large, heavy skillet over medium-high heat and add the oil. When the oil is hot, add the meat and sauté until golden brown, turning with tongs; transfer to a bowl. Add the sausages to the same skillet and brown on all sides, turning to brown evenly. Transfer to a cutting board. Now add the onion and celery to the same skillet, decrease the heat to medium, and cook for 5 minutes, or until translucent. Add the tomato paste and stir constantly for 1 minute, then stir in 1 cup of the wine and the water; simmer until reduced by about half. Add this mixture to the bowl with the boar. Cut half the sausages in half crosswise (leave the remaining sausages whole). Transfer the sausages to the bowl with the boar and wine mixture.

In a small bowl, combine the garlic, thyme, 1 teaspoon salt, and ½ teaspoon black pepper.

Preheat the oven to 325°F. Spoon one-third of the beans into a large, deep casserole (enameled cast iron is ideal). Nestle half the boar and wine-vegetable mixture and half the sausages into the beans. Scatter with half the garlic-thyme mixture. Repeat, layering the ingredients, and cover with a third and final layer of beans. Pour in the broth and remaining ½ cup of wine. Add enough water so the liquid only just barely covers the beans. Cover the pan snugly with the lid or well-crimped aluminum foil and bake for 1 hour. (At this point, you could cool thoroughly, and then refrigerate the dish overnight or for up to 24 hours before finishing.)

In a small bowl, combine the bread crumbs and parsley. Remove the foil/lid from the casserole and spread half of the crumb mixture over the top. Bake uncovered for 1 hour more. Remove from the oven and use a large, flat spoon to gently press the crumb crust down into the beans, so the liquid wells up slightly over the spoon. Scatter the remaining crumb mixture over the top, increase the heat to 375°F, and return the pot, again uncovered, to the oven for about 45 minutes more. At this point, if the top is not golden brown, turn on the broiler and crisp the top for 3 to 5 minutes, watching closely to prevent it from scorching. Allow the passoulet to rest for 5 to 10 minutes, then serve, giving each diner part of the top crust.

NOTE: If using grass-fed pork, reduce the cooking temperature by 10 to 15 percent (that is, braise at 300°F instead of 325°F).

CENTRAL COAST: Longoria Tempranillo, Clover Creek Vineyard, Santa Ynez Valley
FARTHER AFIELD: Red wine from Ribera del Duero, Spain

Various Parts of the Lamb, Grilled on a Brochette with Rosemary and Garlic

For helping me to perfect this dish, huge thanks are due to San Francisco's "King of Meats," my friend, butcher Ryan Farr (I helped him write his first cookbook, *Whole Beast Butchery*). Ryan's guidance was crucial in achieving my ambition: to create a skewer full of lamb-a-licious goodness. When threading the lamb parts onto the skewers, pierce the bacon where it overlaps, to mostly enclose the pieces of liver. This will protect them from drying out on the grill. Don't press the various pieces too snugly together on the skewers, or the heat will not penetrate evenly. SERVES 6 TO 8

8 ounces lamb kidneys, 2½ to 3 inches across at their widest point

12 ounces lamb from the leg, trimmed of fat and cut into 1¾-inch cubes

1 pound lamb shoulder, trimmed of fat and cut into 1-inch cubes

8 ounces lamb liver, cut into 1-inch cubes

4 slices bacon, cut crosswise into thirds

¼ cup extra-virgin olive oil

1 tablespoon red wine vinegar

1½ teaspoons minced fresh rosemary

4 garlic cloves, minced or pushed through a press

4 scallions, white and light green parts only, finely chopped

Fine sea salt and freshly ground black pepper

6 ounces watercress, leaves and tender stems only, about 1½ cups

About 8 ounces vine-ripened tomatoes, cored and cut into small chunks

Anchoïade (recipe follows), for serving

Cut each kidney in half horizontally across the center and remove the membrane. If there is still fat on the exterior, leave a thin layer, to protect the delicate flesh during grilling. Cut each half into 2 or 3 chunks, depending on the size (aim for approximately 1-inch chunks).

In a shallow bowl, combine all the various bits of lamb, bacon, olive oil, vinegar, rosemary, garlic, scallions, ¾ teaspoon salt, and plenty of pepper. Toss to combine, and let stand at room temperature for 30 minutes (or cover and refrigerate for up to 6 hours; return to room temperature before grilling). Toss the mixture occasionally.

Prepare a charcoal or gas grill for medium-high-heat grilling. Lift the bits of lamb from the marinade, and wrap each piece of liver with a piece of bacon. Thread the lamb pieces together onto 12 to 16 long bamboo skewers, dividing the different bits equally and keeping them closer to the pointy end, so they'll be easier to eat. Wrap the blunt ends of the skewers with aluminum foil to come most of the way down the skewer to the meat.

Grill the skewers for 8 to 10 minutes total, turning over with tongs two or three times, until slightly firm and char-marked. If the fire flares up, move the skewers temporarily to a cooler section of the grill. The shoulder, liver, and kidneys should be cooked through, and the leg still medium-rare. Transfer to a platter and let stand for 3 to 4 minutes.

Serve each brochette atop a small pile of watercress and sliced tomatoes, and drizzle with a little of the anchoïade.

Anchoïade

In a mini prep or standard food processor, combine the anchovies, garlic, parsley, plenty of pepper, and just enough of the olive oil to make it move in the processor. Pulse until smooth and then transfer to a small bowl.

NOTE: A little of this outrageously delicious sauce goes a long way.

CENTRAL COAST: Happy Canyon Vineyard "Barrack Ten-Goal," Santa Barbara County (Bordeaux-style blend)
FARTHER AFIELD: Red wine from Bordeaux

2 (2-ounce) cans oil-packed anchovies (or about 25 anchovy fillets from a glass jar), soaked in warm water for 5 minutes, drained, and patted dry

4 garlic cloves, thinly sliced

1 tablespoon coarsely chopped fresh flat-leaf parsley

Freshly ground black pepper

⅓ to ½ cup extra-virgin olive oil

Butterflied Leg of Lamb with Persimmon and Chickpea Couscous

Way out at Starr Ranch, west of Paso Robles, the Starr family produces not only Hachiya and Fuyu persimmons but addictively good dried persimmons and walnuts, not to mention some luscious Rhône varietals and a delectable late-harvest Viognier (dessert wine) called Sweet Chariot. It's one of the most tranquil spots on earth.

Ask your butcher to butterfly the lamb out flat for you. The resulting piece of meat is shaped roughly like a butterfly with a surface that resembles the Himalayas. The plus side of the oddly shaped piece of meat is that it slices like a dream and provides a range of doneness. Very well-done, medium, and pink slices all done at the same time pretty much serve everyone's taste. Because of the odd appearance, I usually slice it in the kitchen. SERVES 8

¾ cup medium-dry white wine, such as Viognier

¾ cup fruity extra-virgin olive oil

1 (6- to 7-pound) well-trimmed leg of lamb, butterflied (see above)

Fine sea salt and freshly ground black pepper

12 small sprigs fresh thyme

COUSCOUS
1¾ cups homemade or store-bought low-sodium beef or chicken broth

5 tablespoons salted butter

Fine sea salt

1¾ cups instant couscous

1 (15-ounce) can chickpeas, well rinsed and drained

1¼ cups dried persimmons (about 4 ounces), diced

2 scallions, white and green parts, very finely chopped

⅓ cup sherry vinegar

⅓ cup extra-virgin olive oil

Freshly ground black pepper

½ cup sliced almonds, toasted just until golden

⅓ cup coarsely chopped fresh mint

2 lemons, cut into wedges

Combine the wine and olive oil in a baking dish or roasting pan just large enough to fit the lamb in an even layer. Season the lamb all over with salt and pepper, then place the lamb in the marinade with the uneven, meaty side down; cover and marinate for 2 hours in the refrigerator. Turn the lamb and marinate for 2 to 3 hours more. Bring to room temperature for 30 to 40 minutes before grilling.

Prepare a charcoal or gas grill for medium-high-heat grilling. Dry the lamb well with absorbent paper towels and, again, season all the nooks and crannies generously with salt and pepper. Tuck the thyme sprigs in here and there, and grill with the uneven side facing the heat source for 11 to 14 minutes, until nicely charred and grill marked.

Turn over and grill for an additional 5 minutes with the fat side down. On a charcoal grill, transfer the lamb to the indirect side or cooler of the grill, with the fat side down. On a gas grill, decrease the heat to medium-low. Cook for an additional 20 to 30 minutes, until done to your liking (about 130°F at the thickest point for medium-rare; because of the irregular thickness of the meat, there will be some rare, some medium, and some well-done slices).

Meanwhile, make the couscous by bringing the broth and butter to a boil in a small saucepan (or a microwave) and add about ⅔ teaspoon salt. In a large, heatproof bowl, combine the couscous, chickpeas, persimmons, and scallions; stir in the hot broth. Cover the bowl and let stand for 5 minutes. Add the vinegar, olive oil, plenty of pepper, half the toasted almonds, and half the mint; fluff with a fork.

Let the lamb rest for 5 to 10 minutes, loosely covered with aluminum foil. Slice across the grain into long, thin slices and serve on warmed plates with a spoonful of the couscous. Scatter with the remaining almonds and mint and serve with the lemon wedges.

NOTE: If using grass-fed lamb, reduce both the cooking time and cooking temperature by 10 to 15 percent (that is, grill over medium heat instead of medium-high heat).

CENTRAL COAST: Jonata "Todos," Ballard Canyon, Santa Ynez Valley (Syrah blend)
FARTHER AFIELD: Châteauneuf-du-Pape, Rhône Valley, France

Seared Baby Lamb Chops in a Sea of Green

Small lamb rib chops with the bones frenched have gained fame and fans as "lamb lollipops," and indeed that's what they look like, complete with handy handle for grasping while you nibble the perfectly tender meat. I'm always one to dispense with tableware, if possible, but be sure to swish the chops through the luscious sauce as you consume them. And, since there will be plenty of sauce, I highly recommend the addition of crusty wedges of artisanal bread, for mopping up the green sea. If you're not averse to forks, serve this dish with mashed potatoes on the side.   SERVES 4

In a pot of rapidly boiling salted water, blanch the scallion greens and parsley for 1 minute; drain and immediately rinse thoroughly with cool running water. Again, drain well, and spread on absorbent paper towels.

Finely chop the scallion whites. In a medium saucepan, combine the scallion whites and wine; bring to a brisk simmer over medium heat. Cook until the liquid has reduced by about half, 10 to 15 minutes. Stir in the cream, decrease the heat to low, and keep simmering until again reduced by about half. Let cool for 10 minutes.

In a blender, combine the blanched scallion greens and parsley, milk, and the cream mixture. Blend at high speed, scraping down the sides as necessary, for 2 to 3 minutes, until very smooth and bright green. Transfer to a double boiler set over hot, but not simmering, water. Stir in ½ teaspoon salt and a big pinch of pepper. Taste for seasoning, cover, and set aside for up to 20 minutes *only*.

Preheat a cast-iron grill pan over superhigh heat (or prepare a very hot charcoal grill). Pat the chops thoroughly dry. Season both sides of each chop with a little salt and pepper. Sear the chops for about 2 minutes on each side for rare, or a little longer, if desired. Let rest on a warm platter for 2 minutes. During the resting time, very gently reheat the green sauce. Divide the sauce among wide, shallow bowls. Crisscross 3 lamb chops in the center of each bowl and serve.

continued on page 198

40 scallions, trimmed of roots and limp or discolored leaves; white and green parts separated

Leaves and tender stems only from 1 bunch fresh flat-leaf parsley

1½ cups medium-dry white wine, perhaps a Rhône-style blend

1½ cups heavy cream

⅔ cup whole milk

Fine sea salt and freshly ground white pepper

12 lamb rib chops, 1 to 1¼ inches thick, ideally with the bones frenched

NOTE: If using grass-fed lamb, reduce both the cooking time and cooking temperature by 10 to 15 percent (that is, grill over medium-high heat instead of super high heat).

CENTRAL COAST: Beckmen "Purisima," Ballard Canyon, Santa Ynez Vallay (Rhône red blend)
FARTHER AFIELD: Shiraz, Barossa, Australia

Warm Sausage and Potato Salad

This rustic, ready-in-moments meal in a bowl is skewed toward the sausage rather than the potato, yet it delivers plenty of crunch (celery and mild red onion), acidity (lemon zest, mustard), and brightness (fresh tarragon). Picnic fare par excellence, just right for a trip up Vineyard Drive west of Paso Robles, where Chateau Margene's elegant tasting room boasts a peaceful patio next to a bucolic pond. Or, sample Tablas Creek's excellent range of Rhône blends and single varietals—such as my favorite, Picpoul—and have your picnic on *their* gorgeous patio! SERVES 6

Prepare a charcoal or gas grill or broiler for high-heat cooking. Grill or broil the sausages, turning occasionally, for about 4 minutes, or until the outsides are crisp. Set aside.

Bring a pot of lightly salted water to a boil and boil the potatoes for 10 to 15 minutes, until tender but not falling apart. Drain and let cool.

Slice the cooked sausages into ½-inch rounds and then crosswise into quarters. Cut the potato halves again, into quarters. Whisk the lemon juice, oil, mustard, tarragon, ¾ teaspoon salt, and plenty of pepper in a large bowl and add the sausages, potatoes, celery, onion, and zest. Toss together well and serve at room temperature.

CENTRAL COAST: Dragonette Happy Canyon Sauvignon Blanc, Santa Ynez Valley
FARTHER AFIELD: Kim Crawford Sauvignon Blanc, New Zealand

1 pound mild or hot precooked pork or chicken sausage (about 4 links)

8 small red potatoes, halved

1 tablespoon juice from 1 lemon and finely grated zest

⅓ cup extra-virgin olive oil

2 tablespoons whole-grain mustard

1 tablespoon minced fresh tarragon

Fine sea salt and freshly ground black pepper

4 celery ribs, cut into ¼-inch dice

½ cup finely chopped red onion

Marcie Jimenez/
Jimenez Family Farm

"I love to feed people," says the ball of nurturing energy known as Marcie Jimenez, who has been doing just that as far back as she can remember. Marcie is a fixture at farmer's markets throughout the Central Coast, bringing produce, pies, and naturally raised meat to ravenous, eager consumers who know she only sells the *best*.

An avid horsewoman in her youth, Marcie was used to the outdoors and cherished its beauty. After growing up right around the corner from me in Santa Monica, she naturally gravitated to the beauty of the Santa Ynez Valley, where her family had bought a farm in 1976. With a degree in animal science from Cal Poly, Marcie knew her destiny lay in farming and ranching. "There is nothing more rewarding than growing your own food, and I've been lucky enough to do that, and be successful at it."

Marcie first started baking pies after her son was born. He is now 25. "I needed something productive to do while staying at home," she says. Local restaurants and gourmet grocery stores loved the pies, and the business took off—in fact, it got too big. "I didn't want to be selling to big companies. I wanted to be at the level where I am talking to the people I'm feeding," she says. So the business was sold and she "got small" again. "All I wanted to do was to make a living with a little farm," she says.

In 2002, Marcie and her husband, Gustavo, bought the family farm from her dad, who at 81 still loves traveling to the Thursday evening farmer's market in San Luis Obispo to sell the new generation of Marcie's pies: blackberry, boysenberry, olallieberry, strawberry, rhubarb,

> *One summer, I looked around at all the squash we were growing, and I said to my husband, "We've got to get some pigs!"*

apricot, peach, and apple. Now Marcie and Gustavo grow "way too many" kinds of produce (she's like a kid in a candy store when the seed catalogs arrive) and raise sheep, goats, rabbits, and a few pigs. Both her kids have worked on the farm and still help out at the 14 farmer's markets where Jimenez Family Farm sells products. (Not all products are sold at all the markets—their production is way too small for that.) Marcie literally glows with pride at the beautiful produce she is able to share with her customers at the market. Marcie always enjoyed raising sheep and goats, but when her son got involved in 4-H, she started to think about larger meat animals. "One summer, I looked around at all the squash we were growing, and I said to my husband, 'We've got to get some pigs!'"

This is a woman with a passion for growing things and feeding people and the convictions to do it the right way: small. So what does the future hold? "I'm very excited about the lamb I am raising now. The breed is called Dorper—a cross between Dorset and a Persian fat-tail. When they are grass fed, they put on just the right amount of fat. The meat is incredibly tasty." Marcie's dad is Greek, so she grew up eating lamb, and she was surprised to discover that not everyone else did. That's why it's so gratifying now when customers clamor for her lamb. "If there is any problem, it's that people don't understand I'm not a grocery store," she says. "I can only sell what I have, and sometimes I have to say 'no.'" Saying "no" to hungry people is clearly not high on Marcie's favorites list.

IF YOU VISIT:
There's no store at the farm, but you can visit www.jimenezfamilyfarm.com, or contact the farm at (805) 688-0957 for information on the farmer's markets where Marcie currently is a vendor.

Corsican Lamb Shoulder
with Olives and Vermentino

Vermentino is the primary white grape variety in Corsica, a rough-and-tumble island off the southern coast of France that closely resembles some rugged sections of California's Central Coast (think Big Sur). Vermentino is also grown in northern Italy and in the Rhône region of France, as well as in the rolling hills around Paso Robles, most notably by Tablas Creek, which has championed the varietal. The bracing acidity and full, slightly citrusy flavor of Vermentino make it a perfect partner for the richness of the lamb shoulder, in the braising pot *and* in the glass. SERVES 6

1 (2½- to 3-pound) boneless lamb shoulder, butterflied into a large, irregular rectangle about 1½ inches thick at the thickest point

Fine sea salt and freshly ground black pepper

½ cup flavorful olives, pitted and coarsely chopped (black or green)

3 ounces feta or fresh goat cheese, crumbled (about ½ cup)

3 garlic cloves, finely chopped or pushed through a press

2 tablespoons coarsely chopped fresh mint, plus a few sprigs for serving

2 to 3 tablespoons extra-virgin olive oil, as needed

½ cup Vermentino or other dry, citrusy white wine

½ cup homemade or store-bought low-sodium chicken broth

Preheat the oven to 450°F. If the lamb is fatty, place a rack in a large roasting pan (grass-fed lamb will be lean enough so no rack is needed).

Lay the lamb on a work surface, fat side down, with one narrow end facing you. With a sharp knife, make crosshatch cuts into the meat about ½ inch deep. Season lightly with salt and pepper, and spread the olives and feta over the interior surface, leaving about one-third uncovered at the far end; scatter with the garlic and mint. Beginning with the end closest to you, roll the lamb up firmly. Tie every 2 inches with kitchen twine to make a compact cylinder about 4 inches in diameter at the thickest point. Pat the outside thoroughly dry. Brush all over with a little olive oil and season generously with salt and pepper.

Place the lamb in the large roasting pan, and roast in the hot oven for 25 minutes. Lower the oven temperature to 300°F and add the wine and broth to the pan. Continue roasting until an instant-read thermometer inserted into the meat registers 155°F, about 35 to 40 minutes more. Transfer the lamb to a cutting board, tent loosely with aluminum foil, and let rest for 10 to 20 minutes.

Tip the roasting pan and spoon off some of the fat. Place the pan over medium-high heat and simmer briskly to reduce the liquid by about half, about 5 minutes. Taste and adjust the seasoning with salt and/or pepper. Remove the strings from the lamb and carve into thick slices. Serve at once, moistened with a spoonful of the pan juices. Scatter the mint sprigs over the top.

NOTE: If using grass-fed lamb, reduce the cooking temperature by 10 to 15 percent. (That is, do the initial high-heat roasting at 425°F instead of 450°F. Braise at 300°F, as directed.)

CENTRAL COAST: Palmina Nebbiolo, Stolpman Vineyard, Santa Ynez Valley
FARTHER AFIELD: Barolo from Italy

Whole Tenderloin of Grass-Fed Beef with Bordelaise Sauce

This dish is worthy of a really important celebration, such as the night I tested it: the "big" birthday of Terry Hoage, a legendary 13-season NFL defensive back who played for the New Orleans Saints, among many other teams, before turning his hand to winemaking. Terry and his wife, Jennifer, make critically acclaimed, small-production Rhône blends and varietals on the west side of Paso Robles, including many whose names tip a hat to his football career, like "Skins" and "5 Blocks." (Because of their "insider" cachet, the wines are often oversubscribed, but those who persevere—and visit the winery—may be able to secure a bottle or two.)

Ask your butcher to trim the silverskin from the beef and tuck the tail underneath, then tie the tenderloin so it's an even thickness throughout. Considering the cost, he or she should be happy to do so. SERVES 6 OR 7

2 tablespoons whole-grain mustard

1½ tablespoons extra-virgin olive oil, plus more for searing

1½ teaspoons dried thyme

1 (3-pound) grass-fed beef tenderloin, at room temperature

Fine sea salt and freshly ground black pepper

Bordelaise Sauce (recipe follows)

Preheat the oven to 450°F. Whisk together the mustard, olive oil, and thyme. Pat the roast thoroughly dry with absorbent paper towels and season all sides generously with salt. Brush the mustard mixture over all sides and place the meat on a rack set in a roasting pan.

Roast the meat on the center rack for 15 minutes, then turn off the oven and do not open the door for 5 minutes more. Then check the temperature in several places. If the temperature has reached 118°F to 120°F, remove the pan from the oven. (If it's still between 110°F and 115°F, leave in the turned-off oven, with the door closed, for 5 minutes more. Remove from the oven and, leaving the meat on the rack, wrap it loosely with aluminum foil; allow to rest for 5 to 7 minutes (the temperature will rise to 125°F to 130°F). Slice ½ inch thick and serve on warm plates with plenty of the sauce ladled over the top.

NOTE: If using grain-fed beef for this recipe, increase the initial oven temperature to 500°F.

Bordelaise Sauce

Place the marrow bones in a wide bowl of well-salted ice water and refrigerate for 30 minutes to firm the marrow. Using a small, sharp knife, cut the exposed marrow crosswise every 2 inches, down to the bone. Pry out the marrow pieces with the knife, working it around the concave bone, ideally in whole pieces. Immerse the chunks again in fresh, well-salted ice water and refrigerate for 2 hours, changing the salted ice water halfway through.

Cut the marrow into ½-inch chunks, and refrigerate until serving time. (Reserve the bones in the freezer for soup or stock.)

In a small bowl, whisk 1 tablespoon of the softened butter with the flour to make a smooth paste.

Place a medium saucepan with sloping sides over low heat and add the remaining 1 tablespoon butter. Add and cook the shallot gently until translucent, about 7 minutes. Add the red wine, thyme sprigs, and bay leaf; adjust the heat so the liquid simmers briskly. Reduce by about half, 15 to 18 minutes.

Discard the thyme and bay leaf and stir in the veal demi-glace, ½ teaspoon sea salt, and a pinch of pepper. Simmer briskly to reduce again, by about one-third. Now whisk in the butter-flour paste and simmer until slightly syrupy, stirring occasionally, 3 to 4 minutes. Decrease the heat to very low. (Or, the sauce may be set aside at this point, covered, at the back of the stove for up to 30 minutes before finishing. Rewarm just to the steaming point before continuing.)

Add the diced marrow to the steaming sauce and warm through just until the edges of the marrow appear translucent, 2 to 3 minutes. Do not allow to simmer.

NOTE: Veal demi-glace is available in better supermarkets and specialty stores. Commercially available veal demi-glace varies in consistency; if the final sauce is too thick, adjust with a teaspoon or two of water. If necessary, you could substitute rich, homemade beef stock that has been reduced by half, but the sauce will have a different flavor and a less rich and unctuous consistency.

CENTRAL COAST: Clos Pepe Estate Pinot Noir, Santa Rita Hills
FARTHER AFIELD: Pinot Noir from Santa Lucia Highlands, California

2 beef marrow bones, sawn in half lengthwise (ask your butcher to do this with a bone saw)

Kosher salt, for soaking the marrow bones

2 tablespoons butter, softened

1 tablespoon all-purpose flour

1 large shallot, minced

2 cups Cabernet Sauvignon or Bordeaux-style blend

2 sprigs fresh thyme

1 fresh or dried bay leaf

¾ cup veal demi-glace (see Note)

Fine sea salt and freshly ground black pepper

Fork-Tender, Wine-Braised Brisket

A beautifully marbled brisket is the perfect candidate for the mysterious alchemy that results when wine and time are combined with a low temperature in the coddling environment of your home oven. The initial caramelization is the key to great flavor here, so give the searing process your full and undivided attention. You'll soon be rewarded with a long, lazy afternoon to pursue your activity of choice—whether it's reading or surfing—while the magic wends its way toward an unctuously perfect result. Like all braises, this dish is even tastier a day or two after cooking, when the flavors have had a chance to develop. SERVES 6

3 tablespoons finely chopped
fresh flat-leaf parsley

2 tablespoons finely chopped
fresh rosemary

2 teaspoons finely chopped fresh sage

4 garlic cloves, finely chopped
or pushed through a press

3 pounds beef brisket, judiciously
trimmed of excess exterior fat

3 slices bacon, cut into
¼-inch strips crosswise

⅓ cup plus 2 tablespoons
all-purpose flour

1 teaspoon paprika

Fine sea salt and freshly
ground black pepper

2 tablespoons butter

1 tablespoon extra-virgin olive oil

1 small yellow onion, thinly sliced

1 fresh bay leaf or 2 dried

2 medium carrots, peeled and
cut into ¼-inch dice

2 celery ribs, cut into ¼-inch dice

1 (750-ml) bottle Syrah
or red Rhône blend

Cooked rice, polenta, or noodles, for
serving (about 1½ pounds before cooking)

In a small bowl, blend together the chopped herbs and garlic. With a small, sharp knife, cut slits all over the brisket and, using a chopstick, push a strip of bacon into each slit. On a large plate, blend ⅓ cup of the flour with the paprika, 1 teaspoon salt, and ½ teaspoon pepper. Dredge the brisket in the flour, shaking off the excess.

In a large, heavy casserole, heat the butter and olive oil over medium-low heat. Sauté the onion for 3 to 4 minutes, until softened. Turn the heat up to medium-high and push the onions to one side. Add the brisket and scatter the garlic-herb mixture, bay leaf, carrots, and celery around the edges of the pan. Brown the brisket on all sides, stirring and taking care not to scorch the herbs and vegetables. Transfer the meat to a platter and preheat the oven to 300°F.

If there is too much fat in the vegetable-herb mixture, drain off as much as you like and sprinkle the remaining 2 tablespoons of flour over it. Stir together for a minute, then add 1 cup of the wine. Bring to a rapid boil and, stirring occasionally, reduce the liquid by half. Add the remaining wine and salt and pepper to taste. Bring the wine to a simmer and return the brisket to the casserole.

Cover the casserole and braise in the oven for 4 or, even better, 5 hours, turning the meat once every 45 minutes. (It may be prepared to this point 1 or even 2 days ahead; cover and refrigerate the meat in the sauce, then rewarm together gently.)

Transfer the meat to a warm platter and, if the sauce is too thin, loosely cover the meat and simmer the sauce briskly for a minute or two, to thicken. Taste for seasoning and adjust with salt and pepper, if necessary. Pour the sauce over the meat and serve generous pieces with plenty of sauce, mounded over rice, polenta, or noodles.

NOTE: If using grass-fed beef, reduce the cooking time by 10 to 15 percent and check occasionally to be sure the meat is not drying out.

CENTRAL COAST: Byron Pinot Noir, Santa Maria Valley
FARTHER AFIELD: Priorat, Spain

Grilled Flat-Iron Steak
with Yellow Pepper–Caper Rouille

Flat-iron steaks are the new darlings of the meat world, but there are only about four per head of beef, so they will always remain relatively rare no matter how popular. The steaks are cut from a very lean area of the shoulder/chuck, which is normally quite fatty. Cooked correctly (think flank steak), this is a delicious and economical cut. Most butchers make "shoulder-tender medallions" from this area of the animal, so ask him or her to cut flat-iron steaks for you, instead. Just like flank steak, flat-iron takes well to marinating. Don't cook past medium-rare, though, or there will be tears.   SERVES 6

Brush the steaks generously on all sides with olive oil, and season generously with salt and pepper; rub in the oregano. Let stand while you make the rouille.

To make the sauce, preheat a broiler to high heat and place a baking sheet on the top rack. Place the pepper quarters on the sheet, skin side up, and broil until charred and blistered, 3 to 5 minutes. Turn over and broil for 1 to 2 minutes more, until tender. Immediately transfer to a bowl and place the bowl inside a plastic bag. Twist to seal and let steam for 10 minutes. Slip off the skins, coarsely chop the flesh of the pepper, and transfer to a food processor with a tiny hole in the feed tube (for making mayonnaise) or a blender. Add the egg yolks, garlic, salt, and ground chipotle; blend until almost smooth. With the motor running all the time, drizzle the olive oil into the feed tube (or blender) slowly, until the oil has all been absorbed and the rouille is thick. Transfer to a bowl and fold in the capers.

Prepare a charcoal or gas grill for medium-hot grilling or preheat a ridged griddle pan over high heat until very hot. Scrape most of the oregano from the steaks and grill for 2 minutes on each side. Move the steaks to a cooler part of the grill (or turn the heat down to low) and continue cooking for 1 to 2 minutes more per side, to your desired doneness. Let rest for 5 minutes, then carve crosswise into thin slices. Fan the slices on warm plates and spoon a river of rouille down the center, or serve the rouille on the side.

continued on page 210

6 flat-iron steaks, 8 to 9 ounces each and about 2 inches thick

Extra-virgin olive oil, for brushing the steaks

Fine sea salt and freshly ground black pepper

About 2 tablespoons coarsely chopped fresh oregano

YELLOW PEPPER–CAPER ROUILLE

1 small orange or yellow bell pepper, quartered lengthwise, seeded, and cored

2 egg yolks

4 large garlic cloves, minced or pushed through a press

¼ teaspoon salt

⅛ teaspoon ground chipotle chile or cayenne pepper

⅔ cup extra-virgin olive oil

⅓ cup capers, drained and chopped

NOTE: If using grass-fed beef, reduce both the cooking time and the cooking temperature by 10 to 15 percent (that is, grill over medium coals instead of medium-hot coals).

CENTRAL COAST: Saarloos and Sons Cabernet Sauvignon "Sons," Ballard Canyon, Santa Ynez Valley
FARTHER AFIELD: Merlot from Napa Valley, California

Malbec-Braised Short Ribs with Creamy Polenta and Meyer Lemon Gremolata

At first glance, the method here may seem complex, but the result is something not even a rib aficionado is likely to have come across before. Inside, the meat is succulent and collagen rich—outside, it's crusty and crisp, almost as if the ribs have been deep fried. This worth-the-effort recipe is best executed with a friend, since it's important to stay with the polenta-making process at all times during the last 30 minutes before serving time. SERVES 6

16 garlic cloves, lightly crushed

Coarse and fine sea salt and freshly ground black pepper

4½ to 5 pounds bone-in short ribs

3 tablespoons extra-virgin olive oil, plus a little more, if needed

1 large carrot, coarsely chopped

1 small white or yellow onion, coarsely chopped

1 large leek, white and light green parts, coarsely chopped

3 sprigs fresh thyme

2 fresh bay leaves or 4 dried

3½ cups Central Coast Malbec or other full-bodied red wine with soft tannins

¼ cup red wine vinegar

1½ cups homemade or store-bought low-sodium beef or chicken broth

GREMOLATA
2 tablespoons finely grated Meyer lemon zest

2 tablespoons minced garlic

2 tablespoons finely chopped fresh flat-leaf parsley

Creamy Polenta (recipe follows), for serving

Place 6 of the garlic cloves and 2 teaspoons coarse sea salt in a mortar, and pulverize to a paste with a pestle (or mince and smash with a large, heavy chef's knife). Rub all sides of the ribs with this paste, and grind some pepper over all sides. Let stand at room temperature for 1 hour.

Place a large, heavy saucepan over low heat and add 1½ tablespoons of the oil. Add the carrot, onion, leek, and remaining 10 garlic cloves. Sauté, stirring, for 5 to 6 minutes, until softened but not browned, then stir in the thyme, bay leaves, wine, and vinegar. Bring to a simmer, then remove from the heat and transfer to a large heatproof bowl or measuring jug. Let cool to room temperature.

Place the ribs and wine mixture in one jumbo-size or two large heavy-duty zip-top bags. Seal well, and refrigerate for at least 8 hours but preferably 24 hours, turning over once or twice.

Preheat the oven to 275°F. Remove the ribs from the marinade and scrape off all the vegetables. Pour the marinade (with all the vegetables) into a saucepan, add the broth, and bring to a brisk simmer. Remove from the heat.

Pat the ribs dry thoroughly with absorbent paper towels and season all four sides with fine sea salt and pepper.

Place a very large, heavy skillet or sauté pan over medium-high heat and add the remaining 1½ tablespoons oil. When it is very hot, add half the ribs and brown for about 2½ minutes on each of all four sides (sauté in two batches to avoid overcrowding; add a touch more oil, if necessary). Transfer the ribs as they are done to a large roasting pan and pour the warm marinade over them. Cover the pan tightly with aluminum foil, and roast for 3 to 3½ hours, turning over halfway through, until fork-tender but not completely falling apart. Remove from the oven, uncover, and let stand for 5 minutes.

With tongs, transfer the ribs to a platter and remove the bones. Trim away any obvious gristle and big pieces of surface fat, without cutting the ribs into very small pieces. (If desired, the beef and cooking liquid may be refrigerated, well wrapped, for up to 2 days before the final grilling. Return the meat to room temperature before the final grilling process.)

To serve, strain the cooking liquid, discarding the vegetables, and skim off the fat (this will be much easier if it's been refrigerated). In a saucepan over high heat, simmer the liquid rapidly for 15 to 20 minutes, until reduced to about 1 cup of very dark liquid. Remove from the heat, taste for seasoning, then cover and keep warm while you grill the ribs.

Preheat a charcoal or gas grill, cast-iron griddle pan, or broiler until very hot. Meanwhile, warm six plates in a low oven.

To make the gremolata, combine the lemon zest, garlic, and parsley in a small bowl.

Sear the chunks of meat for 1 to 2 minutes on all sides until heated through, brown, and beautifully crisp on the outside. Place a mound of soft, creamy polenta in the center of each warm plate, top with a few pieces of crispy meat, and drizzle with a spoonful of the sauce. Scatter a tablespoon of the gremolata over each and serve at once.

NOTE: If using grass-fed beef, reduce the cooking time by 10 to 15 percent.

Creamy Polenta

In a large, heavy saucepan, combine the cream, milk, water, and salt. Place over medium heat and bring to a boil; then lower the heat so the liquid is barely simmering. Add the polenta in a thin stream, whisking all the time. As soon as all the polenta has been added and the mixture is smooth, switch to a wooden spoon. Decrease the heat to low and stir the polenta more or less constantly until thickened to a mounding consistency, 20 to 30 minutes.

Remove from the heat and thoroughly stir in the pepper, butter, and cheese. Serve at once.

CENTRAL COAST: Clos Pepe Estate Chardonnay "Homage to Chablis," Santa Rita Hills (Yes, Chardonnay. Don't look at me; you put the lemon in there! —W.H.)
FARTHER AFIELD: Malbec from Argentina

1 cup heavy cream

1½ cups whole milk

2½ cups water

1 teaspoon fine sea salt

1½ cups polenta or coarsely ground cornmeal

¼ teaspoon freshly ground white pepper

2 tablespoons butter

⅓ cup grated cheese (choose from Italian Fontina, pecorino, or Parmigiano-Reggiano)

Old Creek Ranch

Old Creek Ranch, nestled in the hills above the coastal town of Cayucos, began as a family dairy when Bob and Ruth Blanchard came north from Los Angeles in search of a healthier place to raise their young family. That was in 1949. Three generations and 60 years later, the dairy cattle are gone, replaced by Valencia and navel oranges, lemons, Hass avocados, and an array of livestock. Today, Bob and Terri Blanchard continue to work the family ranch. About 10 years ago, the Blanchards began selling at regional farmer's markets, and now, that's how they sell everything they produce. "No more middleman. We started in Santa Clara and Santa Cruz Counties," says Bob, "and we couldn't believe the demand for our meat and oranges."

Although it's still very much a family enterprise, Bob and Terri have expanded their product line to include stocks, juice, jams, and marmalade. The family is selling everything they produce, and the ranch store has also started selling certified organic produce from neighboring farms. "It all started with the orange juice machine," groans Bob. "Terri found one for sale in an ad from a New York deli and made me buy it. I thought the owner wouldn't be able to ship it, but he just busted up some pallets and nailed a box around it. So then we had a commercial juicer, but because of health regulations, we had to build a facility, with all the requisite sinks and drains and tiles and whatnot." Bob shakes his head. "So then we said, 'might as well get a stove!'"

The ranch now produces a line of beef, lamb, goat, and pork stocks. "We follow Sally Fallon's recipe from *Nourishing Traditions*," says Bob. "We use our own spring water and simmer the stocks for 48 hours. We started selling a few quarts a week, and now we're up to about a hundred."

Today, the farm is home to goats, pigs, sheep, beef cattle, and chickens. The orange groves are organic, and there's a rich ecosystem under the trees, but the wild grasses needed dethatching and some form of fertilization. "So we got chickens, and we have several flocks rotating through the orchards. We're washing a lot of eggs!" Bob is very particular about the ranch produc-

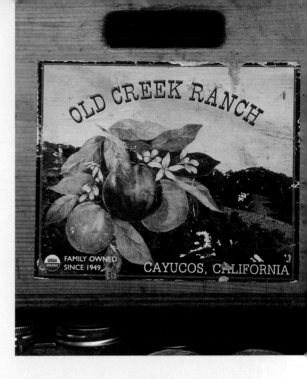

There's a direct line between proper grassland management and the peregrine falcon.

tion and oversees every aspect of it. "Terri used to ride the range with me all the time," he sighs. "She was a real cowboy." These days, Terri finds herself busy with marketing the ranch's burgeoning meat and produce sales.

Growing up, their son Bowman was always adamant about environmental issues. An early job involved managing coastal terraces for grazing, so he learned about entire ecosystems, native grasses, and endangered species like the burrowing owl. Now the Blanchards manage their herds with a rotating paddock system, which mimics the effects of a wild herd of mammals grazing on pastureland. Light grazing prevents the grasses from forming a thatch and choking the soil; uprooting the grasses also contributes to healthy microbial life in the coastal soils. "Healthier wild pastures produce more native seeds, which feed the meadowlarks and blackbirds, which are in turn prey for the endangered peregrine falcon. There's a direct line between proper grassland management and the peregrine falcon," Bob points out with pride.

Certified organic and completely grass fed, the predominantly Angus beef herd is also carefully managed to bring out "old-fashioned" qualities missing from modern breeds. "The big, straight-sided beef cattle you see today are not the same animals that were originally brought here from Ireland, Scotland, and England," says Bob. "They were bred up to produce a lot of lean meat, but they take longer to mature, and the feedlots process them too soon." Bob looks for smaller, fine-boned animals with a larger rumin or "gut." "These animals are more like the ones you see in photos from the 1940s. All of an animal's feeding and energy goes into growth until they reach maturity, then they start marbling up and putting on fat. So a smaller animal with a larger digestive system puts more energy into flavor." Bob also practices reverse breeding in his Dorper sheep and Boer goat herds, looking for the desirable, healthy traits found in smaller-framed animals.

IF YOU VISIT:

Old Creek Ranch meats and produce are sold at various farmer's markets in Santa Cruz, Palo Alto, and San Jose (check at www.cafarmersmarkets. com). You can also buy direct from the home ranch in Cayucos on Tuesdays and Wednesdays from 9 a.m. to 2 p.m. Besides steaks, roasts, and braising cuts, the ranch also offers ground meat, sausages, and jerky. Try the oranges, delectably sweet fresh-squeezed orange juice, and kiwi jam. Bakers will want to pick up some leaf lard—excellent for flaky piecrusts.

12520 Santa Rita Road
Cayucos, CA 93430

(805) 995-1164

www.oldcreekranch.net

Chianti-Style Braised Beef over Buttered Noodles

In the process of writing two in-depth meat books over the past couple of years, I gained a visceral (sorry) understanding of the way different cuts of meat behave in varying circumstances. This made me very happy. Chuck, the cut called for here, has the ability to transform into melting tenderness, whereas various other cuts of beef often sold under the generic label "stew meat" (such as round) will produce tough little nuggets (still tough even if you braise them for days). This comforting, Tuscan-esque dish may be prepared one, or even two, days ahead—in fact, it's even better that way. Just cool, cover, and refrigerate the meat in the sauce, then rewarm together gently. SERVES 4 TO 6

2 tablespoons grapeseed
or vegetable oil

3 slices bacon, cut into
¼-inch strips crosswise

2 pounds beef chuck, cut
into ¾-inch chunks

Fine sea salt and freshly
ground black pepper

1 small yellow onion, thinly sliced

1 fresh bay leaf or 2 dried

2 medium carrots, peeled
and cut into ¼-inch dice

½ small fennel bulb, cored
and cut into ¼-inch dice

4 garlic cloves, finely chopped

2 tablespoons finely chopped
fresh rosemary

2 teaspoons finely chopped fresh sage

4 tablespoons coarsely chopped
fresh flat-leaf parsley

1½ cups Central Coast
Sangiovese or Italian Chianti

1½ cups beef consommé or
homemade beef broth

1 (15-ounce) can crushed San
Marzano tomatoes, with the juice

Cooked noodles, such as
pappardelle, for serving

3 tablespoons cultured,
salted butter, softened

In a large, heavy casserole or pot, sizzle the oil and bacon over medium-low heat until the fat has rendered, 8 to 10 minutes. With a slotted spoon, transfer the bacon to a bowl and reserve. Increase the heat to medium-high, and season the beef chunks generously with salt and pepper. When the fat is nice and hot, add half of the beef and sear until nicely caramelized on all sides, turning only once or twice, 4 to 5 minutes; transfer to the bowl. Sear the second batch and transfer to the bowl as before. Lower the heat slightly; add the onion, bay leaf, carrots, and fennel and sauté until softened and slightly golden, about 8 minutes (add a touch more oil if the mixture seems dry). Stir in the garlic, rosemary, sage, and 2 tablespoons of the parsley; cook for 1 minute more. Add 1 cup of the wine and bring to a rapid simmer. Stirring occasionally, reduce until the pan is almost dry. Add the remaining wine, consommé, tomatoes, ½ teaspoon salt, and plenty of pepper. Return the bacon-beef mixture to the pot and bring to a low simmer.

Partially cover the pot and simmer very gently on the stovetop for 2 to
2½ hours, stirring the braise once every 20 minutes or so, until the meat
is very tender. If the "sauce" is too thin, transfer the meat to a warm
platter and simmer briskly for a minute or two, to thicken. Taste for
seasoning and adjust with salt and pepper, if necessary.

In a warm serving bowl, fold the hot noodles with the butter and remaining 2 tablespoons parsley. Add the meat and sauce and serve on warm
plates.

NOTE: If using grass-fed beef, reduce the cooking time by 10 to 15 percent.

CENTRAL COAST: Rusack Sangiovese, Ballard Canyon,
Santa Ynez Valley
FARTHER AFIELD: Brunello di Montalcino, Tuscany, Italy

Slow-Grilled Goat, Argentinean Style

As Americans learn to take advantage of diverse forms of protein and utilize the whole animal, not just the luxury cuts, goat is gaining in popularity in restaurants and backyards around the country. For me, it feels like a full circle: My first Thanksgiving after college, stone broke and living in Manhattan's Little Italy (right next door to Chinatown), I prepared a big goat couscous in lieu of turkey.

Goat is a bony animal—not like a pig—so allow about 1½ pounds of dressed weight (cleaned and prepared for cooking) per person. The *salmuera*, or basting brine, adds flavor while also keeping the delicate, lean meat from drying out in the fiery atmosphere of the grill. If you get the liver with your goat, wrap it in a protective layer of caul fat and grill it up for an earthy hors d'oeuvre.

About the fire: You will need 15 to 20 pounds of cured hardwood and/or hardwood charcoal to create a bed of glowing coals and then keep the fire at medium-low heat for another 1 to 2 hours. Do not introduce unlit wood or coals to the cooking fire—instead, make a "feeder fire," where you bring additional coals to mature, ash-covered condition before transferring them to the cooking fire. To test this recipe, I worked closely with Paso Robles's most famous carnivore, Argentinean Jaime Harris, who sourced the goat from his network of local ranchers (www.ranchersalliance.com). He grilled our goat on my fantastic Hasty-Bake grill, using a charcoal kettle grill as the feeder fire. SERVES 12 TO 15 AS PART OF A LARGER SPREAD

SALMUERA:

4 cups water

6 garlic cloves, chopped (do not peel)

¼ cup coarse salt

1 cleaned and headless goat, butterflied (20 to 25 pounds, starting with a 45- to 50-pound whole animal), at room temperature

Chimichurri Sauce (recipe follows)

To make the *salmuera*, stir together the water, garlic, and salt until the salt has dissolved. Transfer to an empty wine bottle. Let stand for several hours, or overnight.

In a covered wood-fired or charcoal grill with a minimum 3-foot grilling surface, build a large fire with cured oak, almond wood, or even eucalyptus—popular in Argentina—mixed with some hardwood charcoal (see above). Let it burn down to glowing, medium-low, ash-covered coals. Spoon a little of the *salmuera* over the bone side of the goat, then arrange it on the grill grate with the bone side down. Cover the grill and cook, basting with more *salmuera* occasionally, until the bones are golden and the meat is beginning to shrink away from them, 1 to 1½ hours. Feed the fire occasionally with mature coals, keeping the temperature around 250°F or 275°F. Remove and eat the kidneys, then flip the goat over and spoon a good amount of *salmuera* into the concave cavity of the chest. Continue grilling until the meat in the thickest part of the leg reaches 160°F to 170°F, 30 to 45 minutes more. Keep the grill mostly covered to prevent flare-ups but baste the goat occasionally with the *salmuera*.

Transfer the crispy and golden goat to a large cutting board and cover loosely with aluminum foil; let rest for 10 to 15 minutes.

To carve, grab the forearm, or shank, lift it up, and begin cutting between the ribs and shoulder blade to separate the forearm and shoulder from the chest cavity. Now cut the inside of the elbow away from the forearm to remove the forearm from the shoulder (this will make it easier to remove the meat from the shoulder). Cut down between the rib bones, and cut down the backbone, repeating until you reach the back leg. Now place the leg meaty side down. Holding onto the bone, cut down to the bone to remove all the meat. Repeat with the other side of the animal. Place all the cuts on a platter, adding the rib bones for show, or in case someone might decide to gnaw on one. Serve with chimichurri sauce on the side.

ADVENTURE CLUB

In Argentina, the small intestines of young goats and lambs are well rinsed, then braided and briefly grilled. They plump up nicely with the heat and can be nibbled with a little chimichurri while guests wait for the main event.

Chimichurri Sauce

The classic accompaniment to roasted and grilled protein in Argentina, this sauce is as ubiquitous there as ketchup is in the United States. It's redolent with garlic and fresh oregano, and the high olive oil content adds just the right level of richness to the lean and delicate meat of a young goat. MAKES ABOUT 1½ CUPS

Finely chop or pulse the parsley, oregano, garlic, and salt, scraping and blending with your knife if not making in a small food processor. Stir in the vinegar, oil, black pepper, and red pepper flakes and let stand at room temperature for at least 3 hours. (Or, warm briefly over very low heat, just to release the flavors.) Chimichurri is best used the day it is made, because the parsley will begin to discolor when left in contact with the vinegar.

CENTRAL COAST: Rancho Santa Rosa Pinot Noir "Flying Goat," Santa Rita Hills
FARTHER AFIELD: Malbec, such as Vinalba, Patagonia, Argentina

2 cups packed fresh flat-leaf parsley leaves

1 cup packed fresh oregano leaves

12 garlic cloves, smashed

2 tablespoons kosher salt

6 tablespoons red wine vinegar

1 cup extra-virgin olive oil

1 to 1½ teaspoons freshly ground black pepper

½ to 1 teaspoon red pepper flakes (optional)

CHAPTER 6

From the Dairy

Danika Reed, owner and hands-on proprietor of Vivant Fine Cheese, in Paso Robles, has been "living the cheese life" ever since she reached adulthood. The shop occupies a convenient spot right next door to Paso's finest hotel (to date, at least—things are changing fast), Hotel Cheval, and shares the warm stone hues of that elegant hostelry. Both feature inviting outdoor patios perfect for sipping local wines and nibbling local cheeses.

I dropped in to grill Danika about the local dairy scene, and as we chatted (over cheese, natch), the next-generation Cheese Queen, Danika's two-year-old daughter, Emma, wandered in: "Mom, I want some baguette with goat cheese on it." This apple has fallen close to the tree.

Christine Maguire at Rinconada Dairy (page 232) is certainly the poster girl for Central Coast cheesemakers, but there are also several other small operations, and more on the way as the region takes its place alongside the northern California wine regions as a wine *and* food destination. (At Cal Poly in San Luis Obispo, a potential next generation of artisan cheesemakers is currently studying the art.) Goat cheese may be marginally in the ascendant hereabouts, but sheep's and cow's cheeses— including burrata, crème fraîche, and mascarpone—and sheep's milk ice cream are all produced by small, independent farmers, people who nurture both their animals and their dairy products with equal patience and passion. In this chapter, I've collected some dishes in which dairy is the star. Served cold, warm, melted, or grilled, milk (the gift that keeps on giving) and cheese (milk's leap toward immortality) are this recipe collection's raison d'etre.

Wine pairings by Chris and Shandi Kobayashi of Artisan restaurant, in Paso Robles ("Farther Afield" pairings provided by the author)

Pistachio-Crusted Goat Cheese with French Beans, Radicchio, Endive, Red Grapes, and Sherry Vinaigrette

If goat cheese is beginning to feel overused in California cuisine, just taste one disk of tangy goodness and your enthusiasm will be instantly renewed. At Happy Acres Family Farm in Templeton, Stephanie Simonin and her family produce far more than just impeccable little cheeses—their lotions and lip balms are luscious, and there's an amazingly silky goat cheese ice cream, too. If pistachio oil is not available, use walnut oil, or skip the nut oil and use a fruity green olive oil for the full quantity of oil. SERVES 6 AS AN APPETIZER

¼ cup shelled pistachios

⅓ cup panko (Japanese bread crumbs) or fine dry bread crumbs

3 tablespoons extra-virgin olive oil

3 (3½-ounce) rounds fresh goat cheese, very cold, sliced crosswise through the center to create 6 disks about 1¼ inches thick

SHERRY VINAIGRETTE

2 tablespoons sherry vinegar

1 shallot, minced

1 teaspoon Dijon mustard

½ teaspoon fine sea salt

¼ teaspoon freshly ground black pepper

6 tablespoons pistachio oil or fruity extra-virgin olive oil

6 ounces fine French green beans, trimmed

1 medium head radicchio, quartered, cored, and slivered

2 medium heads Belgian endive, quartered lengthwise, cores trimmed away, and slivered lengthwise

2 cups red grapes, halved

In a food processor, pulse the pistachios into a powder (don't overdo it, or you'll end up with nut butter). In a small, shallow bowl, mix together the ground pistachios and panko. Place the olive oil in another small, shallow bowl. Gently turn each disk of goat cheese in the olive oil to coat all sides, then dredge through the crumb mixture, patting the crust gently to help it adhere. Place on a baking sheet and repeat with the remaining disks. Refrigerate for 1 hour.

To make the vinaigrette, in a large bowl, combine all of the ingredients and whisk until smooth. Set aside.

continued on page 226

Preheat the oven to 425°F. In a small saucepan of rapidly boiling, lightly salted water, blanch the green beans for 2 to 3 minutes, depending on their size. Drain immediately and refresh under cool running water until no longer steaming. Drain on a clean kitchen towel. Transfer the baking sheet of coated cheese to the oven and bake for 5 minutes, or just until the disks are beginning to soften and collapse slightly.

Add the green beans, radicchio, endive, and grapes to the bowl of dressing. Toss thoroughly, until everything is evenly coated with the vinaigrette. With a metal spatula, transfer each goat cheese round to the center of a plate. Mound the salad over and around, and serve at once.

CENTRAL COAST: Silver Horse Albariño, Paso Robles
FARTHER AFIELD: Albariño from Galicia or elsewhere in Spain

Goat-Cheesy Tarragon Mashed Potatoes

In a household that is unapologetically protein-centric, it's crucial to have a great mash on board, and this is mine. I am afraid it is also unapologetically cheesy. What can I say? The amount of milk you use here will be dictated by your personal preference for the consistency of your mash. This flavor profile perfectly complements the proteins known as fish, shellfish, poultry, rabbit, and pork. If serving with red meat, substitute minced fresh thyme leaves for the tarragon. SERVES 6

Bring a large saucepan of lightly salted water to a boil. Add the potatoes and cook, uncovered, for about 20 minutes, or until the potatoes are very soft. Lift the potatoes from the boiling water, and place a metal bowl or the top insert of a double boiler over the water you used to cook the potatoes (pour off a bit, if necessary, to prevent the water from touching the bottom). Adjust the heat so the water below is gently simmering.

Add the potatoes, ½ cup of the milk, butter, salt, and pepper to taste. Steadying the pan with one hand, mash together until smooth, then add the cheese and blend in well. Add a little more of the milk, if desired, and blend in the tarragon. Taste and adjust the seasoning as needed and serve right away.

CENTRAL COAST: Halter Ranch Sauvignon Blanc, Paso Robles
FARTHER AFIELD: Entre-Deux-Mers, Bordeaux, France

4 medium russet potatoes (about 2 pounds), peeled and quartered

½ to ¾ cup whole milk

½ cup (4 ounces) unsalted butter

½ teaspoon fine sea salt

Freshly ground white pepper

10 ounces soft fresh goat cheese, softened, cut into 6 pieces

1 teaspoon minced fresh tarragon (or, if you must, ½ teaspoon dried)

Tomme, Artichoke, and Serrano Ham Soufflé

Many people are frightened of soufflés, and yet they go into a swoon when one emerges, puffed and golden, from the oven. "Ooooh," is the universal cry. I guess that's why soufflé making is perhaps my most popular cooking class. You may have heard that's it's verboten to open the oven door when baking a soufflé. Once it's been in the oven for 30 minutes, however, a quick peek is just fine. Use a long skewer to test the center of the soufflé for doneness: If it comes out clean, the center is set.

SERVES 4 TO 6 AS A LIGHT MAIN COURSE OR LUNCH, OR 8 AS A FIRST COURSE

Preheat the oven to 400°F and place a rack in the center position. Place a baking sheet on the rack. Generously butter the base and all the way up the sides of a 2-quart porcelain soufflé dish. Add the Parmesan and turn to evenly coat the base and sides with a thin coating of cheese.

Place a large saucepan over medium heat and add the butter. When the foam subsides, whisk in the flour. Cook, whisking constantly, until the mixture is bubbling; continue whisking for 2 to 3 minutes, to cook off the taste of the flour (don't let the mixture brown). Remove the pan from the heat and slowly drizzle in the milk, whisking constantly so that lumps do not form. Stir in the wine, return to the heat, bring up to a simmer, and cook, stirring occasionally with a wooden spoon, until the mixture thickens, about 6 minutes; remove from the heat. Stir in ½ teaspoon salt and plenty of black pepper. Whisk in the egg yolks one at a time, constantly whisking until completely blended; set aside. Fold in the Tomme, ham, artichokes, and parsley.

In a large, very clean bowl (preferably made of copper), combine the egg whites and a large pinch of salt. With an electric mixer, beat until stiff peaks form (the whites are ready when they no longer slip if the bowl is tilted). Thoroughly stir about one-third of the egg whites into the egg yolk mixture, to lighten its consistency, then fold the yolk mixture into the remaining beaten whites with a large rubber spatula, taking care not to crush too much air out of the egg whites; do not overmix—a few lumps of egg white here and there are fine.

3 tablespoons unsalted butter, plus more, softened, for soufflé dish

½ cup finely grated Parmesan, Grana Padano, or pecorino cheese, for the soufflé dish

3 tablespoons all-purpose flour

2 cups whole milk

2 tablespoons medium-dry white wine (such as Viognier) or vermouth

Fine sea salt and freshly ground black pepper

9 eggs, separated, plus 1 more egg white

1½ cups coarsely grated Tomme or other sheep's milk cheese (such as Manchego; 6 ounces)

4 ounces Spanish ham (serrano) or prosciutto, finely diced

8 to 10 ounces fully thawed frozen artichoke hearts or canned (drained weight), chopped

2 tablespoons coarsely chopped fresh flat-leaf parsley

Scoop the mixture gently into the prepared dish and lightly smooth the top; place on the baking sheet in the center of the hot oven. Reduce the heat to 350°F and bake for 35 to 40 minutes, until beautifully puffed and golden and only just a little bit wobbly in the center. Serve immediately.

CENTRAL COAST: L'Aventure Estate Rosé, Paso Robles (Syrah, Cabernet Sauvignon)
FARTHER AFIELD: Prosecco Rosé, Veneto, Italy, or Saumur Brut, Loire Valley, France

Frisée with Manchego, Mushrooms, and Walnut Oil

The Gonzales family has been dry farming walnuts on the west side of Paso Robles for 40 years, an area that was nut country for generations before becoming wine country. Their Limerock walnut oil showcases the effect of nothing but natural sunshine and rain: The orchards are low in yields, yes, but the result is an amazingly concentrated walnut flavor. Limerock shares one of the most elegant tasting rooms I've ever seen with Chateau Margene, up Vineyard Drive at Peachy Canyon. It is well worth the pastoral drive, especially if you can score a bottle of Mike and Margene Mooney's impeccable Cab along with a bottle or three of Limerock oil. SERVES 6 AS A FIRST COURSE OR SIDE DISH

Chill six plates in the refrigerator or freezer.

In a large bowl, toss together the frisée, mushrooms, shallot, chives, and half the cheese. Drizzle with the oil and toss gently but thoroughly, until all the ingredients are lightly coated with oil. Drizzle on the vinegar and season with about ⅓ teaspoon salt or to taste and plenty of pepper. Toss again and divide among the chilled plates; scatter the remaining cheese on top.

CENTRAL COAST: Windward Vineyard Estate Pinot Noir "Monopole," Paso Robles
FARTHER AFIELD: Fleurie, Beaujolais, France

4 heads frisée, pale green inner leaves only, cored and torn into bite-size pieces

4 ounces cremini mushrooms, very thinly sliced

1 shallot, finely chopped

1 tablespoon finely snipped fresh chives

5 ounces Manchego, thinly shaved with a vegetable peeler

6 tablespoons walnut oil

4 tablespoons champagne vinegar or white wine vinegar

Fine sea salt and freshly ground black pepper

Rinconada Dairy

The blond, blue-jeaned woman who greeted me the first time I visited Rinconada Dairy in Santa Margarita looked like she'd be right at home running a hip, multinational corporation. Then she introduced me to Dewdrop, the baby goat who lives alongside her dogs inside the house.

"Jim found her on the ground, abandoned by her mother, weighing only 2 pounds. What could we do?"

In the three years since then, Christine Maguire and I have become friends, but I still consider her one of the most deliciously unexpected cheesemakers imaginable.

She and her husband, Jim, a lawyer by day, are no faddish newcomers to the art and commerce of producing food. They've been at it for more than 30 years, since they left their very cosmopolitan life in London—where they met—and a stint in San Francisco. Jim still gets up at 5:30 a.m. to milk the animals before he goes off to work, but Christine has been the hands-on manager, cheesemaker, gardener, and hostess of the dairy's popular farm-stay program, and The Decider ever since her hobby for raising sheep got "a little out of hand" a few decades back. "I'd always had a few sheep, because of my spinning and weaving," she says, "then a friend gave me a goat. I started milking it, and pretty soon I had three goats. But I always swore I'd never make cheese. Bo-ring!"

Christine finds goats "way more adorable than sheep," but sheep seemed like good business—wool, meat, *and* milk—so she bought eight ewes, all pregnant. Suddenly, Christine found herself hand-milking 24 sheep. "Not good." She bought some books, took a cheese-making class at Cal-Poly, and paid a hefty sum for an all-you-might-need package of cheese-making equipment that does the milking all by itself (sort of). Christine was a cheesemaker.

Suddenly, Christine found herself hand-milking 24 sheep.

They bought the 92-acre Santa Margarita spread in 1999, after outgrowing the first homestead ("We were swimming in sheep on 1½ acres!"), but Mother Nature threw a few curveballs, and it wasn't until 2004 that the first wheel of sellable cheese, Pozo Tomme, was produced. Other tremendously tasty sheep, goat, and sheep-goat cheeses have joined the lineup: La Panza Gold, Chaparral, and the new Koby, created for celebrated Paso Robles chef Chris Kobayashi. Most of Christine's cheeses are sold to California (and New York) restaurants and at the Saturday farmer's market in San Luis Obispo, some 30 miles south.

An exciting new development at Rinconada Dairy: chickens. "I couldn't find a chicken I wanted to buy or eat," says this woman—who seems unfamiliar with the concept of "can't be done"—"so I bought some chicks and started raising my own." Christine's chickens are full of old-fashioned rich, chicken-y flavor, golden of skin—and they quickly disappear from any market that's lucky enough to stock a few. This time, the USDA threw the curve ball, so Jim swapped out his farmer's hat for his lawyer's hat, got on the Web and the phone, and discovered that he was right and they were wrong. Grateful diners in the region are now happily munching on Rinconada's poultry, as well as Muscovy ducks, heritage-breed turkeys in the fall, and the pigs that dine on buckets of acorns in the fall and the whey left over from cheese making, which would otherwise be discarded (waste not, want not). Tenacious and unafraid of hard work ("I played a lot when I was younger"), Christine's real secret is love. She loves every animal, the cheeses she creates, the land she cultivates, and her multitalented partner/husband of 35 years. It's a damned tasty recipe.

IF YOU VISIT:
Thinking of a day trip? Don't. Christine is way too busy to show you around. However, if you're interested in a farm stay, join the list of happy visitors who have passed a few days in the simple, comfy accommodations on this working farm. She might even let you lend a hand, but don't get any ideas about adopting Dewdrop.

www.rinconadadairy.com/farmstay.htm

Spaghetti with Sautéed Radicchio and Scamorza

If you've never tasted cooked radicchio, you're in for a serious treat. A little heat tames the bitterness, bringing out a mellow sweetness in this longtime staple California "green." Radicchio tagged along with the huge influx of Italian immigrants to the Golden State's Central Valley in the 1920s, and it has settled in for the duration. This is one of those "while the pasta cooks" dishes that's essential for any socially inclined chef; such preparations work brilliantly as long as everything is measured and prepared before you throw the noodles into the rollicking, salty water.

SERVES 6 AS A FIRST COURSE, OR 4 AS A MAIN COURSE

Fine sea salt

1 pound spaghetti

½ cup full-bodied extra-virgin olive oil

4 garlic cloves, minced or pushed through a press

4 to 6 anchovies, thinly sliced crosswise

1 pound radicchio (about 2 heads), quartered, cored, and slivered

Freshly ground black pepper

½ cup snipped fresh chives

½ cup coarsely chopped fresh flat-leaf parsley

4 ounces scamorza (smoked mozzarella), grated

3 tablespoons unsalted butter, cut into small pieces (optional)

Put a large pot of water on to boil with about 1 tablespoon of salt. Warm the appropriate number of plates in a low oven. When you have all your remaining ingredients gathered and ready, add the spaghetti to the boiling water and immediately proceed to the next step.

In a large skillet or sauté pan over medium heat, combine the olive oil, garlic, and anchovies. Stir and sizzle until the garlic is just beginning to turn brown, 1 to 2 minutes; immediately add the slivered radicchio and ¼ teaspoon salt. Increase the heat to medium-high, grind plenty of pepper over the top, and sauté until the radicchio is wilted and slightly golden in places, 2 to 3 minutes.

Drain the noodles (reserving ¼ cup of the cooking water) and add them to the skillet. Decrease the heat to very low and toss to distribute the radicchio evenly (add a little of the reserved pasta water at this point to help the "sauce" distribute, if you like). Add the chives, parsley, and half the cheese, and again toss well. If desired, enrich the pasta by tossing with the butter until it melts. Immediately mound onto the warm plates and sprinkle with the remaining cheese.

CENTRAL COAST: RN Estate "East Knoll Cuvee," Paso Robles (Syrah, Zinfandel)
FARTHER AFIELD: Primitivo, Puglia, Italy

Crispy Halloumi, Sage, and Rustic Bread Skewers

Who grills cheese on a skewer? As long as you use halloumi, the amazing cheese from Cyprus that just doesn't melt but instead turns crisp and golden, I promise you won't be faced with molten cheese dripping all over your grill. (Please don't try this with any other cheese, though.) In order to achieve even browning in this hugely appealing dish, it's crucial to cut all the cubes square and line up the flat edges. When threading the cheese cubes onto the skewers, press gently while twisting back and forth, to keep the cheese from splitting.   MAKES 4 SKEWERS

To make the flavored butter, combine the butter, lemon zest and juice, garlic, parsley, and a pinch each of salt and pepper in a small saucepan. Warm over low heat until the butter has melted; set aside.

In a large bowl, combine the cheese, bread cubes, sage leaves, and olive oil. Add ¼ teaspoon salt, plenty of pepper, and the ground chile; toss gently. Let stand for 5 minutes, then toss again. (The bread should be thoroughly coated with the oil.)

Prepare a charcoal or gas grill for medium-heat grilling.

Thread a cube of cheese onto a skewer, follow with a folded-over sage leaf, then a cube of bread, and then another sage leaf. Repeat, alternating until the skewer has 5 cubes of bread, 5 cubes of cheese, and 10 sage leaves. Repeat to make a total of 4 skewers. Align all the cubes so the flat sides match.

Using tongs, place the skewers onto the grill so that all flat sides come into full contact with the hot surface. Grill for 2 to 3 minutes on the top and bottom sides only (do not grill on the sides), without moving the skewers—but don't allow the bread to scorch. When you carefully turn each skewer over, try not to let the cubes rotate. When both cheese and bread are golden, transfer to a platter and drizzle with a little of the flavored butter. It's easiest to shove all the ingredients off the skewers and eat with a fork, although perhaps not quite as "rustic" as nibbling straight from the skewers.

CENTRAL COAST: Tolosa Chardonnay "No Oak," Edna Valley
FARTHER AFIELD: Friulano, Friuli, Italy

LEMON-GARLIC BUTTER
4 tablespoons unsalted butter

Finely grated zest, and juice of 1 small lemon

1½ teaspoons minced garlic

1 teaspoon finely chopped fresh flat-leaf parsley (optional)

Fine sea salt and freshly ground black pepper

20 (1-inch) cubes halloumi cheese (about 8 ounces)

20 cubes rustic bread (4 to 5 ounces), crusts removed, cut slightly smaller than the cheese cubes

40 fresh sage leaves, folded over in half

3 tablespoons extra-virgin olive oil

Salt and freshly ground black pepper

¼ teaspoon pure ground chile powder or ground chipotle chile

Bucatini Simmered in Sangiovese with Aged Parmesan

In Italy, variations on this theme are often called *al ubriaco*, "drunken" pasta. If you consider yourself a member of the Adventure Club, make the red wine–glazed pancetta ahead of time, then cut crosswise into ¼-inch strips and sizzle up in a pan before beginning the pasta preparation. Then scatter the garnet-colored porky-smoky tidbits over the ruby red pasta. It's a radically rustic and tasty garnish. Just make sure there's enough wine left for your glasses, as well. SERVES 4 TO 6

Fine sea salt

1 tablespoon extra-virgin olive oil

2 slices thick-sliced pancetta, or Red Wine–Glazed Pancetta (recipe follows), cut into ½-inch strips

3 anchovy fillets, rinsed and coarsely chopped

1 large garlic clove, minced or pushed through a press

¼ to ½ teaspoon red pepper flakes

3 cups Central Coast Sangiovese or Italian Chianti

1 pound bucatini or spaghetti

3 tablespoons salted cultured butter or Irish butter

¾ cup grated best-quality aged Parmigiano-Reggiano

½ cup coarsely chopped arugula leaves

Finely grated zest of 1 lemon

Bring a large, tall pot of water to a boil and add about 1 tablespoon salt.

Place a large sauté pan or deep skillet over medium heat and add the oil. Add the pancetta and stir occasionally until crisp and most of the fat has rendered. With a slotted spoon, transfer the pancetta to a plate; set aside.

Decrease the heat to low and add the anchovies, garlic, and pepper flakes to the pan. Sauté, stirring occasionally, until the garlic is softened, about 2 minutes. Add the wine and ½ teaspoon salt, and increase the heat again to medium, so the wine is simmering gently.

Immediately add the pasta to the boiling water and cook for about 5 minutes, or just until it begins to bend. Grab the pasta out of the water with tongs and transfer it to the pan with the wine, which should be simmering gently. Cook over medium-high heat, stirring frequently, until the wine is almost all absorbed and the noodles are al dente, 5 to 6 minutes more. Stir in the butter and half the Parmigiano and remove from the heat. Add the arugula and lemon zest and keep stirring until the butter and cheese have formed a rich glaze on the deep red noodles. Divide the noodles among warm bowls, scatter with the crispy pancetta and remaining Parmigiano, and serve.

Red Wine–Glazed Pancetta

Preheat the oven to 375°F. In a loaf pan, combine all the ingredients. Move the pancetta slices around so all sides come into contact with the wine mixture. Cover with aluminum foil, crimping securely. Bake for 45 minutes, or until the pancetta is tender and deep red. Let cool in the pan, then cover again and refrigerate in the liquid until ready to serve. To serve, lift the slices from the liquid and pat dry with paper towels. Sizzle in a pan over medium heat until crisp. Reserve the liquid from the pan to use in a soup or braise, or in the recipe at left.

2 fresh bay leaves or 4 dried

½ small yellow or white onion, sliced

8 ounces pancetta or smoked bacon, sliced just under ¼ inch thick

1½ cups fruity red wine, such as Zinfandel

½ cup homemade or store-bought low-sodium chicken or beef broth

NOTE: The quality of Parmesan and butter in this dish bear a direct relationship to the flavor of the finished dish, so be sure to search out the best.

CENTRAL COAST: Niner Sangiovese "Bootjack Ranch," Paso Robles
FARTHER AFIELD: Chianti Classico Riserva, Tuscany, Italy

Clos Pepe

Steve Pepe never intended to make award-winning Pinot Noir. His original goal was to find the best site possible to grow grapes in his retirement—a second chance at an honest job, if you believe what he has to say about it. As a labor attorney for 35 years, Steve spent most of his life defeating time and space. "You are faxing things, e-mailing, couriering documents, sending packages overnight. If there is a problem, you throw more people on it. You never let time or geography get in the way of what you want to do," he says.

Farming posed a unique challenge for an overworked, type A attorney: He needed patience. In an arena dictated by time and geography, Steve had to cede control to Mother Nature. Not that Steve was completely unfamiliar with the rigors of growing grapes. He was the first to plant a large vineyard in his Long Beach backyard—a whopping 70 vines—not quite the idyllic country respite he and his wife, Cathy, also a lawyer, had envisioned for themselves. As disparate as his two professions may seem, law experience did serve as preparation for the challenges ahead. He had gained the ability to calculate the best possible location to realize his and Cathy's dream, and he certainly had the determination. The dream was Pinot Noir.

After scouring the California coast from Mexico to Mendocino for prime cool-climate real estate, it was vineyard manager Jeff Newton of Coastal Vineyard Care who recommended a 40-acre parcel of sloping, loamy hillsides off Route 246, west of Highway 101 in the Santa Rita Hills near Lompoc. Richard Sanford had pioneered the area in 1970. Twenty years later, only a handful of vineyards had established roots there. In 1994, Clos Pepe became the sixth. Today, almost 20 years after that, the number totals 60.

The 29-acre Clos Pepe estate—all but four acres planted to Pinot Noir—has had tremendous influence on the region. Its long-term contracts for vineyard-designate selections are highly prized by well-regarded producers such as Siduri, Ken Brown, Loring, and A.P. Vin. These impeccably farmed grapes are sold by the acre, not by the ton, and cultivated strictly according to the buyers' desires. And Clos Pepe, along with Sanford and Babcock Winery, was instrumental in establishing the Santa Rita Hills American Viticultural Area, effectively putting the region on the map as a premium Pinot Noir producer. And then there is Clos Pepe's devoted winemaker and passionate torchbearer, Wes Hagen.

Steve had to cede control to Mother Nature.

Wes's excitement about his work is nearly impossible to control. As winegrower at Clos Pepe, he has translated Steve's dedication to Pinot Noir into a product wine lovers can appreciate and enjoy. Ironically, Wes never envisioned himself as a winemaker, nor as a vineyard manager. As a teacher and writer, he came to visit his mom, Cathy, and stepfather, Steve, at Clos Pepe one winter and, like so many others in the area, found himself enraptured by its climate, environment, and freedom. After apprenticing at a local winery and learning what he calls the "rhythms of the vineyard," he became the driving force behind Clos Pepe's emergence onto the wine scene. Together, Steve and Wes created an unusually dynamic partnership. They took wine courses together. They make decisions together. They work harvests together—though Steve calls himself their "oldest, slowest, and cheapest employee." Perhaps most important, they act as one another's champion. "Steve loves wine," says Wes. "Before he planted this vineyard he literally dreamed about wine. There was no other option in his life but to make his crazy idea a reality. He literally had to find the greatest place to plant Pinot Noir."

Together their goal has been to consistently produce wine with an intriguing sense of place in their adopted Santa Rita Hills, with chickens, sheep, and a recently established olive orchard, which produces a highly regarded estate-bottled extra-virgin olive oil. A few folks in his area believe it is too cold for olive trees, which Steve chose in honor of his Italian roots. While some call it determination, others call it foolishness. More like seasoned, proven grit.

IF YOU VISIT:

As of this date, tours of Clos Pepe are by appointment only, but Clos Pepe's wines may be purchased locally at Sissy's and Taste of Santa Rita Hills in Lompoc, and at Los Olivos Café in Los Olivos, or ordered online at www.clospepe.com.

Late-Harvest Moscato Panna Cotta with Candied Kumquats

There was a major problem with the development of this dish: There were never any of the jewel-like candied kumquats left when it was time to serve the panna cotta—they'd all been scarfed. Kumquats are often nicer to look at than to eat, due to the exceedingly tart flesh. I assure you, this is the ideal way to prepare (and devour) them. If you don't want to fiddle with unmolding the panna cottas, serve in pretty wineglasses, with a jumble of kumquats on the top. Or, just serve right in the ramekins.   SERVES 8

⅓ cup sliced almonds (about 1½ ounces), lightly toasted

2½ cups heavy cream

1¼ cups whole milk

⅛ teaspoon fine sea salt

2½ teaspoons unflavored powdered gelatin

¼ cup sugar

3 tablespoons late-harvest Moscato or Muscat

CANDIED KUMQUATS
¾ cup sugar

½ cup late-harvest Moscato or Muscat

¼ cup water

12 ounces fresh kumquats, stem ends trimmed, sliced crosswise ¼ inch thick, and all seeds removed

In a large saucepan, combine the toasted almonds, cream, ¾ cup of the milk, and salt. Bring up just to a simmer—watching so it doesn't boil over—and remove from the heat. Let steep for 15 minutes, then strain the liquid through a fine sieve and return to a clean saucepan.

Warm the remaining ½ cup milk in a small saucepan over low heat. Sprinkle the gelatin over the warm milk and let stand for about 3 minutes, or until softened. Add the sugar to the milk-cream mixture, and stir over very low heat until the sugar has dissolved. Stir the gelatin mixture into the cream mixture, and let cool. Stir in the wine and divide the mixture among eight ½-cup ramekins. Cover tightly and refrigerate overnight (or for up to 3 days).

To make the candied kumquats, combine the sugar, wine, and water in a heavy saucepan; bring to a boil. Simmer briskly for 10 minutes, then lower the heat to medium, add the kumquats, and simmer gently for 20 to 25 minutes more, until the liquid has reduced by about three-quarters and thickened slightly. Remove from the heat and let cool. (The mixture will thicken further as it cools, to a marmalade-like consistency.)

Let the panna cottas stand at room temperature for 10 minutes. Run a knife around the edge of each custard and invert onto a small plate. Give a quick downward shake to release the custard. Serve with a spoonful of the candied kumquats on top or on the side.

CENTRAL COAST: Lone Madrone Viognier "Sweet Cheeks," Paso Robles
FARTHER AFIELD: Late-harvest Viognier from Condrieu, Rhône Valley, France

Lavender-Lemon Squares

This simple, sunny dessert is slightly adapted from a recipe provided by Claudia Estrada, the bubbly and charming proprietress of Harmony Lavender Farm in Atascadero. Claudia may always be found at the lavender festivals that dot the Central Coast's summer calendar, along with myriad homemade, lavender-centric products—both edible and decorative (my favorite is the lavender jelly, which is heavenly with roast lamb), all made using the lovingly tended lavender from her own farm.

To make the lavender-infused powdered sugar: The day before you bake, combine ¼ cup culinary-grade lavender buds (or buds from your own plants that have never experienced insecticide) and ⅔ cup confectioners' sugar (about 10 tablespoons) in an airtight container; shake it up to blend. Let stand overnight, then sift to remove the lavender buds.   MAKES 24 SQUARES

Softened butter, for the pan

SHORTBREAD
1½ cups all-purpose flour

½ cup plus 1 tablespoon (4½ ounces) unsalted butter, cut into 10 pieces

6 tablespoons lavender-infused confectioners' sugar (see above)

1½ tablespoons cornstarch

⅛ teaspoon salt

LEMON CURD
4 large eggs (preferably pasture raised), lightly beaten

1 cup granulated sugar

3 tablespoons all-purpose flour

2 teaspoons finely grated lemon zest (preferably removed with a Microplane)

1 cup fresh lemon juice

¼ cup half-and-half

4 tablespoons lavender-infused confectioners' sugar

Preheat the oven to 350°F. Line a 9 by 13 by 2-inch baking dish with aluminum foil, smoothing it flat against the sides and base (make sure there is a little foil overhang at both of the short ends). Butter the foil and set the dish aside.

To make the shortbread, combine the flour, butter, lavender-infused sugar, cornstarch, and salt in a large bowl. Using a pastry blender or two knives, cut the butter into the dry mixture until it resembles coarse bread crumbs. Press this mixture evenly across the base of the prepared dish. Bake for 18 to 20 minutes, until the edges of the shortbread are golden.

Meanwhile, make the curd. In a large bowl, combine the eggs, granulated sugar, flour, lemon zest, lemon juice, and half-and-half. Whisk together until evenly blended. Pour the filling over the hot shortbread crust and bake for 15 to 20 minutes, until the center is set and no longer jiggly. Transfer the pan to a wire rack and let cool completely. Lift the whole dessert from the baking dish, using the overhanging foil to help, and cut into 2-inch squares (or bars).

Immediately before serving, sift or shake a little more lavender-infused sugar over each square. If there are any leftovers, cover with plastic wrap and refrigerate for up to 3 days.

CENTRAL COAST: Adelaida Cellars "Ice Wine, Methode Cryogenic," Paso Robles (Muscat, Viognier)
FARTHER AFIELD: Muscadel from South Africa or Muscat from Alsace, France

Fresh Fig Tart with Honey, Goat Cheese, and Pistachios

In Atascadero, a private garden crafted out of bland suburbanity by our dear friends Jeo and Albion regularly yields a prodigious fig harvest, as well as virtually every fruit, vegetable, and legume that can possibly be cultivated in this forgiving climate. I encourage the boys to open their garden for inspirational tours, because I know of no better (or more stunningly designed) model for sustainability. Even *Sunset* magazine's headquarters in Menlo Park doesn't come close. In my new garden in Paso Robles, two fig trees descended from Jeo's heavy producers are beginning to yield their first fruit—reason for celebration. Here is a delicious, user-friendly way to pair luscious fresh figs with buttery pastry, goat cheese, and bright green pistachio nuts. SERVES 8

Preheat the oven to 400°F.

On a lightly floured surface, unfold 1 pastry sheet. With a lightly floured rolling pin, roll once in each direction to enlarge the sheet slightly, to about 10 by 10 inches square. Cut into quarters to make four 5-inch squares. Transfer the squares to one of two large nonstick baking sheets (or, line the baking sheets with parchment paper or silicone baking liners). Repeat with the remaining sheet of puff pastry, to make 8 squares total. Prick each square all over with a fork, leaving a ½-inch border unpricked.

Distribute the figs over the pastry squares, drizzle with a little honey, and sprinkle with the sugar. Brush the borders lightly with the beaten egg.

Transfer the two baking sheets to the oven and bake for 18 minutes, or until the edges are puffed and golden, switching and rotating pans halfway through the baking time. Remove from the oven and scatter the cheese evenly over each tart. Return to the oven for 3 minutes to soften the cheese, then sprinkle with the chopped nuts and serve.

CENTRAL COAST: Zocker Riesling, Edna Valley
FARTHER AFIELD: Late-harvest Riesling from the Columbia Valley, Washington

2 sheets frozen puff pastry, thawed at room temperature for about 2 hours

12 ripe fresh figs, stemmed and quartered

2 tablespoons honey

1 teaspoon demerara or light brown sugar

1 egg, lightly beaten

3 ounces soft goat cheese, crumbled

¼ cup finely chopped pistachios (salted or unsalted)

Goat and Ricotta Cheesecake with Dates and Salted Orange Caramel

I often prefer to take my after-dinner sweetness in a glass—in the form of a late-harvest Moscato, or one of Rotta Winery's excellent dessert wines—rather than on the plate, so my favorite desserts tend toward the subtle rather than the overly sweet. Cheesecake has always been a favorite, but this tart cheesecake departs from the ordinary with goat cheese and dates, two of California's many proud and exquisite products. If you have never tasted the magic that transpires when caramel marries salt—here, with a jolt of California citrus—prepare for a party on your palate. SERVES 8 TO 10

CRUST
1½ cups gingersnap crumbs (about 26 cookies)

2 tablespoons sugar

Scant 1 teaspoon ground cinnamon

6 tablespoons unsalted butter, melted

FILLING
16 ounces goat cheese, softened

15 ounces whole-milk ricotta

⅓ cup sugar

2 teaspoons best-quality vanilla extract

3 eggs, lightly beaten

14 pitted dried dates, diced

Salted Orange Caramel (recipe follows)

To make the crust, wrap the base and partway up the sides of a 10-inch springform pan with a sheet of heavy-duty aluminum foil, molding it closely to the pan and smoothing the wrinkles. Cut a circle of parchment paper about ¾ inch larger than the base of the pan all around. Spray the inside of the pan with nonstick cooking spray, then press the circle of parchment onto the base, centering it exactly and smoothing the wrinkles firmly onto the metal (the paper will extend up the sides just by half an inch or so; this makes it easy to remove the cheesecake from the base).

In a bowl, combine the gingersnap crumbs, sugar, cinnamon, and enough of the melted butter to just bind the mixture. Use the remaining butter to thoroughly grease the paper-covered bottom and the sides of the springform pan. Scoop the crumb mixture into the pan. With your fingertips, press the crumbs into the corners, evenly across the base of the pan, and about halfway up the sides, turning the pan as you press to make an even layer.

Preheat the oven to 300°F.

To make the filling, combine the goat cheese, ricotta, sugar, and vanilla in a medium bowl and beat with an electric mixer until fluffy. Add the eggs and continue beating until smooth. Fold in the dates and then scoop the filling into the prepared crust.

Bake for 40 to 50 minutes, until the center is almost firm. Let cool to room temperature, then chill overnight before serving.

Run a thin, round-bladed knife around the inside rim all the way down to the base to release the crust. Release the sides of the springform pan and, using the parchment paper, slide the cheesecake from the base onto a flat, round serving platter. Slice into wedges and transfer to individual plates, then drizzle some caramel over the top.

Salted Orange Caramel

Combine the sugar and water in a small, heavy saucepan. Stir over medium-low heat until the sugar dissolves. Increase the heat and boil without stirring until the caramel turns dark amber brown, occasionally swirling the pan, about 8 minutes.

Carefully add the orange juice (the mixture will bubble furiously). Stir over low heat until the caramel has dissolved and the sauce is completely smooth. Stir in the orange zest and salt. Let cool completely. The sauce may be prepared 1 day ahead. Cover and let stand at room temperature.

1⅓ cups sugar

¼ cup water

⅔ cup fresh orange juice

Finely grated zest of 1 orange

1 teaspoon Hawaiian Alaea (orange) salt or sea salt

CENTRAL COAST: PasoPort "Tawny" NV, Paso Robles
FARTHER AFIELD: Malmsey Madeira, Madeira, Spain

San Marcos Honey

At San Marcos Honey, bees are both livestock and livelihood. "You breed them, manage them, try to keep them healthy and happy," says owner Don Cole. The bees are moved to different locations depending on the weather and season. "We put the hives on coastal ranches and mountain locations, starting with orange groves in April, and then avocado groves and wild sage in the hills." The sage season lasts through June, and the bees are then moved into summer pastures with wild sumac and California buckwheat, and the year finishes with overwintering in groves of coastal eucalyptus.

Don caught the beekeeping bug early in life; his father was a hobby beekeeper. "I helped my dad with the bees, and I really got a kick out of it. I think I have an affinity for bees." As a young man in his twenties, he worked as a carpenter but found himself always saving money to build more hives. "I can't explain it; I just enjoy it." Don's favorite tasks are raising queen bees and making comb honey. "In the 1600s, beekeeping was considered an intellectual pursuit, an interesting and complex type of farming." His wife, Anne, handles sales and marketing, and the Coles's two sons are also up to their elbows in honey. Jesse, 25, manages the "honey house," where the bottling, packing, and orders are handled. Jesse is also the family candlemaker. Eli, 22, makes wholesale deliveries and helps manage the hives.

In addition to varietal honeys, the family sells products made from the hives—candles, honeycomb, bee pollen, and propolis tincture. "We have fresh and dried bee pollen," says Don. "It has very high food value, popular with hikers and sports enthusiasts." The propolis tincture is made from "bee glue," the waxy substance that bees collect from trees and resinous plants to line their hive. "Bees add their own enzymes to the propolis, so it's a very effective natural antibiotic," says Don. "It's also really good for your teeth and gums."

San Marcos Honey started as a roadside produce stand. "I'm kind of a frustrated farmer," laughs Don. "I like growing things! Fortunately, I have friends who let me help them out and I get my farming kicks that way, because the honey production takes almost all my time now." The family production is going to stay around 1,000 hives, but now that Jesse and Eli are helping out, Don plans to upgrade equipment and build newer hives.

In the 1600s, beekeeping was considered an intellectual pursuit . . .

"The amount of honey we get from the hives varies dramatically, depending on the vintage," explains Don. "Some years, we get only 30 to 40 pounds, other years maybe as much as 80 to 100 pounds. And there's no way to estimate an upcoming harvest, since the Central Coast can have several dry years in a row, then a very wet year." According to Don, each variety of honey has a unique character. "The orange groves produce the first honey of the season; it's distinctive and fragrant. It smells and tastes like orange blossoms. Sage honey is light, delicate, and doesn't crystallize. We have black, purple, and white sage honeys. And there are several species of eucalyptus in the Central Coast—that honey is amber and complex. Alfalfa is a thick, low-moisture honey. Avocado honey—that's the stout of the honey world. It's dark like a Guinness beer, very molasses-like and rich in minerals like potassium and magnesium. Good for homemade sports drinks. I put it on my hot cereal in the mornings."

Anne also makes a line of "fruited" honeys using local organic fruit from neighboring farms. Try the raspberry, strawberry, or blueberry honey. "The cinnamon honey transforms simple bread into cinnamon toast," she says. The pumpkin-spice honey is truly indulgent, and there may, depending on the season, also be, yes, a *chocolate honey*.

IF YOU VISIT:

San Marcos Honey products can be found at Central Coast farmer's markets in Santa Barbara, Solvang, and Goleta (check times and locations at www.cafarmersmarkets.com), and in a few select natural food stores. Although the farm is not open to visitors, you can call the honey house (805) 681-0312 to inquire about placing orders.

Grilled Peaches Stuffed with Lavender-Absinthe Mascarpone

Head to See Canyon, south of San Luis Obispo and just inland from Avila Beach, for the juiciest, peachiest, most lusciously delicious peaches in the world. The rich, loamy coastal soil and mild climate combine to make the area not just idyllic for human beings, but also perfect for growing all kinds of fruit. In season, See Canyon peaches—especially the dry-farmed fruit—are to supermarket peaches as one of Tablas Creek's fine Rhône-style white wine blends is to Two-Buck Chuck.

It's a little too much trouble to fire up an outdoor grill just for this dish, but it's a natural if you've already used the grill to cook the main course. A ridged cast-iron griddle pan is an easy option. The peaches should not go onto a very hot grill. If you buy dried lavender rather than harvesting it from your own garden, be sure it is rated for human consumption and not as an ingredient for potpourri. SERVES 6 TO 8

In a small bowl, whisk together the mascarpone, absinthe, and honey; refrigerate until serving time. Taste for sweetness and add a little more honey, if desired.

Prepare a gas or charcoal grill for medium-heat grilling and make sure the grate is nice and clean. (Or, preheat a ridged griddle pan over medium heat.)

Brush the cut sides of the peaches with a little honey and place them cut sides down on the hot grilling surface. Grill for 1 to 2 minutes only, until marked by the grill and golden. Transfer to a platter or individual plates and mound 2 tablespoons of the mascarpone mixture into the center of each peach. Scatter a pinch of lavender over each one, and serve.

CENTRAL COAST: Tablas Creek "Vin de Paille," Paso Robles (Grenache Blanc, Viognier, Roussanne, Marsanne)
FARTHER AFIELD: Vin Glacé from the Willamette Valley, Oregon

1 cup mascarpone

1 tablespoon absinthe

1 to 2 teaspoons honey, plus more for grilling the peaches

4 large ripe peaches, halved and pitted

1 teaspoon fresh lavender blossoms, pulled apart

CHAPTER 7

From the Wood-Fired Oven

Since I do not (yet) own a wood-fired oven, I turned for detailed advice and recipes to the premier expert, proponent, and practitioner of wood-oven cooking on the Central Coast, Clark Staub. Clark owns and operates Full of Life Flatbread, a woodsy, convivial restaurant in the small and idyllic town of Los Alamos, between Buellton and Santa Maria, not far from Los Olivos (a region made famous—or, perhaps, infamous—by the movie *Sideways*). His famous flatbreads are distributed in the frozen section of Whole Foods and many other stores in California, and Clark can be seen most weekends towing his colorful tiled oven up and down Highway 101, en route to cater a wedding, winery event, or any other great party. Clark lovingly nurtures and encourages local producers in this region in much the same way Alice Waters once set out to benefit her restaurant's patrons as well as the farmers and growers who supplied her kitchen.

This chapter is less exacting in the instructions than the others, because cooking in a wood oven is more of an art than a science. The process is personal and intuitive, and it will involve a steep and fairly fast learning curve. Those who are new to the practice should first understand a few basic principles. Once you begin to experiment, you'll quickly develop an instinct for the heat and the primitive, living force of the fire itself.

CLARK SAYS:

In a wood-burning oven there are three heat sources that combine to cook the foods: (1) the air temperature inside the oven, (2) the temperature of the oven's floor, and (3) the mass temperature (the temperature of the oven's structure). The air temperature is readily controlled by the amount of flame in the oven and how compactly or sparsely the hot coals are spread out. For example, a pile of coals in the corner of an oven will not have the same effect on the air as coals you have spread out over a wider area of the oven. The air temperature will brown foods and is what we traditionally associate with a wood-burning oven. The floor temperature is a direct result of the air temperature, and will act to bake, crisp, or cook the food from the bottom. Generally, a hotter air temperature over a longer period will make the floor temperature hotter. Also, the floor will always be at its hottest when nothing has been placed onto it, so sometimes we choose to place a new food item directly in the same place that another object (a pizza, a pan, a baking dish) has just vacated. (That spot on the floor will not be as hot as the floor contiguous to it.) The mass heat is the result of all the materials that go into the oven and how long the fire has been heating up the oven prior to baking or cooking. A wood-fired oven made out of masonry (stone, cement, or clay) is generally pretty heavy. Thus, the mass of the oven and the heat stored in it are what create a consistent temperature environment. When one builds a fire, the oven will heat slowly until it reaches temperature. When the baker stops feeding the fire and the flame has diminished, the mass of the oven is what will create a gradual reduction of the temperature.

The first step for any of the recipes in this chapter is to build a fire large enough to heat the oven and build the temperature. I always start with small pieces of kindling, scraps of sticks, and splintered wood, with some larger pieces over it. The fire will catch slowly, but you will also start the important process of building up coals. Another important part of this process is that, by gradually building the oven heat over time, you build mass temperature, and it is the mass temperature that will maintain the chamber heat.

An experienced baker can easily determine the temperature of the oven, but if you are new to this craft, you will probably want to purchase a digital laser thermometer. Point the thermometer at several points in the oven; different surfaces will be at different temperatures. The center of the oven is often cooler than the edges. Roast food items up against the wall to benefit from convection and reflected heat.

The optimal oven temperature to bake a flatbread or pizza is around 700°F. For a roast, gratin, soup, or sauce, you will want a more moderate temperature: around 400°F. When slow roasting a less tender cut of meat, build a small, smoldering fire and aim for 225°F to 250°F. The longer the food stays in the oven at a lower temperature, the more smoky flavor it will pick up. In a standard oven, heat dissipates quickly when you open the door, but in the wood oven the mass provides great consistency of temperature. Use a probe thermometer to gauge the doneness of meat and poultry. And if the outside is starting to char or dry out too much, use aluminum foil to create a heat shield from the fierce heat—especially to protect ears and other extremities of the meat, which will burn easily.

The goal of any responsible wood oven cook is to fully utilize the heat of the fire and the fuel necessary to get it hot enough to cook a pizza. While the oven is heating up (or, when it is cooling off from its highest heat—at 150°F to 225°F or so), roast low-temperature items, like Fennel-Dusted Roasted Grapes or Slow-Roasted Tomatoes. When the oven is at about 400°F, that's the time to make a soup or gratin or to roast small, tender cuts of meat. Pastries like a cooler oven, too, and are perfect for cooking during the waning heat phase (which also often coincides with dessert).

Don't assume the timing given in the recipes will be exact. Instead, watch and nurture your food in the oven, checking and rotating so that each side is equally affected by the direct heat of the oven. I have provided brief instructions for preparing these recipes in a standard home oven, but the flavor will not be as smoky, concentrated, and complex as the results you can achieve in a wood oven.

Wine pairings by Frank Ostini and Anne Twigg of Hitching Post II restaurant, in Buellton

Oven-Roasted Mussels with Chorizo

Clark's take on *moules marinière*, this earthy dish is best prepared in a waning fire, when the temperature is very slowly dropping after high-heat baking of pizza. The broth is to die for. The mussels' juices mingle with the cooking liquid—either wine or beer—while the spicy fat from the chorizo bathes everything with its salty richness. Serve with plenty of crusty bread for mopping. Ideally, drizzle with Yellow Pepper–Caper Rouille (page 209) just before serving. SERVES 6

Ideally, the wood oven should be slowly cooling down from its top heat (700°F) and be in the 500°F to 600°F range for cooking the mussels.

In a large, wide ovenproof casserole or Spanish cazuela, combine the oil, garlic, diced tomatoes, mussels, and wine or beer. Scatter the chorizo and oregano sprigs over the top and fold everything together gently. Place the casserole around the corner from the front door, where the air is slightly cooler than in the center of the oven. Watch the mussels, and when they have all opened, carefully remove the pot from the oven.

Discard any mussels that have not opened and the branches of oregano. Scatter with a little fresh oregano and taste for seasoning. Serve with the same wine or beer used in the cooking process and with the rouille for dipping, if desired.

ALTERNATE METHOD: Roast in an oven at 475°F to 550°F—ideally, convection—or on a charcoal kettle grill set to a similar temperature, regulating the heat so the liquid simmers actively.

CENTRAL COAST: Fiddlehead Sauvignon Blanc "Goosebury," Happy Canyon, Santa Barbara County
FARTHER AFIELD: Sauvignon Blanc from New Zealand

¼ cup extra-virgin olive oil

5 or 6 garlic cloves, minced

10 Slow-Roasted Tomatoes (page 268), stemmed and diced, or 10 drained and slightly crushed canned San Marzano tomatoes

60 small black mussels, scrubbed and debearded

1 (750-ml) bottle dry, crisp white wine, such as Sauvignon Blanc or Pinot Grigio, or about 4 cups light-colored beer, such as pilsner

1½ pounds fresh, soft chorizo, crumbled

Fresh sprigs oregano, plus leaves, for garnish

Yellow Pepper–Caper Rouille (page 209), for serving (optional)

Wood-Roasted Beet Salad with Winter Squash and Beet Greens

Don't worry about the skin of the whole squash blackening and charring in the direct heat of the embers. The hard outer skin of the squash will protect the flesh and the vegetable will steam itself from the inside.   SERVES 6

6 small yellow beets, leafy greens reserved

6 small red or orange beets, leafy greens reserved

Extra-virgin olive oil, for drizzling

Fine sea salt and freshly ground black pepper

6 to 8 small sprigs fresh thyme

1 whole butternut squash (about 2 pounds)

2 small shallots, finely chopped

3 tablespoons balsamic or sherry vinegar

Finely grated zest from 2 oranges

1½ tablespoons fresh orange juice

1½ tablespoons fresh lemon juice

Scant 1 teaspoon ground fennel (ideally, toast fennel seeds and grind in a mortar and pestle)

⅓ cup best-quality extra-virgin olive oil

Coarse sea salt, for finishing

Build a fire in the wood oven and build the temperature up to 350°F to 400°F.

Scrub the beets thoroughly and trim the ends. Divide the beets among two large squares of aluminum foil, keeping the two colors separate so they don't bleed. Drizzle each with olive oil and season with fine sea salt and pepper; add a few sprigs of thyme. Wrap and crimp the tops of the foil to seal the pouches. Place the two pouches on the oven floor fairly near the wall of the oven, so they will benefit from the floor heat as well as the reflected heat of the wall. Using a small fireplace shovel or a stick, create a small nest in the bed of coals for the whole squash, so it's surrounded by hot embers and coals. Roast the squash in the coals for about 45 minutes, or until you can pierce the skin with a knife but there is still slight resistance. You want an al dente squash flesh. The beet pouches should roast for 35 to 45 minutes, until tender when pierced with a knife.

While the vegetables are roasting, discard any tough beet greens, then tear the tender greens into bite-size pieces, discarding any large stems. Keep chilled until serving time.

Remove the pouches and the squash, and let cool. When the squash is cool, brush off any ash and cut in half. Scoop out the seeds and carefully peel the skin off. Dice the squash flesh.

In a large bowl, whisk together the shallots, vinegar, orange zest and juice, lemon juice, ground fennel, and olive oil. Whisk in ¾ teaspoon fine sea salt and plenty of pepper.

continued on page 258

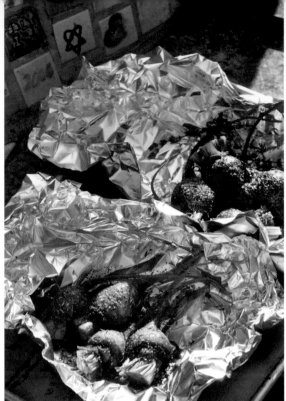

When the beets are cool enough to handle, peel and cut them into wedges. Add the beets and squash cubes to the bowl of dressing and fold together gently until everything is coated with the dressing. Let the mixture stand for at least 30 minutes and up to 1 hour, so the flavors can marry.

Add the beet greens to the bowl and fold to blend. Transfer to a platter or divide among plates and scatter with a little coarse sea salt.

ALTERNATE METHOD: Foil-bake the beets in a 375°F oven—preferably convection—or on a charcoal kettle grill at a similar temperature. Split the squash lengthwise, paint the cut sides with olive oil and season with salt and pepper, and roast, cut side down, along with the beets.

CENTRAL COAST: Margarum "Sybarite" Sauvignon Blanc, Happy Canyon, Santa Barbara County
FARTHER AFIELD: Sancerre, Loire Valley, France

Pig and Fig Pizza

When I got a call from the editors who create Williams-Sonoma's cookbooks—"Would you like to write a pizza book for us?"—I had to shake my head because I was afraid I might be dreaming. Nope—not dreaming. Here's a simple but elemental pizza that sums up my whole attitude toward cooking, living, writing cookbooks, and entertaining friends—and always loving the delightful process. MAKES TWO 12-INCH PIZZAS

Build a fire in the wood oven and build the temperature up to about 700°F. In a small saucepan, reduce the balsamic vinegar over medium-low heat by about two-thirds, until syrupy. Set aside.

Place both dough disks on a lightly floured surface and press them out into rough oval shapes, a little less than ¼ inch thick (if the dough resists your efforts to press it out thin, cover with a towel and leave to rest for about 5 minutes, then persist). Dimple with your fingers every inch or so, leaving the edge untouched, and brush all over with olive oil. Transfer one dough round to a wooden pizza peel liberally scattered with cornmeal. Don't press down on the dough at all as you load and top it, or it will stick to the peel. Immediately scatter the dough with half of the sliced figs, prosciutto, and cheese. Quickly and confidently slide the first pizza onto the floor in the center of the oven and bake for about 5 minutes, rotating occasionally after the first minute or two. Meanwhile, press out the second dough round and transfer to the peel. As soon as the edges of the first pizza are nicely charred and the cheese has melted, remove from the oven. Quickly load the second dough round onto the peel, top as before, and transfer from the peel to the oven. Scatter the first pizza with half the arugula and drizzle with a little balsamic syrup. Cut and serve. Repeat to serve the second pizza.

ALTERNATE METHOD: Bake the pizza at the hottest setting your oven will achieve, preferably set to convection. It will take longer than 2 to 4 minutes, probably 6 to 8. Best results will be obtained with a *fully* preheated pizza stone set on the oven's floor.

CENTRAL COAST: Hitching Post Rosé "Pinks," Santa Maria Valley
FARTHER AFIELD: Chinon Rosé, Loire Valley, France

---

1 cup balsamic vinegar

2 disks (1 pound) Pizza/Flatbread Dough (page 265), after its second rise

Extra-virgin olive oil, for brushing

Coarse cornmeal, for the pizza peel

8 to 10 large, plump fresh figs, stemmed and sliced crosswise about ¼ inch thick

4 ounces thick-cut prosciutto, minced

7 ounces pecorino, coarsely grated

3 ounces small arugula leaves (about 2 cups), tossed with just enough olive oil to coat

Freshly ground black pepper

Alban Vineyards

It is a story that has been told many times, and yet it's worth repeating: John Alban knew at age 17 that he wanted to make wine. His father, a physician, was often given wine as a gift, and he'd share it with his children. The labels bore unique names that John loved to locate on maps spread across the dining room table—he was instantly transported through a bottle of wine. While this might sound like an exciting, transformative time, the real John Alban is way too practical ever to allude to such whimsy. He's dedicated to the actual work of fulfilling his goals, not just waxing poetic about them.

Alban captures all the intensity one might imagine for a person who single-handedly elevated the status of Rhône varietal wines—not only to the California wine-drinking public, but on a national and global scale, as well. When Alban first planted Viognier in Paso Robles in 1985, he nearly doubled the global acreage for the grape. "If we had been conducting this interview just 20 years ago, we'd have had to start by explaining what Rhône varieties *are*," he says. Looking back on those initial years, he laughs in amazement. "I can't emphasize enough that I knew nothing. I had never planted a vineyard or raised a crop before." A city boy, he saw the chance to introduce new varieties—such as the funny-sounding Viognier, Grenache, Syrah, and Mourvedre—to a world that for decades only understood Cabernet Sauvignon and Chardonnay. He sought to bridge that gap, and never imagined just how thirsty and eager the wine-drinking public would be for what he brought to the table.

After studying viticulture and enology at Fresno State and UC Davis, he spent time in the Rhône region in France, gaining an understanding of the soils, climate, and techniques. He searched from Gilroy to the Santa Ynez Valley before settling on a tucked-away parcel in the Edna Valley. It was the diversity of the soils—immedi-

When Alban first planted Viognier in Paso Robles in 1985, he nearly doubled the global acreage for the grape.

ately evident on an ATV ride through the vineyard—that attracted him to the location. Marine and volcanic soils crash into one another below as the limbs of massive old oak trees caress the earth along the creek bed. Just a few acres away, chalky, powdery white soils dominate the hillsides. With 68 acres planted, it is a constant challenge to better understand how each area of his vineyard will perform.

Alban's goal is to create a true designation of place through his final product. He does not introduce anything from the outside into his vineyard. No cover crops are cultivated other than what comes up with the rains. Compost is all produced here. A herd of some 300 sheep perform the first level of weed management, followed by an equally sizable flock of geese, which manages residual growth and insects. Through a rotational grazing system dictated by the seasons, the animals are not given any supplemental feed; they're nourished by what is here, and in turn the vineyard is nourished. If, in jesting, you point out that they seem to be doing all the labor, he jokes back, "They still don't know how to prune."

In Alban's presence, it is easy to understand his dedication to the land and the passion for perfection with which he makes his wines—which regularly garner the highest acclaim from critics across the board. "When I began, I believed that Rhône varieties could become as important to the California wine trade as any other grape," he says. "I wanted to introduce the idea of diversity. My dream was to help people appreciate wine in a whole new way; through its inherent quality rather than by 'birthright.' Today, I understand that I have a certain responsibility to see how far this can actually go."

IF YOU VISIT:
Alban Vineyards does not have a tasting room nor does it have vineyard or winery tours. There is only one way to taste the Alban wines: Sign up for the waiting list for their (regularly sold-out) new releases through their Web site, www.albanvineyards.com.

Fennel-Dusted Roasted Grapes with Sea Salt

Clark Staub calls these concentrated little flavor bombs "fresh raisins." The slow-and-low heat concentrates the sugars and juices of the grapes until they are slightly crisp and imbued with an elemental, essence-of-grape flavor. They are a fantastic garnish for all sorts of dishes (roast pork, atop a pizza or flatbread—the possibilities are endless). The grapes can be placed in the oven shortly after you start the fire, allowing them to increase in temperature as the oven does. Clark likes to pair them with a platter of local cheeses—especially blue cheeses. You can also crush the grapes to extract their sweet, concentrated and slightly smoky juice, then drizzle it over ice cream.

MAKES: 2 TO 3 BUNCHES SHRIVELED AND SOMEWHAT DESSICATED GRAPES

Build a fire in the wood oven and build the temperature to about 200°F. Spread the grape clusters on a large, rimmed baking sheet and brush lightly with the oil. Sprinkle generously with salt and fennel, turning to be sure all sides of the grapes are more or less evenly coated. Place the baking sheet on the oven floor, away from the fire and coals. Keep the coals alive by throwing a small piece of wood on the fire occasionally, but don't let it get too hot. Ideally, roast for 3 to 4 hours, rotating the pan occasionally (the longer they roast, the sweeter and smokier they'll be). The grapes will begin to shrivel and take on a little color. Remove from the oven and serve warm or at room temperature. Or, store in an airtight container in the fridge for 3 to 4 days. Be sure to return to room temperature before serving.

ALTERNATE METHOD: Slow roast the grapes at 185°F to 210°F in an oven—preferably convection—or on a charcoal kettle grill at a similar temperature, managing the temperature so they don't shrivel too fast.

CENTRAL COAST: Longoria Port "Vino Dulce," Santa Barbara County (Syrah)
FARTHER AFIELD: Port from Portugal

2 to 3 large bunches seedless red or black grapes, snipped into small clusters (2 to 3 pounds)

About ¼ cup grapeseed oil

Kosher or coarse sea salt, as needed

Ground fennel (or toasted fennel seeds, ground to a powder in a mortar and pestle), as needed

Slow-Roasted Tomatoes

These are like fresh sun-dried tomatoes, but with a lovely smoky perfume. The process reduces the water content, concentrating the flavor. This is a great dish for off-season tomatoes, because it would be a crime to roast ripe, meaty heirloom tomatoes. This is also the perfect dish to cook in your oven when the heat is either first warming up or is waning from its high point (say, for cooking pizza). Serve the roasted tomatoes warm or at room temperature with burrata, whole in a bowl of pasta with olive oil, sliced on a sandwich, in salad, or on a pizza.

The tomatoes are prepared in almost the exact same way as the Fennel-Dusted Roasted Grapes with Sea Salt (page 263), but since they are larger, they will take longer.

Start with tomatoes on the vine, ideally. Place them in a shallow roasting dish or on a rimmed baking sheet and brush lightly with olive oil, then season generously with salt and pepper and a little oregano. Place the baking sheet on the oven floor, away from the fire and coals. Keep the coals alive by throwing a small piece of wood on the fire occasionally, but don't let it get too hot. Ideally, roast for 3 to 4 hours, rotating the pan occasionally. The tomatoes will begin to shrivel and take on a little color. When the tomatoes are shriveled and partially collapsed but still juicy, remove from the oven and serve warm or at room temperature. Or, store in an airtight container in the fridge for 3 to 4 days. Be sure to return to room temperature before serving.

ALTERNATE METHOD: Slow roast the tomatoes at 185°F to 210°F in an oven—preferably convection—or on a charcoal kettle grill at a similar temperature, managing the heat so the tomatoes don't shrivel too fast.

CENTRAL COAST: Sandhi Pinot Noir, Sanford and Benedict Vineyard, Santa Rita Hills
FARTHER AFIELD: Pinot Noir from New Zealand

Pizza/Flatbread Dough

At Full of Life Flatbread, Clark makes cultured whole-wheat dough (that is, fermented, as in sourdough bread) that has a beautiful, tangy-earthy flavor. Unless you are a very ambitious home baker, you will probably not want to embark on creating a cultured dough. (If you do, look no further than Carol Fields's seminal book *The Italian Baker* for instructions on making your own starter.) You can also ask your neighborhood pizza place if it'll sell you a pound of dough. Or, buy French or Italian bread dough from a bakery. The dough will keep for 24 hours in your refrigerator. Remove from the fridge and let stand for 1 to 2 hours to bring it to cool room temperature, when it will begin to puff up (the length of time required will depend on the weather).

MAKES ENOUGH FOR TWO 12-INCH PIZZAS

Here's my own favorite, foolproof dough, from my book *Pizza* for Williams-Sonoma.

In a large measuring jug, stir the warm water and sugar together, and sprinkle the yeast over the top. Let stand for 5 minutes (it should start to foam). Add the room-temperature water and the olive oil.

In a food processor, combine the all-purpose flour, semolina flour, and salt. Pulse a few times to blend. With the motor running, add the yeast-water mixture quickly in a steady stream, and pulse on and off in 2-second bursts until the dough comes together in a rough mass. (If the dough has not formed a ball within about 12 seconds, remove the cover and sprinkle a teaspoon or two of water or flour over the dough, then process again.) Let the dough rest for 10 minutes, then process again for 25 to 30 seconds longer, holding the top of the food processor with one hand. Turn the dough out onto a lightly floured surface and form into a smooth ball. It should be silky smooth and just slightly tacky to the touch, but not sticky. Place in a large, oiled bowl, turn over once to coat with oil, and cover tightly with plastic wrap. Let rise in a warm place until doubled in bulk and very spongy, 1½ to 2 hours.

Turn the dough out onto a lightly floured surface, punch it down, and knead into a smooth cylinder. Divide into two equal pieces and knead again to form two smooth, slightly flattened disks, dusting with a little flour only if the dough is sticky. Cover with a clean kitchen towel and let rest for 20 minutes. Proceed with your chosen recipe.

¼ cup warm water (110°F)

1 teaspoon sugar

1 package (¼ ounce) active dry yeast

1 cup water, at room temperature

1 tablespoon extra-virgin olive oil, plus more for the bowl

7 ounces all-purpose flour (1 cup plus 7 tablespoons)

11 ounces fine semolina flour (2 cups plus 2 tablespoons)

1 tablespoon fine sea salt

Cass Vineyards and Winery

Steve Cass and his wife, Alice, "discovered" Paso Robles in 1999, when their children were grown. "It wasn't that I was disgruntled with my job," he says, "but 20 years behind a desk is a long time." Steve considers himself a numbers guy and—after all that time at Charles Schwab, during which the company went from 600 to 26,000 employees—it's probably a fair call.

Ted Plemons is a free-spirited, quintessential Californian figure, wild of hair, with flashing eyes and an infectious grin. His enthusiastic discourses on the subject of wine often verge on the raucous. In the past, Ted made people happy by building wonderful houses for them. You couldn't keep him behind a desk for love or money.

At first glance, Steve Cass and Ted Plemons seem like extremely *unlikely* partners. But watch them holding court out at Cass Winery under the sheltering umbrella of the huge oak tree, and it takes only a moment to realize that the two partners are perfectly and symbiotically suited.

Steve's passion for making wine is *all* about lifestyle. His pleasure at being in business purely to make people happy is quietly palpable. "People leave here in a better mood than when they arrived," he says. "I love that." Steve loved wine and, like many people, he saw a wine region that was poised to blast off. Alice was game for a life change. (Son Brian, 16, called his dad "crazy." He now works at the winery, while daughter Kristen works for a large Los Angeles wine distributor.) Steve and Alice bought 146 acres in the rolling, hot-dry canyons east of Paso Robles, blessed by the temperate, breezy influence of the Templeton Gap. They planted 136,000 vines and set about finding a contractor to build a barn.

Among the nine or ten contractors Steve interviewed, Ted Plemons stood out. "He was clearly such an honest guy—he practically wears his heart on his sleeve. Who else would be more trustworthy?" Ted brought in the huge, sturdy barn on time and on budget, and the two became

The two fell in love with the soft, dusty wines Back was making with Rhône grape varieties.

friends, playing "way too much golf" together. On a wine-tasting (and golfing) trip to South Africa in 2003, they went to visit Charles Back at Fairview Wines, in Paarl. The two fell in love with the soft, dusty wines Back was making with Rhône grape varieties. They looked carefully at the whole process and felt that—with the right energy and combination of knowledge—such wines could be made in Paso Robles. Steve had just begun to make wine from his young grapes ("It was dismal," he says), but he wasn't ready to make the financial leap to a real, permitted winery. Ted's enthusiasm and willingness to jump in won the day, and after some serious number crunching, the two became partners in Cass Vineyards and Winery. They've never regretted it. Their South African winemaker, Lood Kotze, has brought accolades, high scores, and happy faces to wine drinkers all across the country. The wine's style is something of a hybrid between the austere French Rhônes and the high-alcohol fruit bombs so common in the region.

Many members of the Cass wine club have become personal friends; lots of them turn out to help with bottling and boxing wine for the biannual shipments. There is a true sense of family among the diverse group of staff, owners, and fans.

The Cass family's other passion is music: Steve and Alice were instrumental in returning the sadly lapsed Paderewski Festival to good health. The festival celebrates the legacy of Ignacy Paderewski, a Polish pianist who fell in love with the area in 1914 and bought 3,000 acres (he was the first to plant Zinfandel here). The reinvigorated festival now sponsors annual exchanges between Poland and Paso Robles, sending local piano students to Poland every other year for master classes and concerts, and welcoming Polish students here in alternating years.

IF YOU VISIT:

Cass is one of the only wineries to serve food (every day), and their weekend events are always celebrations of conviviality. The approachable, food-friendly wines and delightful dishes from gifted, creative chef and busy local caterer Jacob Lovejoy round out the events. (I love the summer Saturday "Tacos and Tunes.")

Tasting room and café open daily, 11 a.m. to 5 p.m.

7350 Linne Road
Paso Robles, CA 93446

(805) 239-1730

www.casswines.com

Smoked Tomato Soup

Make sure there are enough glowing coals so that when new wood is thrown over the hot embers, it will ignite. As soon as the new wood is burning, put on the oven door. This resulting lack of oxygen will extinguish the flame, trapping the smoke in the hot oven. For an added level of flavor, do as Clark Staub does: Caramelize a small, sliced onion until golden and crusty, chop, and add to the pot along with the fennel. MAKES ABOUT 2 QUARTS

SOUP

1 to 3 tablespoons grapeseed oil

2 celery ribs, finely chopped

1 carrot, finely chopped

1 fennel bulb, trimmed, cored, and finely chopped

4 garlic cloves, smashed

2 teaspoons dried oregano

Fine sea salt and freshly ground black pepper

1 whole chipotle chile en adobo, with some of the sauce

3 (28-ounce) cans plus 1 (15-ounce) can peeled Italian plum tomatoes, with the juice

4 cups heavy cream

½ teaspoon smoked paprika (pimentón)

QUENELLES

1 cup heavy cream

2 ounces fresh goat cheese, at room temperature

½ teaspoon freshly ground black pepper

Truffle oil, for serving

Snipped fresh garlic chives or regular chives, for serving

Build a fire in the wood oven and build the temperature to 200°F to 250°F (see above).

Either on the stovetop or on the hearth (in the doorway of the oven), warm a large, shallow fireproof casserole and add a nice slick of oil. Add and sauté the celery, carrots, and fennel until nicely caramelized. Stir in the garlic and oregano. Season generously with salt and pepper, then add the chipotle and all of the tomatoes; stir well and bring up to a low simmer.

Move the casserole inside the wood oven and add a small piece of wood and/or some herb branches to the fire. When the wood ignites, close the door and allow the soup to smoke, uncovered, for 20 minutes. Open the door, standing well away from the opening (the influx of new oxygen may cause the fire to reignite unexpectedly). Carefully reach in and remove the casserole from the oven; let it cool. In batches, puree the soup in a blender and, if you want a very smooth soup, strain through a fine-mesh sieve (or, just leave it thick, for lots of body). Return to the original casserole and, over medium-low heat, warm through. Stir in the cream and paprika and bring to a simmer for 3 to 4 minutes, to blend the flavors. Taste for seasoning and correct with salt and/or smoked paprika.

To make the quenelles, whip the cream in a bowl until it forms soft peaks. Break up the cheese and add it, along with the pepper; whip the mixture until smooth, thick, and speckled with pepper.

Ladle the warm, smoky soup into shallow bowls. Form quenelles of cheese with two soupspoons, then place a quenelle in the center of each bowl. Scatter a few drops of truffle oil and some chives around each quenelle.

continued on page 270

ALTERNATE METHOD: Roast the soup at 250°F to 300°F in an oven—preferably convection—or on a charcoal kettle grill at a similar temperature, managing the temperature.

CENTRAL COAST: Beckmen "Cuvée Le Bec," Santa Ynez Valley (Grenache, Syrah, Mourvedre, Counoise)
FARTHER AFIELD: Red Côtes du Rhône, Rhône Valley, France

Smoky Leek Sauce

In Los Olivos, Shu Takikawa runs a symbiotic family farming and nursery business called The Garden of . . . . . (there are always five dots) and Yes Yes Nursery. Shu's stepdaughter Noey Turk runs the nursery, raising seedlings in a hothouse, which she sells at farmer's markets, and also grows the seedlings for Shu's farm. He raises the vegetables. They also rent vineyard space to Bob and Louisa Lindquist, where they grow the grapes for Verdad. The white part of Shu's leeks is about a foot and a half long, and they get snapped up at the Santa Barbara and Solvang markets as if they were gold. If your leeks are more green than white, use the well-washed green parts to make a brightly flavored green broth.

Shu is originally from Japan, and lots of young farmers—like Jacob Grant of Roots Farm—trained with him before starting their own businesses. MAKES ABOUT 1½ CUPS

On the hearth of a wood oven (just in the doorway where the heat is not too intense), or over medium heat on the stovetop, melt the butter in a flameproof casserole with the olive oil. Add the leeks and stir frequently until nicely softened but not browned at all.

Stir in the garlic and thyme leaves, and sauté until the garlic releases its aroma, about 1 minute. Again, do not allow to brown. Stir in the cream and season with the salt and pepper

Place the pan inside a wood oven at low heat (400°F). Toss the thyme sprigs and stems onto the hot coals and place the oven door over the opening to cut off the oxygen and allow the sauce to pick up a nice smoky flavor.

Let the sauce reduce and thicken for 10 to 12 minutes. When the oven door is removed, the white sauce should have a burnt milk "skin" on its surface. Stir this skin into the sauce. Be careful when you remove the oven door, as the oven chamber has been without enough oxygen to sustain a fire. As you remove the door you are also introducing oxygen to the chamber, and it is likely, depending on how much fuel is in the chamber, that the coals may ignite suddenly.

Taste the sauce for seasoning, and let cool completely.

continued on page 272

1½ teaspoons butter

1½ teaspoons extra-virgin olive oil

5 medium leeks, white and very light green parts only, sliced ½ inch thick

3 small garlic cloves, thinly sliced

2 tablespoons fresh thyme leaves (reserve the woody stems)

1 cup heavy cream

1½ teaspoons fine sea salt

1½ teaspoons freshly ground black pepper

5 sprigs fresh thyme

ALTERNATE METHOD: Soften the leeks in a skillet over low heat on the stovetop, then roast the sauce uncovered in a hot (400°F to 450°F) oven—preferably convection—or on a charcoal kettle grill at a similar temperature.

CENTRAL COAST: Au Bon Climat Chardonnay, "Nuits-Blanches au Bouge," Santa Maria Valley

FARTHER AFIELD: Oak-aged white Burgundy from France

Vine Leaf–Wrapped Sheep's Tomme with Roasted Olives and Lemon

Be sure to roast the packets in a moderate oven, so the cheese in the center will be molten before the outside of the vine leaves become completely charred (a little char is fine—it complements the flavor of the cheese). If you are heating up the oven for pizza, roast the cheese packages before the oven reaches its optimum heat, which would be way too hot.

Although the vine leaves can be discarded, most people like to eat them, as the briny, smoky flavor combines nicely with the soft, spreadable melted cheese. Greek sheep's milk cheese, Manchego, or even Fontina may be substituted for sheep's Tomme. If using Fontina, add a tiny pinch of salt to the packet before wrapping. In season, use fresh vine leaves.

MAKES 4 PACKAGES; SERVES 4 AS A FIRST COURSE, OR 8 AS AN HORS D'OEUVRE

Rinse the vine leaves gently but thoroughly in cool running water and pat dry. Place 2 leaves on a work surface, slightly overlapping, and place 1 piece of cheese in the center. Scatter one-quarter of the garlic, lemon zest, and pepper on the cheese, and wrap up into a secure packet. Place seam side down on a platter. Repeat with the remaining leaves and cheese. Refrigerate for up to 2 hours, if desired.

Let the temperature in the wood oven burn down to 400°F to 450°F. Brush the packets lightly with olive oil and place on a rimmed baking sheet, to contain any escaping cheese. Place the pan on the floor of the oven and roast until the edges of the leaves start to catch fire and the whole package feels soft when gently pressed. The cheese should be only just beginning to ooze from the edges of the leaves. Use a metal spatula to scoop up and transfer to a platter or individual plates. Scatter roasted olives around the cheese and serve with toasted rustic bread.

ALTERNATE METHOD: In a thoroughly preheated cast-iron skillet, roast the cheese packets in a kettle grill at 400°F to 450°F, or in an oven—ideally, convection—set to a similar temperature.

continued on page 274

8 brine-packed vine leaves, base of tough central stems trimmed away

1 pound sheep's Tomme or other semihard sheep's cheese, cut into four 2 by 4-inch rectangles, about 1 inch thick

1 large garlic clove, minced or pushed through a press

Grated zest of 1 large lemon

¼ teaspoon medium-ground black pepper

Extra-virgin olive oil, for brushing

Oven-Roasted Olives (recipe follows)

Toasted wedges of rustic bread, for serving

Oven-Roasted Olives

Toss brine-cured or oil-cured olives with a little olive oil, scatter with some sprigs of fresh thyme and rosemary, and a little lemon or orange zest. Roast in a shallow pan alongside the wrapped cheeses for 10 to 15 minutes, until the olives are shriveled, aromatic, and slightly crisp.

CENTRAL COAST: Alma Rosa Pinot Noir "La Encantada," Santa Rita Hills
FARTHER AFIELD: Red Burgundy, Côte de Beaune, France

Wilted Escarole and White Anchovy Pizza

Here's another dream job: Create the pizza line-up for Santa Monica chef Hans Röckenwagner's new restaurant in Marina del Rey (sadly no longer open). I rose to the occasion with this unexpected combination of salty-sweet-earthy-piquant. To everyone's surprise (except mine), it became the most popular pizza on the menu.   MAKES TWO 12-INCH PIZZAS

Build a fire in the wood oven and build the temperature up to about 700°F.

Combine the olive oil, garlic, and slightly wet escarole in a bowl. Toss to mix evenly. Scatter with the pine nuts and pepper flakes; season lightly with salt and generously with pepper.

Place both dough disks onto a lightly floured surface and press them out into rough oval shapes, a little less than ¼ inch thick (if the dough resists your efforts to press it out thin, cover with a towel and leave to rest for about 5 minutes, then persist). Dimple with your fingers every inch or so, leaving the edge untouched, and brush all over with olive oil. Transfer one dough round to a wooden pizza peel liberally scattered with cornmeal. Don't press down on the dough at all as you load and top it, or it will stick to the peel. Immediately scatter with half of the escarole mixture. Quickly and confidently slide the first pizza onto the floor in the center of the oven and bake for about 5 minutes, rotating occasionally after the first minute or two. Meanwhile, press out the second dough round and transfer to the peel. As soon as the edges of the first pizza are golden and the escarole has wilted, remove from the oven. Quickly load the second dough round onto the peel, top as before, and transfer from the peel to the oven. Drape half the white anchovies over the escarole on the first pizza. Cut and serve. Repeat to serve the second pizza.

ALTERNATE METHOD: Bake the pizza at the hottest setting your oven will achieve, preferably set to convection. It will take longer than 2 to 4 minutes, probably 6 to 8. Best results will be obtained with a *fully* preheated pizza stone set on the oven's floor.

CENTRAL COAST: Flying Goat Crémant "Goat Bubbles," Sierra Madre Vineyard, Santa Maria Valley
FARTHER AFIELD: Crémant de Loire Rosé, Loire Valley, France

2 tablespoons pine nuts, lightly toasted

2 medium heads escarole, brown or wilted outer leaves trimmed away, rinsed, and sliced into ½-inch strips

¼ cup extra-virgin olive oil, plus more for brushing

3 large garlic cloves, very finely chopped

¼ to ½ teaspoon red pepper flakes

Fine sea salt and freshly ground black pepper

2 disks (1 pound) Pizza/Flatbread Dough (page 265), after its second rise

Coarse cornmeal, for the pizza peel

4 ounces white anchovies (*boquerones en vinaigre*)

Leek, Asparagus, and Thyme Flatbread

This recipe is for two flatbreads, while the Smoky Leek Sauce makes enough for four. If you have plenty of helpers or have become a pro at managing multiple flatbreads in the wood oven at once, double all the ingredients here to make four large flatbreads. It's important to work quickly with the dough, so it doesn't lose its oomph and rising power or stick to the peel. All your ingredients and toppings should be prepared and at hand before you begin shaping the dough.

MAKES TWO 12-INCH FLATBREADS

Build a fire in the wood oven and build the temperature up to about 700°F. (If desired, make the Smoky Leek Sauce while the oven is heating up, but be sure it's cool before spreading it onto the dough.) In a small bowl, toss together half of the asparagus, the arugula, lemon juice, a generous pinch of sea salt, and the chives. Set aside.

Working with one disk of dough at a time: Sprinkle a little cornmeal on a pizza peel and stretch and shape the dough into a rough 12- to 13-inch round, trying not to touch the rim. Lift the dough round gently onto the peel. Working quickly, brush a little olive oil over the dough and sprinkle with a little kosher salt. Gently spread half the Leek Sauce over the dough, leaving the edges uncovered. Don't press down on the dough at all as you load and top it, or it will stick to the peel.

Scatter half the smoked mozzarella over the sauce, dot with half the goat cheese, and scatter with half of the scallions and half the remaining asparagus.

Quickly but gently, slide the flatbread from the peel onto the oven floor. Bake for 2 to 4 minutes, rotating with the peel occasionally, until the crust is blistered and the toppings are bubbling. Scatter with half of the salad mixture, cut, and serve. Repeat the process to serve the remaining flatbread.

ALTERNATE METHOD: Bake the flatbread at the hottest setting your oven will achieve, preferably set to convection. It will take longer than 2 to 4 minutes, probably 6 to 8. Best results will be obtained with a *fully* preheated pizza stone set on the oven's floor.

CENTRAL COAST: Buttonwood Rosé, Santa Ynez Valley (Syrah)
FARTHER AFIELD: Bandol rosé, Provence, France

¾ cup Smoky Leek Sauce (page 271)

6 asparagus spears, woody ends discarded, shaved into a bowl of iced water with a mandoline or vegetable peeler

¾ cup baby arugula

Juice of ½ lemon

Fine sea salt

Small handful fresh chives, snipped into ½-inch lengths

2 disks (1 pound) Pizza/Flatbread Dough (page 265), after its second rise

Coarse cornmeal, for the pizza peel

Extra-virgin olive oil, for brushing

Kosher salt

4 ounces smoked mozzarella, cut into small dice or grated

4 ounces soft fresh goat cheese, crumbled

2 scallions, trimmed and cut into 2-inch-long chiffonade

Casa Pau Hana Olive Oil

In Hawaiian, *pau hana* means "no more work," or "work is finished." When Nick and Robin Gladdis decided to sell up in Maui after 13 happy years, move to the Central Coast of California, and make olive oil from trees they planned to plant themselves, that was the general idea. It hasn't turned out quite that way.

First, a garage/workshop/bottling room was built. Planting began in 2002, along with the construction of a home. In 2005, Nick and Robin had their first harvest. In subsequent years, more irrigation was added, as well as a photovoltaic system to provide electricity, and more olive trees. During their free time (both kept their day jobs in the medical industry until 2010), they installed irrigation lines, poured paving slabs, and built a bocce court. Every year, they prune the long lines of silvery trees that march across these golden hills and tend a prodigious patch of tomatoes. On weekends, Nick holds court around the freestanding pizza oven he and Robin built behind their Spanish-style home, topping his ethereal dough with a sauce made from tomatoes grown 10 feet away. Now, the six-acre orchard of Lucca and Arbequina trees is in full production (up to a maximum of 200 gallons a year). Eight years after planting the first few trees, Nick and Robin finally got around to retiring. This is a couple that went "back to the land" without a dusty ponytail or a healthy trust fund, two people who believed that producing something with your hands was a source of pride—worthy of virtually every penny of disposable income and 150 percent of their strength and time. Making such a profound life change takes guts, energy, appetite for risk, and a like-thinking partner. It is, in fact, almost the antithesis of the concept of *pau hana*. It's hard to imagine this dynamic pair ever *not* working.

I asked Nick, "Why olive trees?"

"Everyone here is making wine," he says. "I figured that, with all this wine, eventually there would be a glut and prices would fall. We wanted to grow something else appropriate for the Mediterranean climate." They started off with Lucca olives, which produce a peppery green oil similar in style to Frantoia, then added a contingent of Arbequina, a Spanish fruit that yields a more buttery oil.

Nick set up a truly professional olive oil tasting for us—my first. Each oil is poured into a small blue glass cup—blue, so you will not be tempted to hold the glass up to the light and compare the colors (as I immediately did). Instead, your judgment must be based purely on flavor, and in this first phase of tasting there is no bread in sight. First, you place your palm over the rim of the small glass and swirl, to release the volatile aroma of the oil, then you inhale deeply, as you would sniff a glass of wine. Then, a small sip—and you must not swallow, but rather purse your lips and suck in some air, allowing the oil to gurgle excitedly on your palate. (This has the effect of blasting the peppery character of the oil to the back of your throat and invariably provokes a little cough or two.) Then, Nick heats up some rustic country bread and pours us each a glass of a flowery local Viognier. I sense the buttery presence of lactic acid in the Arbequina oil, and the peppery, Tuscan-esque character of the Lucca. I imagine dressing a clean and simple arugula salad with the Arbequina oil and a little Meyer lemon juice, and drizzling a huge platter of raucous linguine puttanesca with the Lucca oil. The Gladdises are intensely proud of what they've accomplished, and I raise a glass (not the small blue one) to the excellent fruits of their labors.

> This is a couple that went "back to the land" without a dusty ponytail or a healthy trust fund . . .

IF YOU VISIT:

In San Luis Obispo, Casa Pau Hana oils are sold at the Sunday certified farmer's market, and at the Crushed Grape. In Paso Robles, you can find them at Mitchella Vineyard and Winery. The oils are used by various chefs in the region (including Michael Ramos at Meze Wine Café & Market and Clark Staub at Full of Life Flatbread in Los Alamos), as well as farther afield in Flagstaff, Arizona, by Caleb Schiff at Pizzicletta, a wood-fired pizza restaurant.

Visits are by appointment only: (805) 239-5898

casapauhana@hotmail.com

Wood Oven–Roasted Tomahawk Steaks

This outrageous cut of beef from the prime rib section of the animal goes by several different names: cowboy, Flintstone chop, handle-on Delmonico, longbone rib-eye, and tennis racket. It's impossible to estimate how many people two of these monsters will serve, because it depends on the gluttony level of the diners. I have (and will have again, one day) eaten a whole steak by myself, but it's probably more realistic to share one between two diners. They should be good friends, because there will be squabbling about the bone. SERVES 2 TO 4, DEPENDING ON LEVEL OF GLUTTONY

2 tomahawk steaks (about 30 ounces each)

Extra-virgin olive oil, for brushing

Coarse sea salt

Coarsely ground black pepper

Build a hot, relatively young fire in the wood oven to the point where you have a good amount of red embers and coals.

Brush the steaks all over with olive oil, then season very generously with salt and pepper. Wrap the bone with aluminum foil, to protect it from charring.

Depending on your equipment, choose one of the following cooking methods. (Pull the foil off about three-quarters of the way through the grilling time, to allow the bone time to roast but not char.)

Tuscan grill: Rake the hot coals into an even layer about double the width of the grill. Place the grill over the top of the coals, off to one side. Let it preheat for 5 minutes, then place the steaks on the grill. The fat will begin to render and drip onto the coals, causing flare-ups. Try to keep the flame from directly hitting the steak on a regular basis by moving the grill to the other side of the coals, and then back again, shortly after the fat again causes a flare-up. Grill-roast to your desired doneness, turning occasionally.

Large, mesh grill basket with a handle: Place the grill basket directly on the bed of hot coals and let it preheat until it's *very* hot. Pull out the basket, add the steaks, and then grill-roast, moving the basket back and forth between the hot coals and the floor of the oven (to avoid extended flare-ups) to your desired doneness.

Pull the steaks off the heat and let rest for 5 to 10 minutes, then carve and serve.

continued on page 282

ALTERNATE METHOD: Grill the steaks over a white-hot hardwood charcoal fire, using either of the two equipment options given above, moving the steak back and forth when flare-ups occur. Make sure the grilling surface is thoroughly preheated and no more than 2 inches above the hot coals. (Kettle grills will require a work-around to achieve this: Place two bricks in the bottom of the kettle, to raise the lower charcoal grate up much closer to the grilling grate.)

CENTRAL COAST: Qupé Syrah "Bien Nacido," Hillside Estate, Santa Maria Valley
FARTHER AFIELD: Red from the Northern Rhône, France

Acknowledgments

This was a far more collaborative book than any I've written before, and thus many thanks are due to the following:

To Mary Baker, for encouraging me—and opening doors—in the earliest days of the concept; Stacy Jacob, Clark Staub, and Sonja Magdevski for helping with the difficult job of narrowing down the many choices for the profiles (special thanks to Sonja for her all-around selfless enthusiasm and assistance); Chris Taranto, for excellent, knowledgeable guidance on so many levels; and Jen Porter, for her world-class promotional savvy.

To Colin Clark, for his stunning photography, and especially his game willingness to go *way* out of his way to capture more and better images than I could have hoped for. And to Valerie Aikman-Smith, for her expertise in making my food look as wonderful as it tastes.

To the wine pairers—Ali Carscarden, Sonja Magdevski, Cris Cherry, Stephan Asseo, Wes Hagen, Chris and Shandi Kobayashi, Frank Ostini, and Anne Twigg.

To the 25 winemakers and food artisans who took the time to share their passions, their past, and their plans for the future in this book.

To Mark and Maggie at Windward, Jennifer and Terry at Hoage, Jackie at Lone Madrone, Georges and Daniel at Daou, Denis at Domaine Degher, Judy at Starr Ranch, Guillaume and Solène at Clos Solène, Pam at Caliza, Alex and Monica at Villicana, Larry at Via Vega, Neal at Morro Bay Oysters, Debbie at Thomas Hill, and the many other artisans who strive to produce excellent wine and food in the Central Coast region but, because of space constraints, didn't make it into this book.

To Clark Staub, for lending his superior expertise to the wood-oven chapter.

To Carole Bidnick, for being the Jewish mother I didn't get to have; Kirsty Melville, for her confidence in me over the past decade or so; Jean Lucas, for her vision and refreshingly collaborative editing process. Also at Andrews McMeel Publishing—the ebullient Emily Farris, Diane Marsh (for the stunning design), and Lynne McAdoo.

And finally, to my great friend Andrea DeWit, who tested and tasted recipes, styled food, washed dishes, encouraged me, and kept me focused when the going got tough. And to her husband, Michael, for always sensing the perfect moment to open a great bottle.

To my mother, Marcia Légère Binns, for making sure I was born in California.

Metric Equivalents and Conversions

Approximate Metric Equivalents

WEIGHT

¼ ounce	7 grams
½ ounce	14 grams
¾ ounce	21 grams
1 ounce	28 grams
1¼ ounces	35 grams
1½ ounces	42.5 grams
1⅔ ounces	45 grams
2 ounces	57 grams
3 ounces	85 grams
4 ounces (¼ pound)	113 grams
5 ounces	142 grams
6 ounces	170 grams
7 ounces	198 grams
8 ounces (½ pound)	227 grams
16 ounces (1 pound)	454 grams
35.25 ounces (2.2 pounds)	1 kilogram

LENGTH

⅛ inch	3 millimeters
¼ inch	6 millimeters
½ inch	1.25 centimeters
1 inch	2.5 centimeters
2 inches	5 centimeters
2½ inches	6 centimeters
4 inches	10 centimeters
5 inches	13 centimeters
6 inches	15.25 centimeters
12 inches (1 foot)	30 centimeters

VOLUME

¼ teaspoon	1 milliliter
½ teaspoon	2.5 milliliters
¾ teaspoon	4 milliliters
1 teaspoon	5 milliliters
1¼ teaspoon	6 milliliters
1½ teaspoon	7.5 milliliters
1¾ teaspoon	8.5 milliliters
2 teaspoons	10 milliliters
1 tablespoon (½ fluid ounce)	15 milliliters
2 tablespoons (1 fluid ounce)	30 milliliters
¼ cup	60 milliliters
⅓ cup	80 milliliters
½ cup (4 fluid ounces)	120 milliliters
⅔ cup	160 milliliters
¾ cup	180 milliliters
1 cup (8 fluid ounces)	240 milliliters
1¼ cups	300 milliliters
1½ cups (12 fluid ounces)	360 milliliters
1⅔ cups	400 milliliters
2 cups (1 pint)	460 milliliters
3 cups	700 milliliters
4 cups (1 quart)	0.95 liter
1 quart plus ¼ cup	1 liter
4 quarts (1 gallon)	3.8 liters

Metric Conversion Formulas

TO CONVERT	MULTIPLY
Ounces to grams	Ounces by 28.35
Pounds to kilograms	Pounds by 0.454
Teaspoons to milliliters	Teaspoons by 4.93
Tablespoons to milliliters	Tablespoons by 14.79
Fluid ounces to milliliters	Fluid ounces by 29.57
Cups to milliliters	Cups by 236.59
Cups to liters	Cups by 0.236
Pints to liters	Pints by 0.473

Quarts to liters . . . . Quarts by 0.946

Gallons to liters . . . . Gallons by 3.785

Inches to centimeters . . . . Inches by 2.54

Oven Temperatures

To convert Fahrenheit to Celsius, subtract 32 from Fahrenheit, multiply the result by 5, then divide by 9.

DESCRIPTION	FAHRENHEIT	CELSIUS	BRITISH GAS MARK
Very cool	200°	95°	0
Very cool	225°	110°	¼
Very cool	250°	120°	½
Cool	275°	135°	1
Cool	300°	150°	2
Warm	325°	165°	3
Moderate	350°	175°	4
Moderately hot	375°	190°	5
Fairly hot	400°	200°	6
Hot	425°	220°	7
Very hot	450°	230°	8
Very hot	475°	245°	9

Common Ingredients and Their Approximate Equivalents

1 cup uncooked rice = 225 grams

1 cup all-purpose flour = 140 grams

1 stick butter (4 ounces • ½ cup • 8 tablespoons) = 110 grams

1 cup butter (8 ounces • 2 sticks • 16 tablespoons) = 220 grams

1 cup brown sugar, firmly packed = 225 grams

1 cup granulated sugar = 200 grams

Information compiled from a variety of sources, including *Recipes into Type* by Joan Whitman and Dolores Simon (Newton, MA: Biscuit Books, 2000); *The New Food Lover's Companion* by Sharon Tyler Herbst (Hauppauge, NY: Barron's, 1995); and *Rosemary Brown's Big Kitchen Instruction Book* (Kansas City, MO: Andrews McMeel, 1998).

Index